STRUCTURAL UNEMPLOYMENT AND AGGREGATE DEMAND

A Study of Employment and Unemployment in the United States, 1948–1964

Eleanor G. Gilpatrick

THE JOHNS HOPKINS PRESS

to

Essie and Murry Gottesfocht

FOREWORD

by William H. Miernyk

The major soft spot in the American economy in recent years has been a high rate of persistent unemployment. In spite of sustained recovery from the latest postwar recession—a recovery which started early in 1961 and was continuing at the end of 1965—the unemployment rate remained above 4 percent. This is high when compared with the rates which have been achieved by Great Britain and the democratic countries of Western Europe since the end of World War II. In Great Britain, for example, a *local* unemployment rate of 4 percent is regarded as critical. In the United States, by way of contrast, a *national* rate of 4 percent was set as an "interim goal." And even this goal had not been achieved by the end of 1965.

The persistence of relatively high-level unemployment in an economy which was setting new records in terms of production and income precipitated an extensive debate among economists. It seems fair to say that a majority of the participants attributed the bulk of unemployment to inadequate aggregate demand. A small but vocal minority, however, argued that structural changes in the economy were the major causes of persistent joblessness in the face of prosperity. As so often happens when a major issue is debated, supporters of the two schools of thought tended to polarize close to their extreme positions. Many demand theorists argued that even the most intractable, hard-core unemployment would yield to the pressures of further demand stimuli. And the most adamant "structuralists" continued to insist that the problem was not one of inadequate demand, that structural barriers impeded the movement of unemployed workers to jobs. There were, of course, some who took a middle position. As is often true in a lively debate, however, their views attracted less attention than those of the extremists.

In this book, Dr. Gilpatrick subjects the views of both the demand theorists and the structuralists to a careful and painstaking scrutiny. The results of her analysis are not likely to please extremists in either the inadequate demand or structuralist camps. She presents convincing evidence that high-level unemployment since 1957 has been the result of *a combination of* inadequate demand and structural changes. This is something which many economists might have suspected. But Dr. Gilpatrick reaches this conclusion only after a detailed and rigorous analysis.

The unemployment debate was not conducted in an academic vacuum. It had important policy implications. The demand theorists won an important policy victory when the Revenue Act of 1964 was passed. This act called for a reduction in income taxes without a corresponding reduction in federal expenditures. The Keynesian notion of deficit spending under certain circumstances was finally accepted by American policy makers—and by a large segment of the business community—about three decades after it had been advanced by its author.

There can be little doubt that the tax cut had an impact on unemployment. But during the year following, despite continued economic progress, the unemployment rate did not reach the "interim goal" of 4 percent which the advocates of a tax cut were shooting for. True, the rate for married men of prime working age dropped below 3 percent, but the rates for older workers, new entrants to the labor force, and, most particularly, rates for Negroes remained well above the average. By the end of 1965 it should have been evident to even the most casual observer that the demand stimulus was not enough and that further applications of the same medicine could have at least mildly inflationary consequences.

Dr. Gilpatrick shows that one of the major deficiencies of the demand theorists' position is their implicit assumption of homogeneity in the labor force. The labor market does not operate in the same manner as do markets for relatively homogeneous products. Some workers find it more difficult than others to obtain employment even in relatively tight labor markets. It is difficult to see how their joblessness can be attributed to inadequate demand. As average levels of educational achievement have risen in this country, and as technology has progressed, hiring standards have become increasingly stringent; in some cases they have become completely unrealistic. Those responsible for personnel policies in some large corporations have insisted that workers without high-school diplomas need not apply even for routine or menial jobs. As a result many thousands of workers are effectively frozen out of jobs in some industries. There is also, unfortunately, the problem of discrimination, and this can work both directly and indirectly. Even establishments which have removed the color bar to employment, whether on a token or a real basis, may limit the number of Negro employees by unrealistically high employment standards since Negro youth are disproportionately represented among school dropouts. Age is also a barrier to employment, particularly among the unskilled and those whose skills have been rendered obsolete in a given labor market by technological change, the migration of industry, or other causes of shifts in labor demand.

Fortunately for hard-to-place jobless workers our policy makers have been more eclectic than many of the economists who have debated the unemployment issue. They passed the Area Redevelopment Act which created thousands of new jobs. And this was followed by the Economic Development Act. The latter, with its broader focus and larger authorizations, should not only continue but should accelerate the progress started by the ARA. The Manpower Development and Training Act represents a major effort to increase the employability of thousands of disadvantaged unemployed. Programs under this act have been remarkably successful to date in shifting thousands of unemployed workers into productive occupations. And the Office of Economic Opportunity has removed thousands of others from the ranks of the unemployed by placing them either in a trainee status or in productive jobs. Finally, escalation of the Vietnam war in 1965 led to expansion of the Armed Forces which offset to some extent the rising flood of young male workers entering the labor market. Also, all ethical judgments aside, this war has helped sustain the aggregate demand for goods and services, and this in turn has had an impact on the derived demand for labor.

It would be misleading to imply that it is possible to delineate clearly between those workers who are unemployed as a result of inadequate demand and those who are jobless because of structural changes in the economy. In some cases the distinction can be made. If a large number of workers who can meet generally accepted hiring standards are unemployed, as has been the case during each of the postwar recessions, it is evident that insufficient demand is a major cause of joblessness. And when a middle-aged (or older) coal miner with a third- or fourth-grade education is replaced by a coal-cutting machine we have a clear-cut case of structural unemployment. Because unemployment data are not reported in sufficient detail, and because we do not have all of the necessary cross-classifications, it is not possible to estimate with any degree of precision the proportions of the unemployed who are jobless either because of inadequate demand or structural change.

Dr. Gilpatrick recognizes the inadequacies of unemployment data. She has developed a conceptual schema involving complementarity, substitutability, and transferability of skill requirements which provides a convincing demonstration that recent unemployment has been due to both inadequate demand and structural change. From this she derives a series of policy recommendations directed primarily toward the reduction of structural unemployment. The demand side of the unemployment problem is not ignored. Dr. Gilpatrick shows that adequate aggregate demand is a *necessary* condition for effective full employment. But her detailed analysis of the labor market shows that it is not sufficient. Policies designed to stimulate demand and those designed to improve the operation of the labor market are complementary rather than competitive. The issue now boils down to one of priorities in the area of policy determination.

The principle that effective demand must be maintained at a full employment rate is now generally accepted. What remains is the difficult task of working out the details of labor market programs designed to help those who do not find jobs through the market mechanism. European experience shows that unemployment can be reduced to the frictional level in free-market economies. Dr. Gilpatrick's book should help chart the course that must be followed if this goal is to be reached in the United States.

PREFACE

Unemployment has been a major cause of concern in the United States since the close of World War II, particularly since the late 1950's. Despite the fact that business cycle fluctuations have been moderate, each recovery peak from 1948 to 1960 was accompanied by an ever higher unemployment rate. From 1958 through 1963 the yearly rate did not fall below 5.5 percent of the labor force. This meant that in those years an average of at least four million people were looking for work at any one time. Some economists hold the opinion that the minimum level of unemployment has risen over the postwar period and may rise still further.

Investigation of the problem has public support and encouragement. The basic commitment of the federal government to maintain full employment is embodied in the Employment Act of 1946, which states:

> The Congress declares that it is the continuing policy and responsibility of the Federal Government to use all practicable means consistent with its needs and obligations and other essential considerations of national policy, with the assistance and cooperations of industry, agriculture, labor, and State and local governments, to coordinate and utilize all its plans, functions, and resources for the purpose of creating and maintaining, in a manner calculated to foster and promote free competitive enterprise and the general welfare, conditions under which there will be afforded useful employment opportunities, including self-employment for those able, willing, and seeking to work, and to promote maximum employment, production, and purchasing power. [Feb. 20, 1946, c. 33, Sec. 2, 60 Stat. 23.]

This statement of purpose has different and conflicting policy implications. Much depends on diagnosis of the causes of the unemployment, the order of priority of national goals, and the state of economic analysis. All that the Act really does is assure that the subject will be aired each time Congress believes that unemployment is of serious proportions.

The public debates, underway since 1960, largely revolve around the question whether postwar structural changes in technology, final demand, and the location of industry have been the chief contributors to the higher unemployment levels, or whether higher unemployment rates have been due primarily to insufficient spending relative to the productive capacity of the labor force. The fact that the debates have asked the public to choose one position or the other has been unfortunate. The interrelations between the two sets of causes of higher unemployment have been largely overlooked.

This study examines the 1948–64 unemployment experience without arbitrarily rejecting one set of causes in order to accept the other. Its chief aim is to examine the evidence for the position that the rate of structural unemployment has risen in the postwar period in the presence of less than full-employment levels of demand.

The argument proceeds as follows. If structural unemployment has increased as a proportion of the labor force, given the definitions to be outlined shortly, there must have been structural changes which could be translated into changed labor skill requirements. If so, there must be evidence of changed labor skill requirements. But this is not enough. There must also be evidence that the labor force was not able to adapt to changed labor skill requirements, using its four mechanisms, namely, (1) the labor force participation rate, (2) geographic mobility, (3) job mobility, and (4) changed educational levels. Additional points to be covered would be the examination of other possible reasons for higher unemployment rates and some direct evidence of structural unemployment. The interrelationship between structural change and the level of demand also requires examination. Finally, the implications for over-all policy must be spelled out.

Chapter 1 presents a theoretical system of unemployment classifications. It then explores implications for the structural-demand controversy. The emphasis on the theoretical framework derives from a review of the literature which suggests that some of the heat generated in the public debates stems from lack of agreement on the conditions which produce various kinds of unemployment and on the definitions themselves.

Chapter 2 briefly reviews the measurement of unemployment and its recent behavior in historic perspective. Chapter 3 examines the possibility that recent higher rates may be the result of a rise in frictional unemployment. Chapter 4 presents evidence that structural changes have taken place in the postwar period which could give rise to structural unemployment while affecting over-all demand. Chapter 5 examines the effects of these changes on employment requirements. In Chapters 6 and 7 labor's adjustments to changed requirements are studied. These include labor force participation rates and job mobility in Chapter 6, and geographic mobility and educational levels in Chapter 7. Chapters 8 and 9 are attempts to present direct evidence of labor market imbalance, the former dealing with skill shortages and the latter with direct evidences of structural unemployment. Chapter 10 discusses the problem of the minimum unemployment rate that is compatible with stable prices. Chapter 11 offers the study's conclusions and presents policy suggestions which stem from the analysis.

Most of Chapter 1 originally appeared as an article entitled "On the Classification of Unemployment: A View of the Structural-Inadequate Demand Debate," in the *Industrial and Labor Relations Review*, Vol. 19, No. 2 (January, 1966). I would like to thank the editors for permission to use this material.

I wish to acknowledge the helpful criticisms of Professors George H. Hildebrand, Morris A. Copeland, and Alfred E. Kahn, of Cornell University, who helped me avoid several blunders in the doctoral thesis which is the foundation of this book. Professor Robert Ferber of the University of Illinois contributed many hours of serious criticism and comment to the revision of the manuscript. He has given of his time and thought with unstinting generosity; his suggestions for further work have been responsible for many of the improvements but none of the remaining weaknesses of the text. My thanks also go to the numerous people who encouraged me to undertake the study and to carry out the job of revision. These include Professor Adolphe Lowe, Dr. Herbert Striner, Dr. Sar Levitan, Nat Goldfinger, and others. The Industrial Relations Counselors supported a summer of research. I thank Robert Wasson and Jack Gottsegen of the U.S. Department of Commerce for help in incorporating newly revised government series.

I should like to thank Dr. Charles L. Schultze for another kind of help. His work, *Recent Inflation in the United States*, is a touchstone and example for young economists who want to combine economic judgment, theory, and empirical research. It was a goal for emulation and a source of some of the ideas developed here. Finally, I should like to acknowledge my debt to Dr. Knowles and Dr. Kalacheck. Their work is more criticized than praised in this volume, but were it not for their initial investigations and results, much of the work presented here would never have been conceived. This volume, therefore, is offered as another voice in the continuing dialogue which is economics.

Urbana, Illinois   Eleanor G. Gilpatrick
September, 1965

CONTENTS

TABLES

CONTENTS xvii

FIGURES

Structural Unemployment and Aggregate Demand

CHAPTER 1

THEORETICAL FRAMEWORK

This chapter provides a theoretical backdrop for the empirical work to come. It establishes a classification system for unemployment that includes qualitative as well as quantitative and temporal criteria and then examines the "structural-demand" controversy within this framework.

CLASSIFICATIONS OF UNEMPLOYMENT[1]

The amount of labor necessary for any real dollar level of production at a point in time is determined by the physical requirements of the productive technology and the way purchasers choose to allocate their spending among final goods and services. The number of employed individuals which this represents is a function of individual hours worked, the steadiness of employment (or turnover), and the amount turned out per hour of work (productivity) for each final purchase.

Assuming constant prices, the labor supply, or the labor force, is determined by (1) normal and desired hours of work, (2) labor force participation rates of each age-sex category in the population, and (3) the demographically determined composition of the population. The labor force is the sum of the employed and the unemployed. At full employment, with no frictions in labor markets, the labor force equals the employed. The concept of over-full employment is associated with a situation where an inflationary rise in wages draws out a further supply of labor, or where there is bidding for labor beyond the capacity of existing capital equipment or labor supply to respond.

[1] A survey of various definitions in the literature appears in: U.S., Congress, Joint Economic Committee, Subcommittee on Economic Statistics, *Unemployment: Terminology, Measurement, and Analysis*, 87th Cong., 1st Sess. (Washington: U.S. Government Printing Office, 1961).

Thus full employment is reached when the labor force is fully utilized in production at given price levels. There is nothing ambiguous about such a concept as long as the economist is talking about perfectly competitive markets, with homogeneous labor inputs, mobility of labor and capital, flexible prices, and instantaneous market adjustments. But once he accepts a world of imperfect markets, specialized labor and capital, changing tastes and technologies, and incomplete information, he rules out the possibility of instantaneous adjustments. The result is the idea of unemployment existing at full-employment levels. The economist's problem is then to decide how much unemployment is consistent with full employment and to diagnose the causes of additional unemployment as a basis for remedial action.

Concern with diagnosing the causes of original unemployment leads to a theoretical dead end. The diagnosis must be based on reasons for lack of re-employment after disemployment occurs or after new labor force entrants are not newly employed. The reasons for original disemployment are of no concern if re-employment is assured. The movement between jobs would simply be a function of dynamic adjustments. The causes blocking re-employment are the proper targets for policy.

In our framework, unemployment is of two broad types: one caused by inadequacies in over-all demand, the other caused by dislocations in labor market functioning. Within each there is a temporal consideration of long- and short-run unemployment classes. The detailed definitions are as follows.

Frictional unemployment refers to short-term unemployment due to normal market adjustments. It is to this category that economists should limit their requirement that the number of unfilled jobs roughly match the number of unemployed workers. The frictionally unemployed are those unemployed for whom jobs are available within reasonable reach, reasonably suited to their skills, and at current wage levels. The obstacles to employment are short-duration imperfections of market information, business adjustment, or the preference of individuals for unemployment.

Frictional unemployment, as a short-run concept, assumes relative constancy of (1) the state of technology, and therefore labor skill coefficients of output; (2) the aggregate final product mix, an additional factor in over-all labor skill proportions; and (3) the distribution of skills within the labor force and the elasticities of supply of those skills. The skill proportions among the frictionally unemployed should approximate the proportions of the employed or the unfilled jobs because the skills themselves cannot be the cause of the unemployment.

The components of frictional unemployment are generally well known, though not easily measured. *Voluntary unemployment* covers workers who choose to remain unemployed while they await the "right" job, those who quit to get better jobs, and workers fired as a result of misconduct. Another component is *irregular unemployment*, involving unpredictable brief spells of unemployment due to strikes,[2] shortages of materials, and natural disasters. *Seasonal unemployment* refers to regular, recurrent spells of unemployment which show a yearly pattern. For example, the weather cycle affects construction, agriculture, and industries related to agriculture. Style and holiday rhythms affect trade and apparel, and regular yearly retooling occurs in automobiles. Frictional unemployment also occurs as some businesses fail and new ones spring up. We call this last category *business turnover unemployment*. Since frictional unemployment is independent, theoretically, of the level of demand,[3] the definition of full employment is that level of employment where all unemployment is frictional.

A rise in the frictional level of unemployment at full employment could be brought about by an increase in any of the component parts of frictional unemployment, the lessened willingness of people to move about, or deterioration in communication of job information. In addition, it can be due to an increase in the relatively short-run labor force proportions of age-sex groups with high frictional rates of unemployment. But frictional unemployment is short-term. It is unemployment which can be eliminated within a reasonable period of time and without an increase in aggregate demand. Jobs that are reasonably well suited to their abilities are available for the unemployed. Workers are unemployed because they are not aware of other opportunities, they choose to await other opportunities, or they simply require the time to readjust to business changes.

Short-term, demand-linked unemployment is often called *cyclical unemployment* since it appears as a characteristic of business cycle fluctuations. It is that unemployment which is caused by levels of final demand sufficiently low to leave unutilized numbers of labor/force participants with currently used labor skills. Production short of the full-employment level leaves a gap which must be closed through increased business spending, government spending, foreign sales, or a rise in consumption relative to income. In other words, holding technology, labor skills, and the composition of final demand constant, unemployment in this situation is due to short-term *inadequate aggregate demand*.

In the long run the labor force grows and technology changes while new labor skills are learned and others discarded. On the capacity side

[2] In the Census Bureau's Household Survey strikers are classed as unemployed if they are looking for work. We are attempting to make our definitions compatible with this set of definitions.

[3] In actual fact there is evidence, discussed in Chapter 3, that frictional levels also respond to the state of over-all demand.

labor force and productivity growth raises the level of output needed for full employment. If the labor force has kept a constant ratio of its skill composition to required skills in production, unemployment beyond frictional levels is still due to inadequate demand, but the gap between full-employment levels of output and actual levels of output can appear, not only in recessions, but at cyclical peaks. The long-run gap at cyclical peaks, which is a function of the spread between the rate of change of labor force capacity and the rate of change of output, creates what is sometimes called *growth gap unemployment*.

Both forms, cyclical and growth gap, are due to inadequate aggregate demand. The gaps are measured in terms of numbers of dollars of current output needed to employ the given numbers of unemployed after the frictionally unemployed are deducted. A distinguishing feature of unemployment due to inadequate aggregate demand in both the long and short run is that an increase in aggregate spending can provide employment for workers who are capable of accepting the new positions.

Structural unemployment comes about in the long run and can arise regardless of the level of demand. As technology, the composition of final demand, and the location of industry change, these structural shifts affect the composition of labor skill requirements. There is no problem as long as the labor force is itself able to adapt to the new requirements. Where this is not the case the structurally unemployed are victims of one situation or another: Either their skills are no longer used in output and also are not transferable to other occupations, or their skills are required in smaller proportions to output and complementary skills needed for output are in short supply. The two basic changes—technology and final demand product-mix—are aggregate in nature. Localized increases in structural unemployment can also occur where there are shifts in location of industry, there is an exhaustion of raw materials, or the two aggregate phenomena are concentrated regionally. The key to the structural problem is the mismatching of specific labor skill demands and supplies where there is (1) limited transferability of skills and (2) limited substitutability among skills.

When technical change involves the absolute uselessness of a skill, such as the blacksmith or the railroad fireman, no amount of increase in demand or the increased supply of any other skill will provide employment for the displaced workers unless they are qualified and willing to do some other work. The less adaptable the skill endowments and the less elastic the technical coefficients with respect to substitution of other skills, the more the workers approach a condition of "pure" structural unemployment. If, for example, the new technology requires education above the high-school level, those displaced who have had less education are structurally unemployed.

On the other hand, if the technological change creates new coefficients which simply increase the proportions of one kind of skill to the detriment of others, and if the one in greater demand is not available in adequate supply in the population, then all those with skills which are the complements of the one in short supply will be structurally unemployed. The owners of the displaced skills will face "pure" structural unemployment at current levels of demand, but they are structurally unemployed because of skill shortages at higher levels of demand. In the presence of a sufficient supply of the newly required skills, an increase in aggregate demand could employ more of the displaced skill.

When there are nontransferable skills and relatively fixed coefficients, greater increases in demand and a greater supply of the newly demanded skills are both required to employ the displaced skills than before the technological change. If, on the other hand, the less needed skills are transformed into more needed skills, a much smaller increase would be needed to send the displaced workers back to work. (The displaced workers need not be trained for the more needed skills themselves, as long as training permits some movement of existing labor force members along the skill continuum, leaving vacant jobs behind for entrants or displaced workers.)

Structural unemployment resulting both from the obsolescence of skills and the smaller proportions of certain skill requirements in production can be counteracted through worker retraining. But the form resulting from changes in proportions can also be alleviated by providing for an increase in demand together with an increase in the supply of the newly needed skills. The skill availabilities of those not in the labor force, but potential entrants, are therefore important. The labor force reserve helps determine the elasticity of supply of the skills. At the same time it is possible to classify inexperienced labor force entrants as structurally unemployed when their skills are either inadequate or in excess of current requirements.

When we divide structural unemployment between obsolete skills and nontransferable skills which are wanted in smaller proportions and whose complements are in short supply, we clarify a point of diagnosis. That is, skill shortages and obsolescence of skills are additive symptoms; either situation alone can produce structural unemployment. The disease is the result of a mismatching in the labor market, and the sequence of diagnosis must be: (1) proving the existence of structural change, leading to a change in labor skill requirements, and (2) showing the inability of the labor force to adapt quickly to the changed requirements—despite the existence of a price mechanism. Then it is necessary to survey the skills of the unemployed and, in addition, compare them with the skills needed in unfilled jobs.

LABOR SKILL COEFFICIENTS OF
PRODUCTION AND UNEMPLOYMENT

The major distinction made here with regard to frictional, structural, and "demand" unemployment derives from our view of technical labor coefficients. By such coefficients we do not mean the ratio of a composite labor unit[4] to a composite capital or output unit. Rather, we mean the proportions of various distinct kinds of labor employed with respect to distinct units of output and in conjunction with given units of capital. The possibility of structural unemployment as we define it depends on two things: (1) relative inelasticity of specific labor skill coefficients in at least some sectors or areas of the economy, and (2) relative nontransferability of at least some labor skills.

We suggest, a priori, that the more mechanized an industry, the more fixed the specific labor skills required per unit of capital or per unit of output. This may be more obvious with respect to direct labor, but to the extent that producers do not willingly throw their profits away it may be true of some indirect labor as well. It also seems possible that as labor skills require more specific training they are less transferable; that is, that transferability of skills is a decreasing function of training time. If the proportion of more highly trained employed workers rises as a percentage of total employment, we have a decline in over-all labor skill transferability.

In the Bureau of Labor Statistics (BLS) employment data the separation of workers into categories of production and nonproduction employees has inadvertently encouraged the idea that the number of employed nonproduction workers is not related to output requirements. But this is analogous to the statement that fixed capital has no relationship to output. On the other hand, if we deny the perfect substitutability of labor and capital it should be equally clear that one kind of labor is not completely interchangeable with other forms of labor. This is especially true once the particular machine is purchased. As Domar points out, " . . . in advanced industrial countries it is more meaningful to think of the machine as the main determinant of output, with the worker attached to it, rather than the other way round. . . ."[5] We would expand the term "machine" to include all capital used for the production of goods and services.

Theodore Schultz may or may not be correct in treating the improvement of human skills as a form of investment, but he does point up the

---

[4] For example, John Maynard Keynes, *The General Theory of Employment, Interest and Money* (New York: Harcourt, Brace, and Company, 1936), pp. 41–42.

[5] Evsey D. Domar, "Full Capacity vs. Full Employment Growth: Comment," *Quarterly Journal of Economics*, LXVII, 4 (Nov., 1953), p. 559.

error in treating labor as a homogeneous input: "The failure to treat human resources explicitly as a form of capital, as a produced means of production, as the product of investment, has fostered the retention of the classical notion of labor as a capacity to do manual work requiring little knowledge and skill, a capacity with which, according to this notion, laborers are endowed about equally."[6]

The history of thought on the impact of technological change has concerned itself chiefly with the destabilizing effects of labor displacing productivity increases. Summaries of the theoretical arguments appear in the work of Adolph Lowe,[7] Sylos-Labini,[8] and Fukuoka[9] among others. The questions raised are essentially related to whether, when labor is economized by technological change, there is an automatic mechanism which will retain (or restore), in the short run, a full-employment equilibrium. This is a problem in economic dynamics.

The answer has been optimistic where the assumptions involved included perfectly competitive markets, homogeneous factors, and a high elasticity of substitution of factors. The long-run problem of dynamic equilibrium has been raised as one involving the full-employment growth rate and its compatibility with a rate of growth necessary to keep capital investment on a steady path.[10] The quality of labor inputs required or supplied is not generally raised.

The pessimists' answers to the question of labor displacement and stability generally stem from their denial of the elasticity of substitution of factors. The technical coefficients are considered relatively fixed. Thus, if workers are displaced at a point of fully utilized capital, the problem is one of equipping the displaced workers with "working places." When innovations are capital-saving, the problem is further complicated by a lower demand for investment goods and the working places are still unsupplied. What is in question is the automatic adjustment of the system through interchangeable factors, divisible units, and flexible prices. Whether one assumes relatively fixed coefficients and nontransferable skills will partly determine whether one calls the effects of technological displacement a matter of inadequate demand. Whether one admits the

[6] Theodore M. Schultz, "Investment in Human Capital," *American Economic Review*, LI, 1 (March, 1961), p. 3.

[7] Adolph Lowe, "Technological Unemployment Reexamined," in Eugen Rentsch Verlag, *Wirtschaft und Kultursysteme* (Erlenbach-Zurich, 1955), pp. 232–33.

[8] Paolo Sylos-Labini, *Oligopoly and Technical Progress* (Cambridge: Harvard University Press, 1962), pp. 112–18.

[9] Massao Fukuoka, "Full Employment and Constant Coefficients of Production," *Quarterly Journal of Economics*, LXIX, 1 (Feb., 1955), pp. 25–29.

[10] See Daniel Hamberg, "Full Capacity vs. Full Employment Growth," *Quarterly Journal of Economics*, LXVI, 3 (Aug., 1952), pp. 444–49.

possibility of structural and/or demand unemployment is clearly related to one's view of the nature of economic adjustment.

It is usually assumed that at any level of technology there exists a variety of ways to turn out a given commodity combining varying amounts of labor and capital. Since the neoclassicists assume infinite divisibility and homogeneity of both labor and capital inputs, then, once the technological possibilities are given, the relative prices of the factors determine the quantities that will be employed. Thus the coefficients (or the ratios of capital and labor to output) are variable. This is a short-run concept since it must hold technology constant. There is no room for overhead costs because inputs and outputs relate to the same time period and must be varied instantaneously.

The concept of flexible coefficients and substitutability of factors in the short run can go along with the idea of "neutral" technological change in the long run. Then if there are changes in the *observed* coefficients, these can be attributed to the effects of factor prices. For example, Kendrick and Sato use the long period change in the labor share to measure the elasticity of substitution of labor and capital.[11]

Those who suggest the existence of fixed coefficients in the short run point out that once a machine is bought its labor requirements are given rather rigidly, and the machine will not be replaced by another machine unless the saving in variable costs compensates for the additional depreciation costs of the new machine over time. But, if coefficients are fixed in the short run, nonetheless they can be variable over time. Labor-saving or capital-saving techniques, the composition of demand, and the ages of capital equipment all can vary the over-all capital/labor ratio as may changes in factor costs. This is the setting in which labor displacement raises problems because we deal now with problems of factor shortages and redundancies as well as the closing of the income circuit.

Though many economists accept the possibility of fixed capital/labor coefficients, and though the specificity of capital embodied in overhead costs is recognized as an economic fact, labor is still usually treated as a homogeneous composite. This is easy to do when additional skill is accounted for by calling it additional labor in terms of wage units.[12] This approach ignores the possibility that where there is a change in technology not only may the over-all capital/labor ratio be readjusted, but the coefficients relating to various kinds of labor may be altered. Once this eventuality is admitted there exists the possibility of bottlenecks on the labor side with resulting unemployment of both capital and labor, with

---

[11] John W. Kendrick and Ryuzo Sato, "Factor Prices, Productivity, and Economic Growth," *American Economic Review*, LIII, 5 (Dec., 1963), pp. 974–1003.

[12] As in Keynes, *General Theory*, pp. 41–42.

the exception of the skills in short supply. This is analogous to the case where the full-capacity growth rate is above the full-employment rate,[13] because the labor bottleneck can theoretically induce a cut-back in output and then investment, and start a downward spiral. The inadequacy in this kind of labor growth, however, cannot be cured by more demand or by lowering the savings ratio. It requires eliminating the bottleneck. Even if we eliminate technological change, a shift in demand between industries can accomplish the same effect by rearranging the aggregate coefficients.

The nonhomogeneity of labor and the fixity of technical coefficients is mentioned and dropped in several places in the literature. Keynes not only saw that employment could vary at the same level of dollar output given a shift in taste[14] but he also recognized that it is possible to reach bottlenecks in resources in the presence of widespread unemployment.[15]

Fukuoka quotes a selection from Kaldor which asserts that once capital equipment is in existence there is a strong complementarity between equipment, labor, and raw materials. We would like to insert some mention of the specificity of labor into the following passage: ". . . in so far as a change of technical coefficients is actually observed, it should be regarded as a dynamic transition from one set of coefficients to another rather than as a smooth substitution along the static schedule."[16]

Professor Lowe raises the point we make directly but does not elaborate it since he believed at the time that skills were becoming more interchangeable: "The place to look for technical obstacles is rather a high degree of specificity on the part of the displaced labor force, that may delay its shift to other occupations and thus extend the period during which technological [un]employment persists."[17]

In the course of commenting on the possibility of a difference between the full-employment and the full-capacity growth rates, Domar raises and dismisses the possibility of a downturn due to labor shortages. But he did not envision the possibility, in 1953, as the statement below indicates, that the shortage may not be in total labor but in a *particular kind* of labor. He comments that, if the full-capacity rate exceeds the full-employment rate,

a good part of the resulting capital could not be used for lack of complementary factors, i.e., essentially for lack of labor. Faced with such prospects, investment falls and a depression begins. Thus we come to a most interesting and startling, but not equally substantiated

[13] We use these terms as they are defined by Hamberg in "Full Capacity."
[14] Keynes, *General Theory*, pp. 286–87.
[15] *Ibid.*, pp. 296–300.
[16] Fukuoka, "Full Employment," p. 30.
[17] Lowe, "Technological Unemployment Reexamined," p. 244.

as yet, conclusion that labor becomes unemployed because it is short.
. . . The last war has shown that labor can be "stretched" to a
remarkable extent.[18]

Yet, in the same article, Domar's advice to the underdeveloped world
is to accumulate capital but to be sure that "it is of the right kind and its
usefulness is not inhibited by the absence of a properly trained labor
force and of other requirements."[19]

UNEMPLOYMENT CLASSIFICATIONS
AND THE STRUCTURAL-DEMAND CONTROVERSY

In 1961 the Joint Economic Committee held a series of hearings to
ascertain whether the 1957–60 unemployment rates could be attributed
to structural changes or inadequate demand. The study done by James W.
Knowles and Edward D. Kalacheck, the Knowles-Kalacheck Report,[20]
was commissioned at this time. The study has been regarded as a definitive
work and its position—that inadequate total demand was the culprit—
was adopted by the Subcommittee on Economic Statistics.[21] At roughly
the same time the Council of Economic Advisers, with Walter Heller as
chairman, also denied the significance of structural unemployment,[22] as
did many other economists who testified.[23] Our reading of the literature
suggests that several conflicting sets of unemployment definitions were
used by economists and these, in turn, affected the witnesses' position in
the controversy. Frictional and structural unemployment were sometimes
used as synonomous terms.

[18] Domar, "Full Capacity," pp. 560–61.

[19] *Ibid.*, p. 562. Of course, Domar's main point is that the inflexibility of the economist's model produces threatening dangers which the real world seems able to avoid.
Whether the real world is now facing greater real dangers is our current concern.

[20] U.S., Congress, Joint Economic Committee, Subcommittee on Economic Statistics,
Higher Unemployment Rates, 1957–60: Structural Transformation or Inadequate Demand,
87th Cong., 1st Sess. (Washington: U.S. Government Printing Office, 1961) [to be
referred to as the Knowles-Kalacheck Report].

[21] U.S., Congress, Joint Economic Committee, Subcommittee on Economic Statistics,
Employment and Unemployment: Report, 87th Cong., 2nd Sess. (Washington: U.S. Government Printing Office, Feb. 2, 1962).

[22] Council of Economic Advisers, "The American Economy in 1961: Problems and
Policies," *January 1961 Economic Report of the President and the Economic Situation and
Outlook: Hearings,* Joint Economic Committee, 87th Cong., 1st Sess. (Washington:
U.S. Government Printing Office, 1961), pp. 309–92 [to be referred to as the Heller
Report].

[23] U.S., Congress, Joint Economic Committee, Subcommittee on Economic Statistics,
Employment and Unemployment: Hearings, 87th Cong., 1st Sess., Dec. 18, 19, 20, 1961
(Washington: U.S. Government Printing Office, 1962).

The study by Knowles and Kalacheck defines the inadequate demand position as that in which "the rate of growth in final demand has been low relative to the actual and normal rates of growth in potential supply made possible by increases in capital stock, labor force, and productivity."[24] This concept seems to suggest more than a cyclical inadequacy in demand and can include inadequacies at cyclical peaks. Some theorists, however, ascribe the persistent high rates since 1958 to an abortive recovery in 1959–60.[25]

Many "structuralists" have not stated their own position clearly and have allowed themselves to be backed into a box in which they must prove the adequacy of over-all demand in order to make their case. This is the way in which Knowles and Kalacheck presented the issue in their study.[26] A later article by N. J. Simler also asserts that the structuralists, including Curtis, Fackler, and Killingsworth, "appear to be saying that the rise in unemployment rates has taken place despite the presence of a generally adequate level of aggregate demand and a tolerably sufficient number of job opportunities."[27] The structuralists are asked to prove that increases in job vacancies match increases in unemployment. However, this is an argument for a rise in frictional unemployment, not structural, as we define it. On the other hand, proof of inadequate demand is an unfortunate way to dismiss charges of labor market imbalances.

If we suppose that demand is below full-employment levels, we can conceive of concomitant technological changes which make certain skills more demanded at the expense of others. Then job vacancies would appear for the newly sought skills, but the scarce skills' complements would be left unemployed. These unemployed are structurally unemployed, but job vacancies would match only the skills in short supply.

In the Heller Report a changed demographic composition of the labor force was one of the assumed sources of structural unemployment. The position of the structuralists was summarized as follows: ". . . the new unemployment is concentrated among workers who are intrinsically unemployable by reason of sex, age, location, occupation or skill."[28] We disagree, not with the position as stated, but with the tests. The tests that were offered sought, essentially, to determine how much unemployment came from changes in the proportions of the above-named categories, holding given unemployment rates constant. The study did not equate

[24] *Higher Unemployment Rates*, p. 6.

[25] *Employment and Unemployment: Hearings.*

[26] *Higher Unemployment Rates*, p. 9.

[27] N. J. Simler, "The Structural Hypothesis and Public Policy," *American Economic Review*, LIV, 6 (Dec., 1964), pp. 985–86.

[28] Council of Economic Advisers, *January 1961 Economic Report*, p. 329.

structural unemployment with a rise in unemployment rates in these particular groups, but rather with larger proportions of these groups (with normally higher rates than other groups) within the labor force.

The theory implicit in the test is that specific group unemployment rates could remain unchanged while the groups' labor force shares changed—thus affecting only the over-all rate through a shift in weights. But it is likely that changes in a group's labor force proportions make the group relatively more or less able to find employment. If the skill and experience of the group is held constant, its competitive position relative to other groups is affected when its labor force share changes since labor demand is for specific requirements. Particularly with age, the existing differences among the unemployment rates largely reflect different group endowments with respect to skill and experience. Thus when a group's relative labor force share changes, its competitive position changes. Changes in group unemployment rates are therefore the likely result both of shifts in labor force proportion and of shifts in the demand for specific kinds of labor skills. The Heller test was inappropriate for structural unemployment.

To the extent that voluntary unemployment reflects factors inherent in youth and women (youth are experimenting and gaining practical experience, and women have fluctuating home responsibilities), the approach has some validity. Changes in labor force composition in favor of these groups, however, would increase frictional unemployment and would raise the frictional minimum unemployment rate at full employment. It would not cause structural unemployment in the sense described in this study.

Another use of the term structural unemployment suggests that it is the economic structure of the labor market itself which may be causing higher unemployment rates. That is, trade union power, minimum wage laws, the pressure on employers to maintain relative wage standings, and social insurance all combine to raise the effective wage level above the marginal efficiency of many workers and new entrants. Clarence Long calls this "creeping unemployment." [29] This view is echoed in the work of Demsetz [30] and Gallaway. [31] It assumes that employers would not displace those at the bottom rungs of the skill ladder or the highly unionized if there were less unionization or no socially supported wage floors. These authors, however, have not successfully explained the exceptions from their models;

[29] Clarence D. Long, *A Theory of Creeping Unemployment and Labor Force Displacement* (Baltimore: Johns Hopkins University) [mimeo.; no date—either 1960 or 1961].

[30] Harold Demsetz, "Structural Unemployment; A Reconsideration of the Evidence and the Theory," *The Journal of Law and Economics*, IV (Oct., 1961), pp. 80–92.

[31] Lowell E. Gallaway, "Labor Mobility, Resource Allocation, and Structural Unemployment," *American Economic Review*, LIII, 4 (Sept., 1963), pp. 694–716.

high unemployment rates in less organized industries, uncovered employment, and among new entrants, nor have they faced the fact that technological change can alter labor requirements as a result of capital-saving innovations as well as labor-saving innovations.

STRUCTURAL CHANGE AND AGGREGATE DEMAND

Charles Killingsworth, speaking as a panel chairman at the December, 1964, proceedings of the Industrial Relations Research Association, decried the fact that the structuralists' position has been assumed to reflect the Federal Reserve Board's concern with inflation. This has generated the requirement that the structuralists prove the adequacy of over-all demand. The structural position has been identified with nonliberal views and with opposition to tax cuts and other aggregative techniques, but a growing number of commentators have been concerned with the possibility that these problems are coexistent.[32] Little has been said about the possible reinforcement of the two sets of causes.

Let us consider the two major structural changes: a shift in the composition of final demand (from goods to services) and technological change. If changes in the level of output were related to the rapidity of the shift, or if the distribution of income were so related, then high levels of unemployment, even if due to inadequate demand, could generate structural unemployment by accelerating the shift.

Another source of interaction of structural change and demand could come about in any market suffering from both skill shortages and inflexible prices, given relatively fixed coefficients. With the introduction of new technology, individual firms could displace workers with skills in less demand; but eventually the shortage of other, complementary skills could hold back production and income so that prior levels of demand, being reduced through labor displacement, would not be maintained through investment or consumption. In this case the structural change itself brings about a decline in demand, and skill shortages which lead to underutilized capacity will lower the demand for investment goods as well.

Technological changes which are capital-saving may affect labor skill requirements. In addition, an increase in capital productivity will affect

[32] These include trade union circles, the Department of Labor, and Robert Nathan (in the American Bankers Association, *Proceedings of a Symposium on Economic Growth, February 25, 1963* [New York: American Bankers' Association, 1963]); National Planning Association (*The Rise of Chronic Unemployment*, Planning Pamphlet No. 113 [Washington: National Planning Association, April, 1961]); William Haber ("Unemployment: Inadequate Demand or Structural Imbalance," *Michigan Business Review*, XVI, 5 [Nov., 1964], pp. 10–15), among others, and more recent views expressed by the Council of Economic Advisers.

the amount of capital demanded at any given level of output, and so the composition of final demand. Changes in the composition of final demand can also further affect capital demand in that different industries have differing degrees of capital intensity and varying "break-even" points with respect to capacity utilization. These affect the aggregate capital/output ratio and the level of investment demand.

These comments suggest that the two kinds of unemployment causes can reinforce each other or offset each other, depending on the particular combinations of circumstances. In addition, the unemployment categories themselves are not rigidly separated. There is interaction among structural, frictional, and "demand" unemployment.

Workers who are seasonally unemployed, for example, may not be recalled as promptly when demand is low. The amount of voluntary unemployment is affected by the relative availability of alternative jobs. In booming demand periods marginal business enterprises that use older techniques may become profitable. These could employ workers who appear to be structurally unemployed at lower demand levels.

N. J. Simler describes how inadequate demand unemployment may induce structural unemployment if the former levels are not quickly reduced.[33] If one assumes that the longer a worker is unemployed the more his skills deteriorate, then prolonged periods of inadequate demand can induce obsolescence of skills as the longer-term unemployed are less and less desirable from the employer's point of view. This leaves a core who may be unemployable even at higher demand levels.

The same level of unemployment can be the result of any combination of frictional, structural, and inadequate demand unemployment. As a further complication, a massive program to retrain workers, without a boost in over-all demand, would merely transform the structurally unemployed into those unemployed due to inadequate demand.

[33] Simler, "The Structural Hypothesis and Public Policy."

CHAPTER 2

UNEMPLOYMENT AS A POSTWAR PROBLEM

This chapter briefly examines the nature of unemployment measures, places the data in an historical framework, and discusses the analytical methods of attack used in later chapters.

THE MEASUREMENT OF UNEMPLOYMENT

Various methods and concepts could be used to measure and define unemployment. The definitions employed in the published figures are very much in keeping with the Employment Act's emphasis on activity. The base population is potential workers: the noninstitutional population fourteen years old and over. The labor force is the sum of those working (the employed) and those looking for work (the unemployed).[1] Thus the labor force concept expresses actual labor availability and not potential labor supply.

The estimation of the size of the labor force and unemployment takes place monthly in the Current Population Survey conducted by the Bureau of the Census, the "Household Survey." The classification of individuals is based on activity during the calendar week that includes the fifteenth of the month. The survey is the single source of data in our present system of labor force statistics that gives a comprehensive head count of individuals.[2]

[1] The "total labor force" includes the Armed Forces, while the "civilian labor force" does not.
[2] The survey was begun in 1940, under the Works Progress Administration, and in 1942 the Census Bureau became responsible for it. In 1959 the analysis and publication of the data became the responsibility of the Bureau of Labor Statistics. The method used is a personal interview system based on a stratified area probability sample.

According to this system, persons fourteen years old or over are either (1) not in the labor force, (2) employed, or (3) unemployed. Although an individual could possibly be in all three categories in a survey week, he is counted only once. The system therefore uses an order of priorities: being in the labor force comes before not being in; working comes before looking for work; looking for work comes before having a job attachment but not working; and looking for work comes before not working or not looking.

The *employed* are in one of the following classes: (1) all persons who did any work (even one hour) for pay or profit during the survey week; (2) all persons who did at least fifteen hours of unpaid work in a family-operated enterprise (farm or nonfarm); (3) all persons who had a job but were temporarily absent because of illness, vacation, bad weather, an industrial dispute, or other personal reasons, provided they were not looking for work at the same time. As can be seen, the global figure for employment does not recognize involuntary part-time employment, but recent supplementary data provide this information.

The *unemployed* are: (1) all persons who did no work for pay during the survey week (or worked without pay for fourteen hours or less in a family-owned enterprise) and who were looking for work; (2) all persons who were not at work and would have been looking for work except that (a) they were waiting to be called back from a lay-off within the next thirty days, or (b) they were waiting to report to a new job within the next thirty days (and were not students in the survey week),[3] or (c) they volunteered that they would have been looking for work except that they were temporarily ill or believed no work was available in their line or area. Looking for work includes any of the following activities: registration at an employment agency, being on call at a personnel office or professional register, placing or answering ads, writing letters of application, canvassing employers, being interviewed by prospective employers, working without pay to get experience and training, and awaiting the results of work efforts undertaken in the previous sixty days.

The *civilian unemployment rate* is the number of unemployed as a percentage of the civilian labor force; this is the global figure in common use. It is clearly defined but open to misinterpretation. It does not take account of need, part-time unemployment, or degree of labor force attachment. It does not include those who leave the labor force in discouragement, while it does include unemployables and casual workers as long as they seek employment.

---

[3] Groups (a) and (b) were classed as employed until 1957. The global series has been revised for the years 1947–56 to conform to the new definitions, but many component series remain unadjusted.

The layman has every right to inquire whether the phenomenon of higher unemployment rates is a function of the data and perhaps not a real economic problem. One answer is that, aside from a few revisions in coverage and the changes in definition in 1957,[4] the Household Series "uses the same basic concepts and methodology for the entire period from 1947 to the present."[5] Another answer is that the public data have often been under attack and therefore under review practically since they have been collected, and there has never been evidence of any manipulation of the concepts or data gathering procedures for partisan purposes. A recent public examination of the data and the methodology employed in collecting them, the "Gordon Report,"[6] came up primarily with proposals to broaden coverage rather than with criticism of the concepts and methodologies used.

ALTERNATIVE MEASURES OF UNEMPLOYMENT

The seriousness of the unemployment problem must be evaluated in terms of its behavior over time, using definitions and measures consistently over the period. The global rate displayed levels at least as high as 1954 recession rates of unemployment for each year from 1958 to 1963. We can compare this behavior with other rates which include or exclude workers who might be treated differently in alternative unemployment measures.

Table 1 presents the civilian unemployment rate and five alternative measures which we shall discuss briefly. The total labor force rate (Column 2) includes the Armed Forces and is lower than the civilian rate, as one would expect, but moves with it. The difference is very small. This is

[4] The sample design has been broadened several times. In 1960 figures for Alaska and Hawaii were incorporated, and in 1953 and 1962 Census data were incorporated.

[5] Raymond T. Bowman and Margaret E. Martin, "Special Report on Unemployment Statistics: Meaning and Measurement," *The American Statistician*, XVI, 4 (Oct., 1962), p. 22.

[6] President's Committee to Appraise Employment and Unemployment Statistics, *Measuring Employment and Unemployment* (Washington: U.S. Government Printing Office, Sept., 1962). Other critical or explanatory sources include: Stanley Lebergott, "Unemployment Statistics for Fiscal and Monetary Policy," *Proceedings of the Fourteenth Annual Meeting* (New York: Industrial Relations Research Association, 1961), pp. 16–27; National Bureau of Economic Research, *The Measurement and Behavior of Unemployment* (Princeton, N.J.: Princeton University Press, 1957); U.S., Congress, House, Subcommittee of the Committee on Education and Labor, *Unemployment Statistics: Hearings*, 85th Cong., 2nd Sess. (Washington: U.S. Government Printing Office, 1958); *Unemployment: Terminology, Measurement, and Analysis*; U.S., Bureau of Labor Statistics, *Concepts and Methods Used in Household Statistics on Employment and Unemployment from the Current Population Survey*, BLS Report No. 279, June, 1964; and U.S., Bureau of Labor Statistics, *How the Government Measures Unemployment*, May, 1962.

TABLE 1: Selected Unemployment Rate Measures, 1947–64

(percentages)

Year	(1) Civilian labor force	(2) Total labor force	(3) Experienced wage and salary workers	(4) Experienced workers	(5) Married men	(6) Labor force time lost
1947	3.9	3.8	—	—	—	—
1948	3.8	3.7	4.2	3.0	—	—
1949	5.9	5.8	6.7	5.1	3.4	—
1950	5.3	5.2	6.0	4.9	4.6	—
1951	3.3	3.2	3.7	2.9	1.5	—
1952	3.1	2.9	3.3	2.5	1.4	—
1953	2.9	2.8	3.2	2.4	1.7	—
1954	5.6	5.3	6.0	4.6	4.0	—
1955	4.4	4.2	4.8	3.8	2.6	—
1956	4.2	4.0	4.4	3.4	2.3	5.1
1957	4.3	4.2	4.5	3.8	2.8	5.3
1958	6.8	6.6	7.2	6.2	5.1	8.1
1959	5.5	5.3	5.6	4.9	3.6	6.6
1960	5.6	5.4	5.7	5.0	3.7	6.7
1961	6.7	6.5	6.8	5.9	4.6	8.0
1962	5.6	5.4	5.5	4.9	3.6	6.7
1963	5.7	5.5	5.5	4.9	3.4	6.8
1964	5.2	5.0	5.0	4.4	2.8	—

NOTE: Census of Population data introduced in 1953 and 1962. Alaska and Hawaii included in 1960. Data in columns (1), (2), (3), and (6) have been adjusted to reflect changes in the definitions of employment and unemployment adopted in 1957. Data in columns (4) and (5) have not been so adjusted for the years 1947–56.
Experienced rates prior to 1958 based on data for January, April, July, and October of each year. Experienced workers have had at least two full weeks of employment.
Married men included are those living with their wives. Data for 1949 and 1951–54 are for April; 1950 for March.
Time lost assumes unemployed lost 37.5 hours per week; those on part-time for economic reasons lost difference between 37.5 hours and time actually worked.

SOURCE: U.S., Office of the President, and Department of Labor, *Manpower Report of the President, 1965* (Washington: U.S. Government Printing Office, 1965), pp. 193, 207; and U.S., Office of the President, *Economic Report of the President, 1964* (Washington: U.S. Government Printing Office, 1964), p. 234, and *1965*, p. 217.

because the Armed Forces, in the 1947–64 period, were never more than 5.4 percent of the labor force (as in 1952) and are counted as employed. In computing the unemployment rate, therefore, only the denominator is affected by their inclusion.[7]

The self-employed and unpaid family workers are not dependent on the decisions of others for their employment status and can more often manage some employment during a given period. Thus these groups have a low rate of unemployment because of the nature of their job attachments.

[7] Although the difference between the rates is small, the size of the Armed Forces can affect the rates themselves to the extent that young men in service would normally be employed, unemployed, or not in the labor force in the absence of conscription.

Some critics say that the unemployment rate used at present really under-states the general picture. For these critics, the rate in Column 3 serves better. This covers only experienced wage and salary workers and thereby also excludes workers with no previous job attachment. This rate is greater than the global rate but has moved closer to it as the self-employed have declined as a percentage of the labor force and as the inexperienced unemployed have grown in number. But, again, the year-to-year pattern is very similar to the over-all rate.

If we eliminate only those unemployed who have not had at least two weeks of full-time work experience, the resulting unemployment rate, the experienced worker rate (Column 4), is below the over-all rate. But, here too, the yearly movements show responses similar to the global rate.

For those who consider secondary wage earners such as dependent youth, wives, and the aged to be transients in the labor force, another measure exists which includes only men who have family responsibilities. This is the unemployment rate for married men living with their wives. As Column 5 indicates, the years 1949–50 and 1952–53 show a rise in this rate while other measures fall. It is possible that this was due to mobility before and after the Korean mobilization and could be considered a frictional rise. From 1953 this rate, while lower than the global rate, followed much the same pattern. Rising levels of unemployment at cycle peaks are not just related to workers with transitory attachments to the labor force; it appears here as well.

Labor force time lost (Column 6) is an entirely different measure in that it does not count people, but hours. This method takes account of time lost by workers who work only part-time for economic reasons, but until 1964 it did not adjust for those who are unemployed but looking only for part-time work.[8] The annual data are available from 1956. This rate shows the highest absolute level of unemployment, but the yearly movements are in phase with the pattern of the other rates.

The similarity of movement of the various rates suggests that unemploy-ment changes are extremely interrelated; thus the levels may be different but the movements are similar over the cycle and in their trend. Inclusion of what may be considered marginal groups in the over-all rate does not

---

[8] The method used assumes that 37.5 hours per week are lost by the unemployed, and the partially unemployed lose the difference between their actual time worked and this figure. Potential manhours are calculated by adding manhours actually worked plus hours imputed to employed persons with a job but not at work, plus manhours lost by the unemployed and workers on part-time work for economic reasons. In 1964 a new series was begun which takes the place of the rate reported in Column 6. It is called labor force time lost through unemployment and part-time work but reflects whether unemployed persons sought full- or part-time jobs. See the Department of Labor's *Monthly Report on the Labor Force*, issues from 1964.

distort the pattern because these groups have been included from the start. Exclusion of those who leave or do not enter the labor force because of discouragement also has been consistent over time. The rates all show a continuing high level of unemployment after 1958, and all show rising peak period unemployment since 1953.

A question for any current study of unemployment must be, "How will you measure structural unemployment?" The problem of available data is second only to the conceptual issue. The structurally unemployed include those out of work because of shortages in complementary skills plus those with obsolete skills. Those out of work due to inadequate demand are the sum of those in scarcest supply who are out of work plus those who would be used as their complements in production, less the frictionally unemployed. The latter would be those for whom unfilled jobs existed within a reasonable distance that were reasonably suited to their skills. The structurally unemployed could not be employed unless (1) there were an increase of skills in short supply, and possibly demand as well, to utilize the short-skill holders, or unless (2) their skills were changed, or (3) their skills were again demanded in greater proportions.

The actual enumeration would be next to impossible, even if adequate job vacancy and skill requirement data existed. The observed marginal increments vary considerably from the average because of changing final demand and the nature of the various production functions; thus the direct measurement problem is enormous. The approach this study intends to take is an indirect one. It will measure the symptoms of structural unemployment, rather than its actual amount, by looking for departures from regular patterns that might appear in relation to over-all demand.

COMPARISONS WITH OTHER COUNTRIES

An indication of the seriousness of recent unemployment is a comparison of the United States' rate with other countries' rates. The President's Committee asked the Bureau of Labor Statistics to make a comparative study covering the year 1960 in cross-section and the time series for 1951–61.[9] Eight industrialized countries were selected for study: the United States, Canada, France, the Federal Republic of Germany, Great Britain, Italy, Japan, and Sweden. The basis for comparison was rates of unemployment, rather than numbers, since population and the labor force figures were vastly different in each country.

[9] President's Committee to Appraise Employment and Unemployment Statistics, *Measuring Employment and Unemployment*, pp. 223–70.

The conclusions of the study cover the following points. (1) The method of measurement has been a minor factor in determining the differences in national rates of unemployment. (2) The United States' rate in 1960, 5.6 percent, was high relative to the other industrial countries studied, with the exception of Canada. The composite rate for the seven countries with a combined labor force more than twice the United States' was 2.1 percent. (3) "The unemployment position of the United States and Canada relative to that of other countries worsened appreciably" during 1951–61 while it either held steady or improved substantially for the other countries.[10] (4) The degree of strength of cyclical patterns seemed to be unimportant. (5) "Demographic factors such as the growth of the labor force and its sex and age composition are of limited help in explaining this country's higher unemployment rates."[11] (6) An important relationship appears to exist between average annual rates of economic growth and the change in the unemployment rates over the period 1951–60.

The report concludes that countries with lower rates of unemployment experienced faster growth in the 1950's and their workers had more stable attachments to their jobs. Great Britain proved an exception, but, although its rate of growth was as low as that of the United States, its labor force grew more slowly. The international comparison did not establish the reasons for the higher rates in the U.S. and Canada because it admittedly left out of its investigation many possible causes, some institutional and some structural. It did contribute to the impression that U.S. unemployment is of serious proportions.

HISTORIC EMPLOYMENT AND OUTPUT DATA

Figure 1 presents the civilian unemployment rate since the turn of the century. The rates from 1900 to 1939 are retrospective estimates, largely compiled by Stanley Lebergott.[12] Seen in historic perspective, the postwar period cannot be said to display dramatic levels of unemployment. Certainly the levels of the Great Depression, rising as high as 24.4 percent, are not part of the 1947–64 experience. The trough year rates of 1908, 1915, and 1921 were also above the troughs of 1949, 1954, 1958, and 1961. Figure 1 makes clear, however, that the general direction from 1945 to 1964 appears to be upwards in contrast to the 1900–29 period, which showed little peak year trend. The lowest peak year rate attained after 1945 was 2.9 percent in 1953 (or 2.5 percent using the old definitions).

[10] *Ibid.*, p. 235.
[11] *Ibid.*
[12] National Bureau of Economic Research, *The Measurement and Behavior of Unemployment*, pp. 215–16.

But rates as low as 0.8 (1906), 1.9 (1926), and 3.2 percent (1929) were achieved without a war-time economy.

The postwar years have displayed other symptoms that point to the existence of a problem. If the unemployment rates are listed by turning point dates and compared with business cycle dates, as in Table 2, we get some idea of the responsiveness of the rate to over-all conditions. Using the entire post-World War I period from 1921 to 1964, by calendar years, we see that the unemployment rate has led at the onset of recession only in the 1957 and 1960 downturns. This is corroborated by the seasonally adjusted monthly data available for the post-World War II period. Recovery, or the lower turning point, does not appear delayed, using the yearly data, except in 1928 and in 1933, when we had an obviously serious problem. The monthly data show, however, that there was a greater recovery lag in unemployment in 1958 and 1961 than in earlier post-World War II years.

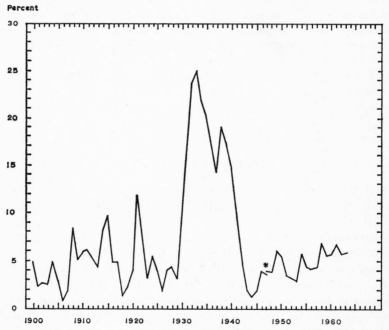

FIGURE 1: Civilian Unemployment Rate, 1900–64. (Source: 1900–46, Lebergott, in National Bureau of Economic Research, *The Measurement and Behavior of Unemployment* [Princeton, N.J.: Princeton University Press, 1957]; 1947–64, U.S., Office of the President, and Department of Labor, *Manpower Report of the President, 1965* [Washington: U.S. Government Printing Office, 1965], pp. 193, 207.)

* New series using definitions of employment and unemployment adopted in 1957.

TABLE 2: Business Cycle Dates for Real National Output and the Civilian
Unemployment Rate, 1921–61

Calendar year dates			Monthly dates		
NBER standard reference dates	Unem- ployment rate specific dates	Unem- ployment relative to reference dates	NBER standard reference dates	Unem- ployment rate specific dates	Unem- ployment relative to reference dates
Peaks (onset of recession)			**Peaks (onset of recession)**		
1923	1923	coincident			
1926	1926	"			
1929	1929	"			
1937	1937	"			
1944	1944	"			
1948	1948	"	Nov., 1948	Oct., 1948	lead 1 month
1953	1953	"	July, 1953	Aug., 1953	lag 1 month
1957	1956	lead 1 year	July, 1957	Apr., 1957	lead 3 months
1960	1959	lead 1 year	May, 1960	Feb., 1960	lead 3 months
Troughs (onset of recovery)			**Troughs (onset of recovery)**		
1921	1921	coincident			
1924	1924	"			
1927	1928	lag 1 year			
1932	1933	lag 1 year			
1938	1938	coincident			
1946	1946	"			
1949	1949	"	Oct., 1949	Oct., 1949	coincident
1954	1954	"	Aug., 1954	Sept., 1954	lag 1 month
1958	1958	"	Apr., 1958	July, 1958	lag 3 months
1961	1961	"	Feb., 1961	May, 1961	lag 3 months

NOTE: NBER refers to National Bureau of Economic Research.
Monthly unemployment rate dates are based on seasonally adjusted data as of January,
1964. The peak month is the lowest unemployment rate or, when the rate is stable at its
lowest point, the last month at its low point. The trough is determined in a similar way.

SOURCE: National Bureau of Economic Research and *Monthly Report on the Labor Force*,
Jan., 1964, p. 34.

This suggests a greater stickiness in unemployment, which might be
related to the briefness of the 1953–57 and 1957–60 cycles, except that the
expansion after 1961 is now of record length (September, 1965) and the
unemployment rate remained at 5 percent or above until January of 1965.

Naturally, the role of output must be introduced. To what extent have
changes in real output been related to changes in the unemployment rate?
The answer is that the two variables are intimately connected. Using the
revised series from the National Income Division of the Commerce
Department (NID), percentage changes in real GNP were correlated with
point changes in the unemployment rate over the interval 1929–30 to

1962–63. The product-moment correlation coefficient is -0.916, significant at the 1-percent probability level.[13]

The regression equation is $x_1 = 1.27 - 0.37\, x_2$; where x_1 is the point change in the unemployment rate and x_2 is the percentage change in real GNP in 1958 dollars. Thus unemployment can be expected to rise at a zero rate of output growth by about 1 percent of the labor force and decline by only 0.4 percent of the labor force for each percentage rise in output above 1.3 percent.[14] Since the standard error of estimate for the unemployment rate is a point change of ± 1.2, however, deviations within the range of reasonable probability include changes in the unemployment rate as high as those charged by the structuralists.

In the postwar years 1947–48 to 1962–63 no calculated rate changes are much beyond one standard error and there is no tendency toward a systematic direction of error. The predicted value for 1963–64 is off by only 0.1 point. (The older series, however, shows underestimation of unemployment in thirteen out of the sixteen observations.)

When the sixteen observations covering the years 1947–48 to 1962–63 are regressed separately, the new NID data yield an r of -0.88 (-0.87 adjusted), while the old data yield an r of -0.91. For the more recent period the point change in unemployment is accounted for by the equation $x_1 = 1.46 - 0.36\, x_2$ (standard error $= 0.61$), but the two equations do not differ significantly.

The regression equations suggest that the sluggishness of output has been roughly responsible for persistent unemployment, but within the bounds of 1 to 2 percent of the labor force the structural position is compatible as well. It is also necessary to note that a high and significant coefficient of correlation shows only relatedness, not the direction of causation. We do not know to what extent unemployment itself has held back production. If there are structural skill shortages, output can be held back; if there is high unemployment, demand can be affected. The relationship between changes in the unemployment rate and changes in output does not provide a diagnosis of unemployment.

THE TIME PERIOD

Another reason that current levels of unemployment must be viewed as a problem stems from the institutional setting. There is no justification

[13] In 1947–48 the data incorporate the new unemployment definitions. There are two overlap years. The difference in the point changes between the new and the old series is 0.1 in 1947–48. It is of course questionable to use measures of significance in time series analysis since normal distribution must be assumed, and each point is one observation out of each universe.

[14] Using the older series for real GNP in 1954 dollars, $r = -0.925$, and $x_1 = 1.33 - 0.39\, x_2$; thus the generalization holds.

for the attitude that unemployment rates acceptable at an earlier time are acceptable today. To take this position would be to assert the inadequacy and lack of purpose of the institutional changes that have been adopted since the mid-1930's, changes geared to dampen severe unemployment and the cycle.

The period of the 1920's is sometimes used as a comparison base with the period after 1945. But the resemblance is not a basic one, despite the fact that over-all patterns of consumer expenditures were superficially similar, both periods witnessed rapid technological change, and both are postwar periods. A glimpse at Figure 1 will indicate that the direction of unemployment rates from 1921 to 1928 was downwards, while the reverse is true from 1945. In the intervening period the Great Depression saw fiscal and monetary policy used increasingly as an aid in steadying prices and employment; the present personal and corporate income tax structure, unemployment benefits, minimum wage and hours laws, and the existence of a strong trade union movement were all absent in the 1920's. While both periods witnessed technological change, it is reasonable to suggest that the nature of the changes was radically different. Not only have the skill and educational levels of the labor force vastly changed, but so have the educational requirements in industrial production. The difference between these two periods is further emphasized by the changed role of government.

It was only after 1946 that the federal government declared that the maintenance of full employment was a major policy aim. At the same time, government expenditures were nowhere near the magnitudes reached in World War II and thereafter, either in absolute figures or in relative terms. This means that, on one hand, a larger share of demand is not open to fluctuations due to business conditions, but, on the other hand, a large part of our resources are tied up with public policy decisions and are subject to politically induced shifts.

If we face a problem with respect to unemployment, its magnitude is relative to the care we have taken to avoid it. But we also need not prove the uniqueness of the 1947–64 period in order to show reason for concern. For seven years running, 1958–64, the annual unemployment rate exceeded 5 percent. No precedents are required to command the judgment that the American economy has shown unsatisfactory performance during this lengthy period.

To date, the two major empirical tests of the structural unemployment position have been confined to the years 1957–60.[15] It was within this period that structural unemployment was assumed to have appeared, if at all. But the tests cannot be considered adequate under this limitation.

[15] The Knowles-Kalacheck Report and the Heller Report, referred to earlier.

The period is short and comes too late to show the changes that may have occurred earlier or that may have been accumulating over time. Any accumulation of structural unemployment earlier than 1957 would be masked by 1957 unless the rate of structural unemployment were continuing to increase. Certainly a rising rate of structural unemployment need not be claimed to reject a simple demand hypothesis. On the other hand, rejection of the demand position need not mean that higher unemployment rates after 1957 are solely the result of more structural unemployment. If the peak years 1957 and 1960 both experienced accumulated structural unemployment as well as inadequate demand, then the two years could both be markedly different from comparable earlier years, and similar to each other. In the chapters that follow, the entire period 1948–64 will be examined.

CHAPTER 3

HAS THE FRICTIONAL RATE OF UNEMPLOYMENT RISEN?

A possible explanation for recent high rates of unemployment other than structural change or inadequate demand is that the frictional rate of unemployment has risen autonomously. This could bring about an upward shift in the aggregate unemployment rate, all other things being equal, but need not be a major cause for alarm. A society might consider high levels of frictional unemployment an acceptable cost for relative security and freedom for its workers to move from job to job, or to move less than required by normal business needs.

Short of a head-count of workers and unfilled jobs, there are no data for a direct test of this third hypothesis; instead, several indirect tests can be substituted. The first is to investigate whether any of the component parts of frictional unemployment show signs of having risen autonomously. The second is to consider frictional unemployment to be closely approximated by short duration unemployment and to examine the behavior of the short-term unemployment rate. The third is to consider whether there has been a change in the proportions of the labor force by sex and age such that composition alone has caused the over-all rate to rise. A fourth test is to search for signs of inadequate or excessive geographic mobility. This latter approach will be explored in a later chapter.

THE COMPONENTS OF FRICTIONAL UNEMPLOYMENT

First, we look at the signs which would indicate that component rates of frictional unemployment have risen. Among the components—irregular, voluntary, seasonal, and business turnover—there are rough indicators for the latter three. The first, irregular, does not constitute a regular component of a frictional rise, by definition.

Voluntary Unemployment

An autonomous rise in the voluntary unemployment rate can come about if (1) voluntary labor mobility rises at every level of unemployment, and if (2) such job moves involve periods of unemployment no shorter than before the rise. The mobility involved could be between employers, industries, occupations, areas, or labor force statuses. High voluntary mobility might raise the unemployment level in periods of tight labor supply, but in a period of rapid change it might be a substitute for unemployment as workers who are able to make a successful shift from a declining industry or area leave working places behind them for less mobile workers. In this case, less over-all mobility could lead to higher unemployment rates.

One available measure of job mobility relates to moves within manufacturing and does not indicate whether unemployment is a concomitant part of the job change; this is the turnover rate for manufacturing establishments.[1] Turnover rates in manufacturing establishments are presented in Table 3. A declining trend has appeared, superimposed over a cyclical pattern of declines in trough years. The net accession rate (Column 5) is negative in 1949, 1953, 1954, 1957, 1958, and 1960. This includes the three upper and three lower turning points of the business cycle; it may indicate a one-year lead in the downturn compared with the unemployment rate.

The decline in turnover cannot be equated with a decline in mobility because it also reflects the employment trend in manufacturing. The data reflect the movement of people into and out of existing jobs in manufacturing, rather than the movement of people from job to job, or into and out of industries. They are not separated by occupation and thus reflect total employment in the industry rather than just blue-collar workers. The indicator for voluntary mobility would be the quit rate

[1] Turnover data are collected by the state agencies that participate in the Employer Survey of the BLS. It covers 223 manufacturing industries. The information comes from personnel records in reporting establishments and refers to the entire month. The tabulations are presented by industry, state, and area, as rates per 100 employees. The breakdowns used are: total accessions and new hires, total separations, quits, and lay-offs. The data refer to all employees including supervisory, managerial, part-time, and temporary workers. Beginning with January, 1959, transfers to another establishment within a company are included, making a break in the series. See Donald Dewey, "Labor Turnover as an Index of Unemployment in the United States, 1919–58," *The Journal of Industrial Economics*, LXVII, 4 (Nov., 1953), pp. 559–63; Lebergott, "Unemployment Statistics for Fiscal and Monetary Policy;" and *Measuring Employment and Unemployment*.

TABLE 3: Labor Turnover Rates of All Employees in Manufacturing Establishments, 1947–64

		(Rates per 100 employees)				(6)
Year	(1) Civilian unemployment rate	(2) Total accessions	(3) Total separations	(4) Quits	(5) Accessions less separations	Quits rate as percentage of separations rate
1947	3.9%	6.2	5.7	4.1	0.5	71.9%
1948	3.8	5.4	5.4	3.4	0.0	63.0
1949	5.9	4.3	5.0	1.9	(0.7)	38.0
1950	5.3	5.3	4.1	2.3	1.2	56.1
1951	3.3	5.3	5.3	2.9	0.0	54.7
1952	3.1	5.4	4.9	2.8	0.5	57.1
1953	2.9	4.8	5.1	2.8	(0.3)	54.9
1954	5.6	3.6	4.1	1.4	(0.5)	34.1
1955	4.4	4.5	3.9	1.9	0.6	48.7
1956	4.2	4.2	4.2	1.9	0.0	45.2
1957	4.3	3.6	4.2	1.6	(0.6)	38.1
1958	6.8	3.6	4.1	1.1	(0.5)	26.8
1959	5.5	4.2	4.1	1.5	0.1	36.6
1960	5.6	3.8	4.3	1.3	(0.5)	30.2
1961	6.7	4.1	4.0	1.2	0.1	30.0
1962	5.6	4.1	4.1	1.4	0.0	34.1
1963	5.7	3.9	3.9	1.4	0.0	35.9
1964	5.2	4.0	3.9	1.5	0.1	38.5

NOTE: Beginning in 1959, transfers between establishments of the same firm are included in total accessions and separations. Data for Alaska and Hawaii are included beginning 1959.
Parentheses indicate negative figures.

SOURCE: *Economic Report of the President, 1964*, p. 244, and *Survey of Current Business*, Aug., 1965.

(Column 4). (Those who are fired for misconduct might be added since these can be termed "voluntary" actions, but the data are not available.) The quit rate too shows both cyclical sensitivity and a secular decline.

To search for evidence of an autonomous change in voluntary mobility, therefore, we adjust for (1) labor demand in the manufacturing sector and (2) unemployment in the over-all economy. This is done by expressing the quit rate as a percentage of the total separation rate (Column 6). Next, figures in Column 6 are regressed against the civilian unemployment rate. The scatter of points from 1947 to 1963 yields a fairly straight line, except for the years 1947, 1948, and 1950. These years display a quit rate as a percentage of the separation rate far above later experiences, taking the level of over-all unemployment into account.

The coefficient of correlation was computed first for seventeen observations and then without the markedly different three years. In the first instance r is -0.80; in the second r is -0.94, both significant at the 1-percent probability level. Thus voluntary mobility in the form of quitting in manufacturing is a higher percentage of total separations when over-all unemployment is low. There has been a fairly close, inverse linear relationship between voluntary mobility in manufacturing and over-all demand in the postwar period.

Deviations of actual observations that are systematically different in sign from the computed values would indicate an underlying change in the relationship. That is, all positive deviations in one continuous time period and all negative deviations in the other would suggest an autonomous shift. The deviations of the actual from the observed x_1's were computed for the years 1951 to 1963, using the equation based on the fourteen observations: $x_1 = 77.17 - 7.41\ x_2$, where x_1 is the quit rate as a percentage of the total separation rate and x_2 is the civilian unemployment rate. The signs of the deviations are randomly mixed. Only one deviation is beyond two standard errors of estimate, 1957, when actual quits as a percentage of separations were lower than expected. The equation predicts the figure for 1964 within 0.1 point. The years 1947, 1948, and 1950, therefore, may reflect an earlier, higher level of voluntary mobility rates in manufacturing, but there is no evidence of any autonomous change since 1951.

The behavior of the quit rate may reflect two opposing tendencies. First, declines may be related to the aging of the blue-collar work force as total accessions drop. Since quit rates are higher among younger workers, this factor, added to the decline in blue-collar jobs, would tend to lower the quit rate. On the other hand, the increase in jobs for white-collar workers in manufacturing would help to lower the age of the work force and tend to raise the quit rate as young clerical, technical, and professional workers move from job to job.

Scant data exist about aggregate voluntary job mobility.[2] The two years for which comparable studies have been made (1955 and 1961) represent noncomparable levels of economic activity. The former year was a relatively high employment year, while the latter was a recession year. No generalization can then be made about any secular change. In 1955, voluntary job changing was shown to be "a relatively minor factor in

---

[2] See: U.S., Bureau of Labor Statistics, *The Extent and Nature of Frictional Unemployment*, Study Paper No. 6, Study of Employment, Growth, and Price Levels, Joint Economic Committee, 86th Cong., 1st Sess. (Washington: U.S. Government Printing Office, Nov. 19, 1959); Gertrude Bancroft and Stuart Garfinkle (BLS), "Job Mobility in 1961," *Special Labor Force Report*, No. 35, Aug., 1963; Robert L. Stein (BLS), "Unemployment and Job Mobility," *Special Labor Force Report*, No. 3, April, 1960; and BLS Bulletins: No. 1359, *Private Pension Plans and Manpower Policy*, May, 1963, and No. 1407, *Labor Mobility and Private Pension Plans*, June, 1964.

unemployment [and job shifting] . . . was more likely to be an effect of unemployment rather than a cause." [3] Because jobs had become tighter since, there is no reason to expect rising voluntary unemployment caused by mobility increases.

According to the BLS, 1955 voluntary unemployment was estimated to be about 10 percent of total unemployment.[4] This would place it at about 0.4 percent of the labor force in 1955. From 1955 to the recession year of 1961 voluntary causes of job shifts declined in every age-sex group except men over sixty-five years.[5] Thus it is safe to infer that voluntary mobility has not contributed to higher unemployment rates. But the lubricating effect of such mobility may also have diminished; this will be examined in greater detail in a discussion of structural unemployment. A BLS study, however, makes the point that "despite the apparent low mobility of workers in some depressed areas and industries, there is probably no widespread reluctance of workers to change jobs where good jobs are available." [6]

Seasonal Unemployment

The average annual rate of unemployment is an average of twelve monthly observations; thus high seasonal components in monthly unemployment will raise the average rate. But a seasonal decline in the demand for workers does not necessarily result in an increase in unemployment. Many of the fluctuations in agriculture and trade are taken up by unpaid family workers, summer workers, students, and housewives who leave the labor force during slack periods. Some temporary part-time peak demand can also be taken up by multiple job holding.

Increased aggregate seasonality could be based as much on a major shift toward very seasonal industries as on deepening seasonality in specific industries. On a priori grounds the shift from goods such as agriculture and construction to services such as trade and recreation might be offsetting.

The BLS measured the seasonal component in total unemployment for 1957 and 1960;[7] therefore the results indicate only whether there was a rise in this part of frictional unemployment over the three years. Each monthly seasonal factor in unemployment for major industrial groupings

---

[3] *The Extent and Nature of Frictional Unemployment*, p. 50.

[4] *Ibid.*, p. 39.

[5] BLS Bulletin No. 1359, p. 11.

[6] *Ibid.*, p. 1.

[7] *Unemployment: Terminology, Measurement, and Analysis*, and *The Extent and Nature of Frictional Unemployment*.

and for inexperienced workers was calculated, using the BLS's seasonal adjustment technique. The month with the lowest seasonal factor in each series was assumed to have zero seasonal unemployment. Deviations from this factor in the other months were counted as seasonal unemployment. The seasonally unemployed in each month for each series were added to arrive at a month's total of seasonal unemployment. The twelve-month average of these was the aggregate annual average.[8]

In 1957 the seasonal component was about 26 percent of the unemployed.[9] With an unemployment rate of 4.3 percent, the seasonal unemployment rate would be 1.1 percent of the labor force. In 1960 the seasonally unemployed were 21 percent of the unemployed.[10] With an unemployment rate of 5.6 percent, the seasonal unemployment rate would be 1.2 percent of the labor force. The difference from 1957 to 1960 was thus no more than 0.1 percent—practically nil. At least between 1957 and 1960 seasonal unemployment did not show an autonomous rise.

Business Turnover Unemployment

The number of businesses in a community can remain constant when either new businesses are equal in number to those which are discontinued or when there is no change in the businesses in existence. In the former case frictional unemployment may result from the movement of workers from old to new businesses; in the latter case no frictional unemployment would result, for there would be no business turnover. Thus, all things being equal, especially size of firm, the larger the number of businesses discontinued and replaced, the higher the rate of frictional unemployment.[11]

Table 4 presents a rough measure of the phenomenon to be examined. It presents a count of new and discontinued businesses without regard to employment size but excludes firms in agriculture and those supplying professional services. Agricultural new businesses have been declining, presumably, while the latter have been increasing. If it is assumed that size is held constant, the new-to-old ratio must be at least unity for pure

[8] The figures are considered conservative. They assume zero seasonal unemployment in one month, whereas there may be a seasonal component in every month, and the categories are so broad as to probably wash out compensating fluctuations in the components.

[9] *The Extent and Nature of Frictional Unemployment*, p. 52.

[10] *Unemployment: Terminology, Measurement, and Analysis*, p. 82.

[11] Business turnover could result in structural unemployment, but the displaced would have to be unqualified for openings in the new firms; however, structural unemployment is also compatible with zero business turnover. On the other hand, if new businesses could not provide as many jobs as were in the old businesses, the culprit would be inadequate demand, with or without structural unemployment.

TABLE 4: New and Discontinued Businesses, Annual Totals, 1947–62

Year	(1) New businesses (thousands)	(2) Discontinued businesses (thousands)	(3) Ratio of new to discontinued	(4) Net business increase (thousands)
1947	461	239	1.9	222
1948	393	282	1.4	111
1949	331	306	1.1	25
1950	348	290	1.2	58
1951	327	276	1.2	51
1952	346	276	1.3	70
1953	352	299	1.2	53
1954	366	319	1.1	47
1955	408	314	1.3	94
1956	431	342	1.3	89
1957	398	335	1.2	63
1958	397	347	1.1	50
1959	422	346	1.2	76
1960	438	384	1.1	54
1961	431	389	1.1	42
1962	430	387	1.1	43

NOTE: Excluded are firms in the fields of agriculture and professional services. Self-employed persons are included only when they have an established place of business or at least one paid employee.

SOURCE: *Economic Report of the President, 1964*, p. 289.

frictional turnover to occur; the ratio of the new to the old will vary over the cycle. The test for an autonomous rise in frictional unemployment, then, has as a necessary condition that the number of discontinued businesses rise, holding the ratio of new-to-old constant and at least equal to unity.

The data in Table 4 cannot be conclusive because (1) there is no adjustment for business size, so that the number of workers affected cannot be measured; (2) we do not know whether workers displaced from discontinued businesses are qualified to enter the new businesses; and (3) we do not know whether inclusion of agricultural firms and professional services would change the results. The data show a secular increase in both new and discontinued businesses, as is to be expected in a growing economy. The ratio of new-to-old shows a cyclical sensitivity; years of similar ratios show a rise in business turnover without any gains in the rate of net business formation.

The recession ratio 1.1, of new to discontinued businesses (Column 3), appears in each trough year but also appears in 1960 and 1962; yet real output grew in these two years. This suggests greater capacity in the remaining businesses. Both new and discontinued businesses increased in number over the four observations of 1.1 in 1949, 1954, 1958, and 1960, but net businesses declined from 1960 levels in 1961 and 1962. There is a spurt in net business formation in 1955 and 1956 as well as a rise in turnover, while a decline in net, but not gross, turnover appears after 1959. Since we know neither the skill requirements involved nor the number of workers, the only conclusion which can be made is that some rise in frictional unemployment may have occurred due to business turnover since the mid-1950's but this may easily have been structural rather than frictional.

When the conclusions regarding the frictional components of unemployment are combined, there is evidence of a possible rise in business turnover unemployment balanced by a probable decline in voluntary unemployment, and no more than a 0.1-percent rise in seasonal unemployment between 1957 and 1960. There is therefore no justification for the argument that the frictional level of unemployment at full employment has risen.

FRICTIONAL UNEMPLOYMENT MEASURED BY DURATION

By its very nature frictional unemployment is brief. Therefore, one might equate short-term unemployment, say, five weeks total duration, with frictional unemployment. However, the data presented in the Household Survey enumerate the unemployed by currently accumulated time of unemployment and not by length of completed spells. Some of those reported will be continued into longer unemployment and these must be separated out.

Stein and Kellogg were able to isolate persons whose unemployment in any one month was less than five weeks in duration and not continued into the following month.[12] This is because the Household Survey follows 75 percent of its respondents into at least a second month for interviewing. The short-term unemployed thus isolated can be considered to be frictionally unemployed if one also assumes that the spells were terminated by employment rather than by departure from the labor force. The group is probably not totally inclusive, however, because five weeks is an arbitrary cut-off period and frictional unemployment may last somewhat longer. In Table 5 the group isolated by Stein and Kellogg is shown as a percentage of the civilian labor force, in Column 2.

Columns 1 and 2 indicate that the short-term unemployment rate is higher in cyclical low periods and reflects the influence of over-all business

[12] *Unemployment: Terminology, Measurement, and Analysis*, p. 96.

TABLE 5: Ratio of the Short-Term Unemployment Rate to the Aggregate Unemployment Rate, 1948–61

Year	(1) Civilian unemployment rate	(2) Short-term unemployment rate[a]	(3) Ratio of short-term rate to total rate (2) ÷ (1)
1948	3.8%	1.6%	0.42
1949	5.9	1.9	0.32
1950	5.3	1.6	0.30
1951	3.3	1.5	0.45
1952	3.1	1.5	0.48
1953	2.9	1.4	0.48
1954	5.6	1.7	0.30
1955	4.4	1.5	0.34
1956	4.2	1.6	0.38
1957	4.3	1.5	0.35
1958	6.8	1.8	0.26
1959	5.5	1.6	0.29
1960	5.6	1.7	0.30
1961	6.7	1.8[b]	0.27

[a] Number with cumulative unemployment less than five weeks in a given month who were not continued in unemployment in the next month—as a percentage of the civilian labor force.
[b] First half data, seasonally adjusted.

SOURCE: U.S., Congress, Joint Economic Committee, Subcommittee on Economics Statistics, *Unemployment: Terminology, Measurement, and Analysis*, 87th Cong., 1st Sess. (Washington: U.S. Government Printing Office, 1961), p. 96, and *Manpower Report of the President, 1964*, p. 195.

conditions; however, the ratio of the short-term rate to the over-all unemployment rate (Column 3) behaves differently from the short-term rate itself. The peak year ratios are higher than those in cycle troughs. Observed frictional unemployment thus supports the a priori expectation that it is relatively more important at cyclical peaks even though it declines as an absolute rate. At peaks, voluntary unemployment and an influx of new entrants increase as the cyclical component declines.

Has the ratio of the short to the over-all rate risen autonomously over time when account is taken of the trend in the over-all rate? To answer this question Column 3 was regressed against Column 1. The r obtained is -0.95, significant at the 1-percent probability level. The deviations of the actual from the estimated ratios were computed using the equation $x_1 = 0.6266 - 0.0569\, x_2$, where x_1 is the ratio of the short-term rate to the over-all rate and x_2 is the over-all rate. The evidence suggests, if anything, a decline rather than a rise in the frictional rate. With a standard error of 0.022, only one year falls outside 2 standard errors, the year 1955, when the frictional ratio was below the expected. Counting all the observations from 1948 to 1954, five out of seven are under-estimates, while from 1955 to 1961 five out of seven are over-estimates. This suggests a decline in the frictional rate from 1955, independent of the over-all rate. The evidence is not strong but it does raise the possibility that structural problems may have affected the switch from short- to long-term unemployment, over and above the effects of inadequate demand.

The BLS, investigating the relative contributions of longer duration and numbers of new spells to the higher unemployment rates, indicates that between 1948 and 1956 there "was no increase in the rate at which new spells of unemployment were being generated."[13] In other words, the difference between the 1948 and 1956 rates was due to an increase in duration; thus, if one assumed little or no increase in demand-deficiency unemployment between 1948 and 1956, a rise of 0.4 percent in the over-all unemployment rate could be considered the effect of structural causes.[14]

The over-all unemployment rate rose by 1.4 percent of the labor force between 1956 and 1960. The BLS estimates that two-fifths of that rise was due to longer duration and three-fifths due to more spells of unemployment.[15] If Table 5 is used as a basis, only 0.1 of this can be attributed to frictional unemployment; however, it cannot be assumed that the longer duration unemployment was totally attributable to structural unemployment, nor structural totally excluded from the increased spells. Nonetheless, on this premise new structural unemployment between 1948 and 1960 would claim 1.0 percent of the labor force and new inadequate demand would account for 0.7 percent.

CHANGES IN THE COMPOSITION OF THE LABOR FORCE

Another source of frictional unemployment, as indicated in Chapter 1, is a sharp change in the composition of the labor force. Presumably such a change would independently raise the aggregate rate if the component rates were constant but there were a shift in favor of age-sex-color components which have higher rates. This approach implies that the unemployment rates of component groups are independent of the groups' relative sizes and that the relative sizes of the groups are independent of their unemployment rates. In other words, the reasons for unemployment adhere to the age-sex-color characteristics of individuals.

The idea that the unemployment rate of a group is independent of the demand and supply balances with respect to labor skills probably comes

[13] *Ibid.*, p. 70.

[14] This says nothing about the 3.8-percent unemployment existing in 1948. At least 1.6 percent was due to unemployment terminated before five weeks. But frictional unemployment can be of longer duration.

[15] *Unemployment: Terminology, Measurement, and Analysis*, p. 80.

from the view that labor force changes arise primarily from demographic sources. But participation rates are certainly more flexible. There is no reason to believe that participation will not respond to demographic changes as well as to demand changes. As Table 6 indicates, over-all demographic factors affecting labor force size can be easily offset by the labor force participation rate. In past recession years, 1948–49, 1953–54, 1957–58, and 1960–61, the civilian population fourteen years and over grew by 0.9, 1.2, 1.4, and 2.0 percent, respectively. Participation rates changed 0.1, −0.1, −0.3, and −0.3 percentage points in the corresponding years. As a result the civilian labor force grew 1.1, 1.0, 1.0, and 1.4 percent—a much more stable response to recession conditions.

A method called "standardizing" is used to separate the effects of changes in labor force composition on the aggregate rate from changes in the component unemployment rates themselves. The method applies the proportions of a base year to the actual rates of the year in question to see the difference in the resulting over-all rate. For the period 1948–56 the BLS found that "changes in the age-sex, industrial and occupational composition of the labor force had no significant impact on the over-all rate

TABLE 6: Changes in the Civilian Noninstitutional Population, the Civilian Labor Force, and the Civilian Labor Force Participation Rate, 1947–48 to 1963–64

Year	Noninstitutional civilians 14 years and over	Civilian labor force	Civilian labor force participation rate
	Percentage change		Point change
1947–48	1.1	2.1	0.5
1948–49	0.9	1.1	0.1
1949–50	1.0	1.6	0.3
1950–51	(0.3)	(0.3)	0.0
1951–52	0.6	0.1	(0.3)
1952–53	1.7	1.3	(0.2)
1953–54	1.2	1.0	(0.1)
1954–55	1.3	2.1	0.5
1955–56	1.3	2.6	0.7
1956–57	1.5	0.6	(0.5)
1957–58	1.4	1.0	(0.3)
1958–59	1.3	1.1	(0.1)
1959–60	1.7	1.8	0.1
1960–61	2.0	1.4	(0.3)
1961–62	1.6	0.4	(0.7)
1962–63	1.7	1.4	(0.1)
1963–64	1.6	1.1	0.1

NOTE: Parentheses indicate negative figures.
SOURCE: Derived from *Economic Report of the President, 1965*, p. 214.

of unemployment or on the average duration of employment."[16] Other evidence discussed by Raymond Bowman and Margaret Martin indicates that between 1957 and 1960 changed age-sex composition accounts for less than two-tenths of a percentage point rate increase.[17] Beyond this, Jane Meredith states that changes in the composition of the labor force would also not contribute to longer duration unemployment. The shift has been "in favor of groups with relatively few long-term unemployed, offsetting even the small effect of labor force growth in the uptrend."[18] Labor force growth itself "has been an almost negligible factor in explaining the uptrend in long-term joblessness. [Assuming] no change in long-term unemployment as a percent of the labor force, even very large increases in the labor force would add only a small number of persons to the long-term unemployed."[19]

We tested the effects of a changed sex composition in the labor force from 1948 through 1962, with 1960 as the base. Female unemployment rates are generally higher than male, and male participation rates have declined in favor of female. If the sex composition of the civilian labor force were determined by the same participation rates as those in 1960 for every year, keeping the civilian population figures and the male and female unemployment rates unchanged, would the aggregate unemployment rate have been different? The answer is *no* for each year except 1951 and 1953. But in both cases the higher female participation rates in 1960 would have added only 0.1 point to the aggregate rate of unemployment. The effect of having fewer males in the labor force because of lower participation yielded fewer male unemployed. The effect of a higher female participation rate was more female unemployed. But the absolute differences canceled each other, even though the rate changes and accelerations have been different.

The Heller Report, mentioned earlier, tested for the effects on the over-all unemployment rate of changes in labor force proportions by sex, age, education, occupation, and color. Their test is applicable in this framework for investigating a rise in frictional rather than structural unemployment.[20] Group unemployment rates for 1953 were applied to the actual 1960 labor force, and the 1960 specific group unemployment rates were applied to the 1953 labor force. It was found that between the

---

[16] *Ibid.*, p. 70.

[17] Bowman and Martin, "Special Report on Unemployment Statistics," p. 20.

[18] Jane L. Meredith (BLS), "Long-Term Unemployment in the United States," *Special Labor Force Report*, No. 17, June, 1961, p. 603.

[19] *Ibid.*

[20] The tests covered the periods 1957–60 and 1953–60. The shorter period is too late to show possible autonomous rises which may have occurred earlier. We refer mainly to the results using the 1953–60 period.

second quarter of 1953 and the second quarter of 1960, from 12 to 22 percent of the increased unemployment was due to changes in age and sex, color and sex, occupation and sex, or industry and sex.[21] The results, rather than refuting the importance of structural unemployment, have helped to show that there has not been a significant autonomous rise in frictional unemployment.

CONCLUSIONS

The evidence presented in this chapter substantially denies the possibility that the rise in unemployment rates since the mid-1950's was due to an autonomous rise in the frictional rate. The alternative is that the rise was due to some combination of long-run inadequacy in demand and changes in labor requirements to which the labor force was unable to adjust. The remainder of this study examines the alternatives.

[21] Council of Economic Advisers, *January 1961 Economic Report*, pp. 379, 387–88.

CHAPTER 4

STRUCTURAL CHANGE

This chapter investigates two questions. The first is whether the post-war period shows evidence of structural changes that could have been the basis for a rise in the rate of structural unemployment. The structural changes considered are (1) technological change, (2) shifts in the composition of output, and (3) regional effects of industrial change. If these structural changes produced a shift in the labor skill mix, they would be a precondition for a rise in structural unemployment. The second question is whether the structural changes are related to the level of demand. If they are related, a rise in structural unemployment would be possible along with a rise in unemployment due to inadequate demand.

TECHNOLOGICAL CHANGE

Innovation usually is undertaken because it will save inputs of either labor or capital or both—at some expected level of output. When technological innovation occurs, it is embodied in capital equipment which becomes part of the fixed stock of plants and machines.[1] This capital equipment is a relatively long-lived factor of production which is combined directly or indirectly with labor. The innovation expressed in the equipment and plant requires a specific minimum skill level for its utilization in production. Thus, regardless of which factors are saved, a possible by-product of technological change is changes in the kinds of human skills required for the production of goods and services.

[1] Innovations such as Taylorism (efficiency improvements) may be considered as exceptions. However, such innovations move the firm to a level of efficiency which is usually taken for granted by the traditional concept of the production function used in economic analysis.

40

Productivity of Capital

Recent technological change appears to have altered the kinds of skills needed in production but may also have been capital-saving in real value terms. If this is true, it is possible not only that (1) there have been changes in the proportions and elasticities of substitution of labor skills required in production, but also that (2) the real dollar volume of capital stock required for output (and thus investment demand) was reduced. This section examines evidence to support this view.

Investment is necessary for the introduction of technological change, but it is not a sufficient sign of such change. Capital expansion is possible with given technology. On the other hand, net investment is not a prerequisite for technological change; replacement alone can be its vehicle. However, structural unemployment is more likely when a rapid change in technology takes place because it makes possible rapid shifts in labor proportions. Thus, a period of rapid capital growth could be the initiating period for structural change.

Technological change can raise the ratio of output to capital, but so can changes in output. Thus, we examine changes in the ratio of output to capital on the aggregate level by taking account of output changes. Change in the output-to-capital ratio at given rates of change of output is the phenomenon sought.

The period of heavy capital investment need not show an immediate improvement in the output-to-capital ratio. It may only provide for future realization of capital savings. This is because investment in new technology may be made ahead of demand or in a mistaken expectation of increases in demand. If this occurs, it is possible to find a jump in the output-to-capital ratio after the period of heavy investment. In the interim old stocks can be retired.

The impact of capital-saving innovation on demand comes through the effects on investment requirements subsequent to the initial installations of the new technology. The same level of output, all things being equal, would call for less capital. Thus the investment component of demand is depressed. [2] We look for evidence of this phenomenon by examining capital growth relative to output growth.

The period 1954–56 may have initiated a series of major technological changes. Columns 3 and 4 of Table 7, which refer to the new NID output series, show heavy capital investment. The effect on capital stock is not yet fully known, but the old series (Column 6) suggests a similar accelera-

---

[2] Moreover, if capital stocks embodying the new technology are not used at full capacity when installed, the pressure of output on further investment demand will be delayed.

TABLE 7: Percentage Changes in Real GNP, Components, Capital Stock, Employment, and Ratios of GNP to Inputs, 1947–48 to 1963–64

Year	Gross national product old[a] (1)	Gross national product new[b] (2)	Producer durables[b] (3)	Non residential structures[b] (4)	Change in ratio new equipment to new structures[b] (5)	Real capital stock[c] (6)	Employment[d] (7)	Change in Ratio of GNP to Capital stock[a c] (8)	Change in Ratio of GNP to Employment[b d] (9)
1947–48	3.8	4.5	4.5	6.0	(1.4)	4.5	2.0	(0.6)	2.4
1948–49	(0.1)	0.1	(12.1)	(3.3)	(9.1)	3.4	(0.9)	(3.3)	1.0
1949–50	8.7	9.6	9.7	6.7	2.6	3.9	2.3	4.5	7.2
1950–51	7.5	7.9	2.8	11.0	(7.2)	4.6	4.0	2.7	3.7
1951–52	3.4	3.1	(3.5)	(2.8)	(0.6)	3.8	1.2	(0.4)	1.9
1952–53	4.4	4.5	4.9	8.8	(3.9)	3.7	1.3	0.7	4.7
1953–54	(1.6)	(1.4)	(5.0)	2.0	(6.9)	3.4	(1.9)	(4.8)	(1.0)
1954–55	8.2	7.6	13.1	6.6	6.2	4.7	2.7	3.4	4.8
1955–56	2.1	1.8	4.0	14.2	(8.8)	5.0	2.4	(2.8)	(1.2)
1956–57	1.9	1.4	1.0	(1.6)	2.6	4.3	0.4	(2.3)	1.7
1957–58	(1.8)	(1.2)	(14.1)	(8.8)	(5.6)	2.2	(1.8)	(3.9)	0.6
1958–59	6.8	6.4	11.6	(2.4)	13.9	2.0	2.3	4.7	4.0
1959–60	2.6	2.5	6.1	7.4	(1.2)	1.4	1.6	1.4	0.9
1960–61	1.8	1.9	(5.1)	0.0	(5.3)	1.0	0.3	0.8	1.7
1961–62	6.4	6.6	12.8	2.9	9.9	1.6	1.9	4.5	4.6
1962–63	3.4	3.8	6.6	0.6	6.2	1.4	1.2	2.0	2.5
1963–64	—	5.0	13.3	5.0	8.0	—	2.2	—	2.8

[a] Real values based on constant 1954 dollars, old NID series.
[b] Real values based on constant 1958 dollars, revised NID series.
[c] Gross fixed business capital in 1954 billions at year end, based on Bulletin F lives, using old NID investment series.
[d] Based on Household Survey (new definitions), but including the Armed Forces.
Parentheses indicate negative figures.
SOURCE: Derived from U.S., Department of Commerce, Office of Business Economics, *Survey of Current Business*, Aug., 1965, p. 27; Nov., 1964, p. 30 and correspondence; and *Economic Report of the President, 1965*, p. 214.

tion in the accumulation of capital.[3] In addition, investment in equipment rose sharply relative to investment in plant in 1954–55 (see Column 5).

Private industry was taxing capacity in 1955.[4] Most major manufacturing industries were operating at or above their preferred rates of capacity use, according to the McGraw-Hill survey.[5] Only transportation equipment operated at more than 2 points below its preferred rate. This explains the major rise in real capital stock in 1954–56. However, demand

[3] Capital stock data are gross fixed business stocks in 1954 billions at year end, assuming capital stock service lives based on Bulletin F (1942 edition) of the Internal Revenue Service and before the revision of the NID series. The figures were calculated by the Office of Business Economics. Use of gross stock figures assumes that a unit of capital is capable of constant output levels until it is retired like the one-horse shay.

[4] For discussion of this period see: Bert G. Hickman, *Growth and Stability of the Postwar Economy* (Washington: The Brookings Institution, 1960); Charles L. Schultze, *Recent Inflation in the United States*, Study Paper No. 1, U.S., Joint Economic Committee on Employment, Growth, and Price Levels, 86th Cong., 1st Sess., Sept., 1959 (Washington: U.S. Government Printing Office, 1959).

[5] Hickman, *Growth and Stability*, p. 130.

was disappointing after 1955. Between 1955 and 1957, ferrous and nonferrous metals, motor vehicles, rubber products, and textiles all experienced drops in output. In 1956 only producer goods industries such as iron and steel, nonferrous metals, paper and pulp, stone-clay-and-glass, and petroleum refining were operating above preferred capacity levels. By 1957 none of fifteen major manufacturing industry groups was operating at preferred rates, and most were 10 or more points below preferred rates. [6]

The old GNP and capital stock series indicate that in 1955–56, 1956–57, and 1957–58 the output-to-capital ratio fell but then rose continuously through 1963. This suggests that the benefits of the new equipment installed between 1955 and 1957 were realized only as old equipment no longer needed was retired, especially since demand had not risen sufficiently to utilize the new capacity.

The 1958 recession seems to have provided an opportunity for producers to "firm up" output-to-capital ratios by allowing the retirement of obsolete equipment and by introducing cost-cutting savings without much retaliation from labor or competitors. Supporting evidence lies in the fact that of the fifteen manufacturing industries mentioned above, eight reported improved capacity rates in 1958 over 1957. These included iron and steel, nonferrous metals, electrical machinery, motor vehicles, stone-clay-and-glass, food and beverages, textiles, and miscellaneous manufactures. None, of course, was operating at preferred rates. [7]

The impact of technological change was tested by using rough, aggregate data. [8] The relevant figures are presented in Table 7, Columns 1, 6,

[6] *Ibid.*
[7] *Ibid.*
[8] The results discussed below can be considered only indicative for two major reasons. First, capital stock data, even for the aggregate economy, are still in a primitive stage of development. Second, these data do not incorporate the effects of changes in the new investment components of GNP. Not only is capacity difficult to measure, but estimating service lives of stocks is a difficult task. The data used here are based on the Internal Revenue Service's Bulletin F life estimates. These are longer than those currently used for depreciation purposes and minimize the output-to-capital ratio and any effects on the ratio of shorter service lives associated with accelerated obsolescence. Another problem is that government capital stocks are not represented in the gross stock figures, while government product should not necessarily be deducted from gross output figures. The calculations used here divide gross national product in 1954 dollars (old NID series) by gross private business stocks in 1954 dollars. For a description of the stock data, the conceptual problems and other measures, see George Jaszi, Robert C. Wasson, and Lawrence Grose, "Expansion of Fixed Business Capital in the United States," *Survey of Current Business*, Nov. 1962, pp. 9–18, 28. Changes in the GNP and investment series had not yet been used to recompute the gross capital stock series at the time this book went to press. The changes, however, should affect both GNP and gross investment in the same direction. Whether the effects on the rate of change of the output-to-capital ratio relative to the rate of change of output have been offsetting is not yet known. For a discussion of conceptual changes in the investment series see *Survey of Current Business*, Aug., 1965, pp. 12–13.

and 8. Percentage changes in the output-to-capital ratio (Column 8) were regressed against percentage changes in real output (Column 1) in order to explore the relationship of the two variables and seek evidence of a structural shift. Theoretically, in the short run, the relationship should be close. Since stocks are given, the productivity of capital should increase with output until capacity is taxed. Evidence of a technological change would come through a shift in the relationship, providing there was not a gradual, smooth transfer between technologies.

The scatter of 16 points, 1947–48 to 1962–63, shows two distinct, almost straight lines. These are clearly separate time intervals, one from 1947–48 to 1957–58 (eleven observations), and the other from 1958–59 to 1962–63 (five observations). For the entire sixteen observations a co-efficient of correlation of 0.87 is obtained, significant at the 1-percent probability level. When the periods are separated, the coefficients are 0.98 for the eleven observations and 0.996 for the five observations (both significant at the 1-percent level). The adjusted coefficients are 0.86, 0.98, and 0.994, respectively. Separating the periods has improved the coefficients. [9]

The slopes of the lines are almost the same, so that an upward shift is apparent in the "capital productivity" function. This is supported by the fact that the difference between the two constants in the equations is statistically significant at the 1-percent probability level.

Thus, there is some evidence that capital productivity has been improved by technological change over and above changes in output. Therefore there is reason to believe that capital equipment may have been altered enough to affect labor skill requirements and that capital requirements may have been altered enough to affect demand.

This latter possibility is tested by regressing percentage changes in capital stock (Table 7, Column 6) against percentage changes in output (Column 1). The coefficient of correlation for the entire sixteen observations is 0.20, not significant at the 0.05 probability level. The adjusted coefficient also shows no significant difference from zero. For 1947–48 to 1957–58 the coefficient is 0.61 (0.55 adjusted), significant at the 5-percent probability level. The coefficient of correlation for 1958–59 to 1962–63 is 0.90 (0.86 adjusted), significant at the 0.05 level. There is clearly an improvement in the correlation from separating the two periods. As before, there is no appreciable difference in the slopes of the two lines, but

---

[9] The regression line for the period 1947–48 to 1957–58 is: $x_1 = -3.38 + 0.83 x_2$, where x_1 refers to changes in output-to-capital, and x_2 refers to changes in output. In the period 1958–59 to 1962–63 the line is $x_1 = -0.66 + 0.80 x_2$. Thus, output had to rise about 5 percent in the earlier period for capital productivity to rise 1 percent; more recently, only a 2 percent rise was required.

the difference in the constant term is statistically significant at the 0.01 level.[10]

For the early period changes in output explain less than half the changes in capital stock. This relative looseness is explained by the theoretical distinction between induced and autonomous investment, such that the latter moves independently of output. The only deviation as large as two standard errors comes in 1955–56, when the capital stock increased 1.2 percent more than expected from the regression equation. Moreover, the changes 1953–54 through 1956–57 all are above the expected rates of increase of capital stock. This supports the view that technological innovation was occurring. The data not only suggest a downward shift in the relationship of capital growth to output growth, but the higher coefficient of correlation in the later period suggests that capital growth is now more responsive to output growth.

Part of the explanation of this marked change in capital productivity comes from the flexibility of the new techniques. Many people think of automation in terms of Detroit automobile production. They associate it with massive operations and continuous, round-the-clock operation. "Detroit" automation uses techniques involving the repetition of a sequence of operations which is self-stopping, uses computerized data, and is geared to long production runs and large firms. Changes are costly. But there are numerically controlled machine tools which can be geared to short production runs. Control tapes are used which can be cheaply prepared for runs as small as 100 units.[11] In addition, the application of electronic devices has made it possible for decision-making about investment, inventory control, and innovation to be handled by the machines themselves.[12]

From 1947–48 to 1956–57 the ratio of new equipment to new plant investment fell by an average of 2.7 percent per year. But from 1957–58 to 1963–64 this ratio *grew* by an average of 3.7 percent per year.[13] It is

[10] The regression equation for 1947–48 to 1957–58 is: $x_1 = 3.52 + 0.13\, x_2$. (x_1 refers to changes in capital stock; x_2 represents output changes.) The equation for the later period is $x_1 = 0.88 + 0.14\, x_2$.

[11] Yale Brozen, *Automation, The Impact of Technological Change* (Washington: American Enterprise Institute for Public Policy Research, March, 1963), p. 35. As a case in point, an ad in the November issue of *Fortune*, 1958, ran as follows: "Flexible automation? The term sounds contradictory. A short time ago it would have been. But Clearing's concept of *flexible* automation out-dates previous thinking that automation necessarily confines production to tremendously long runs—a large investment in single-purpose equipment. . . . Many different parts can be produced on a line such as this. Change-over is quick. . . ."

[12] Herbert Striner, "Prepared Statement Before the Senate Subcommittee on Employment and Manpower, May 23, 1963," (Mimeo.; released by the W. E. Upjohn Institute for Employment Research), pp. 2–4.

[13] See Table 7, Column 5.

reasonable to deduce that the increase in the ratio of equipment to plant permits a more flexible use of capital. This suggests less cyclical vulnerability in the labor-to-output and capital-to-output ratios and also more sensitivity of investment to demand growth. The higher correlation coefficients in the post-1958 series bears this out.

About half of all capital spending in manufacturing in 1957 was for modernization or replacement, rather than expansion. By 1959–60, about two-thirds went for modernization or replacement. Knowles and Kalacheck cite this point to show the inadequacy of over-all demand. [14] However, it actually may indicate that technological change made it possible to expand capacity through replacement outlays. Not only were the technological changes a vehicle for changing labor skill requirements and proportions, but a structurally induced decline in the demand for capital relative to output may have been a major result. [15]

Productivity of Labor

There has been much discussion of the role of technological change in connection with structural unemployment, but confusion arises when growth in labor productivity is identified with technological change. Labor productivity can increase as demand increases without a change in technology, particularly where indirect (overhead) labor is involved. If labor is displaced as productivity rises more rapidly than demand, structural unemployment could result, but only if the skills of the displaced could not be utilized when demand subsequently increased.

On the other hand, aggregate labor productivity need not accelerate when one set of skills is substituted for another. Structural unemployment can occur without marked increases in labor productivity. This is especially true if technical change is capital-saving with respect to output. On an industry level, however, increases in labor productivity accompanied by decreases in output signal technological displacement, if not structural unemployment, since the normal relationship would go the other way. Where output grows and labor productivity grows faster with a fall in employment, the precondition for structural unemployment may also exist. In both cases inter-industry adjustments are required.

[14] *Higher Unemployment Rates*, p. 45.

[15] After this chapter was written a major study by Bert G. Hickman appeared, *Investment Demand and U.S. Economic Growth* (Washington: The Brookings Institution, 1965). It concluded that a decline in business fixed capital investment demand played a key role in the persistent economic slack during 1957–63 (p. 3), that "the real business fixed investment share would have fallen steadily during 1956–63 even if actual GNP had equaled potential throughout the period" (p. 9), and that "the strongest and most pervasive source of declining unit capital requirements is technical change" (p. 10).

Both aggregate and industrial changes in labor productivity are examined in this section.

Private sector output and manhours are normally the aggregate variables chosen for measuring labor productivity. The output measure and the hours measure are not totally inclusive, since government employment and output are omitted. Use of manhours data has other limitations. Data used for comparisons, such as unemployment rates, refer to individuals; hours worked are not uniformly interchangeable with persons. For these reasons the aggregate data used here are the ratios of total real GNP in 1958 dollars (new NID series) to total employment based on the Household Survey but including the Armed Forces. This ratio is called "employed person productivity." It measures the yearly average amount of real output per employed person. A shift toward part-time employment can lower the ratio, therefore, without such a change being reflected in a ratio using manhours.[16]

The behavior of labor productivity is variable over the cycle. It usually increases at a decreasing rate near cyclical peaks as capacity is pushed beyond efficient levels and as less efficient firms and facilities are able to operate at a profit. Similarly, worker productivity rises most rapidly in the early phases of cyclical recoveries when overhead labor and capital are spread over a greater output and because the more efficient firms are earlier entrants in the upswing.[17]

When changes in employed person productivity (Table 7, Column 9) are regressed against changes in real output (Column 2), a correlation coefficient of 0.88 is obtained for the first sixteen observations, significant

[16] The reader may be interested in comparing the average annual rates of change for the postwar cycles of three measures of labor productivity. The first is output per employed person, the second and third are based on private manhours, but the second uses Household Survey data and the third primarily establishment data. All three series are based on output figures prior to the 1965 revisions of the NID output series. Sources for the latter two measures are found in the BLS leaflet, *Indexes of Output per Man-hour for the Private Economy, 1947–1964*, Jan. 29, 1965. Notice the effect of increases in part-time work in the third cycle on employed person productivity.

	Average Annual Rates of Productivity Change		
	Employed person	Household manhours	Establishment manhours
1948–53	3.5	4.4	3.8
1953–57	2.0	2.8	2.5
1957–60	1.8	2.4	2.7

[17] See Thor Hultgren, *Changes in Labor Cost During Cycles in Production and Business*, Occasional Paper 74, National Bureau of Economic Research, 1960; and Clarence D. Long, "The Illusion of Wage Rigidity," *The Review of Economics and Statistics*, XLII, 2 (May, 1960), pp. 140–151.

at the 0.01 level.[18] This is a lower coefficient of correlation than that obtained for capital productivity growth, probably because of the greater proportionality of labor inputs to output. The scatter of 16 points shows no shift in the relationship comparable to that of capital productivity.

The regression equation is $x_1 = 0.23 + 0.60 \, x_2$, where x_1 is the percentage change in productivity and x_2 the percentage change in output. The 1963–64 figure is accurately predicted within one-half a standard error. There is only one deviation greater than two standard errors. This comes in 1955–56 when the change in employed person productivity was 2.5 percent below the predicted change. In 1955–56 there was a major rise in the employment of overhead labor, a companion to the capital boom. Thus, investment both in human and nonhuman capital appeared to be "ahead of demand." The regression equation suggests that employed person productivity rises even at zero output change, but rises less than proportionately with output thereafter.

Employment changes are closely related to output changes. The correlation of employment changes (Column 7) with output changes yields an r of 0.84, significant at the 1-percent level. The regression equation, $X_e = -0.36 + 0.42 \, X_2$ suggests that employment falls at zero output change (because productivity rises). Again, no shift in the relationship is evident and the 1963–64 prediction is accurate within half a standard error. Deviation from the regression line beyond two standard errors again comes only in 1955–56, when employment rose 2 percent above the predicted rise. This supports the explanation for the under-achievement of productivity, that is, an increase in overhead labor of unusual proportions. A shortfall of employment in recession years and in the first recovery year seems to mark the entire period and suggests the well-known fact that manhour increases precede employment increases in recovery.

Using the old NID output series to regress changes in employed person productivity against changes in capital productivity, we again find a shift at the 1957–58 point. The resulting equations, which can be only indicative because of the underlying data, suggest that in the earlier period labor productivity growth outpaced capital productivity growth. This resulted in an increase in the capital-to-labor ratio, i.e., there had been an increase in capital relative to labor. Since 1958 it seems that the gains have been about the same for each. In the 1958–59 to 1963–64 period the rates of change of capital and labor productivity were nearly equal, and changes in aggregate factor proportions were neutral. Further implications with respect to income shares may be interesting to investigate.

---

[18] Correlating changes in the old NID output data with employed person productivity data gives similar results: $r = 0.84$.

There is no evidence of a major shift in the relation of changes in aggregate employed person productivity to output changes; structural unemployment would have to be attributed to technological change causing changes in skill proportions such as the decline in direct labor or because of sectoral dislocations.

A high, negative relationship between changes in the unemployment rate and changes in labor productivity would help support the demand position because it would mean that at high rates of productivity growth displacement is absorbed. Such is not the case.

The correlation between point changes in the civilian unemployment rate and Column 9 of Table 7 (1947–48 to 1962–63) yields an r of -0.66, significant at the 0.01 level; the 1963–64 prediction is accurate within half a standard error. This degree of correspondence, however, explains only 44 percent of the variance, and with a standard error of 1.0 in the unemployment rate, unemployment changes as large as 2 percent of the labor force remain unexplained.

One concludes that the aggregate evidence, crude though it is, supports the position that investment in the 1954–56 period was the vehicle for bunched technological changes. These may have produced major changes in the proportions of labor skill requirements rather than total labor inputs, and could have created a precondition for structural unemployment in the presence of inadequate demand.

Changes in Unit Job Requirements by Industry

An examination of labor requirements on a disaggregative basis is also in order, since over-all data do not reveal component changes. For example, the positive relationship of productivity changes and output on an aggregate level masks the introduction of new technology in declining industries or in firms where the motivation is not expansion of capacity but competitive cost savings.

Ewan Clague and Leon Greenberg examined labor displacement within manufacturing for the periods 1953–59 and 1947–57, and found evidence of technological displacement.[19] Their definition of technologically induced displacement cannot be considered a measure of structural unemployment, however, since no attempt was made to trace the reemployment experience of the displaced workers nor the experience of entering labor force members. In the framework of this study their test establishes a precondition for structural unemployment. This section applies the Clague-Greenberg definition of technological displacement to

[19] Ewan Clague and Leon Greenberg, "Technological Change and Employment," *Monthly Labor Review*, Vol. 85, No. 7 (July, 1962), pp. 742–46.

the nine broad industry groups of the entire economy. Evidence of technological displacement by industry would add support to the argument that technological change made possible an increase in structural unemployment.

Technological displacement is assumed to exist in an industry when labor requirements decrease, employment declines, and output increases or remains steady. It is also assumed to exist where output, employment, and labor requirements all decrease; the employment decline attributed to technology is that accounted for by the fall in labor requirements; the remainder is attributed to a decline in demand. When employment increases or labor requirements increase, no technological displacement is considered to have occurred. [20]

The Clague-Greenberg analysis referred to manhours; this study uses wage and salary jobs in nonagricultural industries and employed persons in farm occupations. [21] The output measures are gross product by industry (value added) in 1954 dollars. [22] The reciprocal of employed person productivity is called unit job requirements. This is equal to employment (as given in the industry series used) divided by industry gross

[20] The assumptions are extremely crude. It is difficult to generalize in the absence of specific industry and firm production functions. When the technique is applied to broad industry groupings it ignores changes in unit job requirements due to a changed composition of output in the industry.

[21] Nonagricultural employment is based on the BLS establishment series and excludes self-employed and unpaid family workers. The agricultural data is based on the Household Survey for agricultural occupations. Both series count both full- and part-time employees. Employment data for government include the Armed Forces.

[22] Gross product by industry is computed by the Office of Business Economics (OBE) in the Department of Commerce. The total of gross product by industry is equal to GNP less a small item attributed to "rest of the world" and a small residual. The real gross product data presented in this chapter are derived from published series. A revised series planned for publication by OBE in mid-1966 has not been made available to researchers prior to publication. However, OBE indicates the following differences in the two series:

1. The industry classification of the revised series will be based on the *1957 Standard Industrial Classification (SIC) Manual*. The changes from the former classification scheme result in an upward revision in the totals for manufacturing and services and a downward revision in the trade totals. In terms of rate changes, only trade is affected upward by these classification changes.

2. The conceptual revisions incorporated recently into the national income and product accounts principally affect the totals for finance, insurance, real estate, and services. The statistical revisions principally resulted in raising the totals and annual rates of change in physical output since 1960.

3. The introduction of new procedures to develop estimates of real gross product by industry will have varying effects upon specific industries. However, the totals mentioned below for service producers were not substantially revised. Those for goods producers will probably indicate smaller rates for 1953–57, while for 1957–60 they will only be marginally higher than for 1953–57. Procedural changes will also dampen the change rates for utilities.

product.[23] Unit job requirements and annual percentage changes in these requirements are presented in Table 8.

An initial surprise in the data comes from an examination of the job requirements of the various industries. Contrary to popular belief, and in spite of the large numbers of part-time workers in some of the service-producing industries, as late as 1963 the latter group did not generate more jobs per dollar of gross product than did the goods-producing industries.[24] There are wide variations, however. In 1948, about 207,000 jobs in the goods-producing sector were required to turn out a billion dollars of real gross product.[25] Only 163,000 jobs including Armed Forces employment were required for the same value of product in the service-producing sector. Despite the more rapid fall of unit job requirements in the goods sector, it just matched the service sector (including the Armed Forces) in 1963. Both sectors required 131,000 workers per billion dollars or real output. Thus, if technological displacement of goods workers is found, different skill requirements by industry would add to the problem of different absorption rates by industry.

The unit job requirements in government are the highest in the service sector,[26] but were not above those in agriculture until 1958. Not only are the skills used by the two not easily substitutable, but the loss in agricultural employment has been more rapid than the gain in government employment. (See Table 9.) Two of the service-producing industries with most rapid output growth were (1) transportation, communications, and public utilities (abbreviated to utilities) and (2) finance, insurance, and real estate (abbreviated to finance). (See Table 10.) But these were meager sources of jobs. The employment share of the first is actually declining, while the latter's share is still only a small part of total civilian employment. Trade, and the industry group called "service industries," are among the more highly job intensive service-producing industries. Both have been increasing their share of employment, but much of this has been in the form of part-time employment. Technological change can threaten further job gains in both. Trade has actually been declining in its share of real output, falling from 18.3 percent in 1948 to 17.6 percent in 1963.

[23] The employment series incorporate the 1957 changes in SIC definitions while the gross product data do not. This adds a further element of crudeness to the unit job requirements concept.

[24] Goods-producing industries are defined as agriculture, mining, manufacturing, and contract construction. The rest are service-producing. This discussion anticipates the effects of shifts in final demand which will be examined later in this chapter.

[25] Data in this paragraph are based on calculations using gross product and employment data by the two broad industry groupings, goods- and service-producers.

[26] Government real gross product is by definition equal to wage and salary costs plus the small addition of other components of value added in government enterprises.

TABLE 8: Unit Job Requirements by Industry, 1948–63

Year	Manu-fac-turing	Agri-cul-ture	Contr. con-struc-tion	Mining	Gov-ern-ment[a]	Utili-ties[b]	Trade	Fi-nance[c]	Serv-ice indus-tries
A. Thousand jobs per billion dollars of real output[d]									
1948	181	392	162	112	267	158	170	57	177
1949	176	407	158	118	268	158	169	54	178
1950	165	367	157	102	267	140	153	52	174
1951	161	365	153	96	273	131	159	51	178
1952	158	337	154	94	274	133	158	52	179
1953	157	305	153	87	275	131	156	54	176
1954	157	298	151	82	276	125	157	54	177
1955	145	293	151	75	272	112	149	53	175
1956	148	299	154	73	272	108	150	53	171
1957	146	282	152	74	275	105	150	51	171
1958	145	256	151	74	277	101	151	50	169
1959	137	257	152	69	278	93	144	50	167
1960	138	237	152	66	278	89	147	49	165
1961	134	227	151	61	280	84	145	48	164
1962	126	213	155	58	274	79	140	47	164
1963	123	196	157	55	273	75	137	46	164
B. Percentage changes									
1948–49	(2.8)	3.8	(2.5)	5.4	0.4	0.0	(0.6)	(5.3)	0.6
1949–50	(6.2)	(9.8)	(0.6)	(13.6)	(0.4)	(11.4)	(9.5)	(3.7)	(2.2)
1950–51	(2.4)	(0.5)	(2.5)	(5.9)	2.2	(6.4)	3.9	(1.9)	2.3
1951–52	(1.9)	(7.7)	0.7	(2.1)	0.4	1.5	(0.6)	2.0	0.6
1952–53	(0.6)	(9.5)	(0.7)	(7.4)	0.4	(1.5)	(1.3)	3.8	(1.7)
1953–54	0.0	(2.3)	(1.3)	(5.7)	0.4	(4.6)	0.6	0.0	0.6
1954–55	(7.6)	(1.7)	0.0	(8.5)	(1.4)	(10.4)	(5.1)	(1.9)	(1.1)
1955–56	2.1	2.0	2.0	(2.7)	0.0	(3.6)	0.7	0.0	(2.3)
1956–57	(1.4)	(5.7)	(1.3)	1.4	1.1	(2.8)	0.0	(3.8)	0.0
1957–58	(0.7)	(9.2)	(0.7)	0.0	0.7	(3.8)	0.7	(2.0)	(1.2)
1958–59	(5.5)	0.4	0.7	(6.8)	0.4	(7.9)	(4.6)	0.0	(1.2)
1959–60	0.7	(7.8)	0.0	(4.3)	0.0	(4.3)	2.1	(2.0)	(1.2)
1960–61	(2.9)	(4.2)	(0.7)	(7.6)	0.7	(5.6)	(1.4)	(2.0)	(0.6)
1961–62	(6.0)	(6.2)	2.6	(4.9)	(2.1)	(6.0)	(3.4)	(2.1)	0.0
1962–63	(2.4)	(8.0)	1.3	(5.2)	(0.4)	(5.1)	(2.1)	(2.1)	0.0

NOTE: See Chapter 4, n. 21–23.

[a] Includes members of the Armed Forces.

[b] Transportation, communications, and public utilities.

[c] Finance, insurance, and real estate.

[d] Real gross product (value added) by industry in 1954 dollars is denominator; wage and salary employees in nonfarm establishments or farm occupations in agriculture is numerator.

Parentheses indicate negative figures.

SOURCE: Derived from *Manpower Report of the President, 1965*, pp. 202, 233, 258.

TABLE 9: Distribution and Percentage Changes of Employment by Industry, 1948–64

Year	Manu-fac-turing	Agri-cul-ture	Contr. con-struc-tion	Mining	Gov-ern-ment[a]	Utili-ties	Trade	Fi-nance	Serv-ice indus-tries
A. Percentage distribution of employment[a][b]									
1948	29.5	14.9	4.1	1.9	10.7	7.9	17.6	3.5	9.9
1949	28.0	15.2	4.2	1.8	11.3	7.8	18.0	3.6	10.2
1950	29.0	14.1	4.4	1.7	11.4	7.7	17.8	3.6	10.2
1951	29.9	12.6	4.8	1.7	11.7	7.7	17.8	3.6	10.2
1952	30.0	12.0	4.7	1.6	11.9	7.7	18.0	3.7	10.3
1953	31.1	11.0	4.6	1.5	11.8	7.6	18.1	3.8	10.4
1954	29.4	11.5	4.7	1.4	12.2	7.4	18.5	4.0	10.8
1955	29.5	11.4	4.9	1.4	12.1	7.2	18.4	4.1	11.0
1956	29.2	11.1	5.1	1.4	12.3	7.2	18.4	4.1	11.1
1957	29.1	10.3	5.0	1.4	12.9	7.2	18.5	4.2	11.4
1958	28.0	9.8	4.9	1.3	13.8	7.0	18.8	4.4	11.9
1959	28.3	9.5	5.0	1.2	13.9	6.8	18.9	4.4	12.1
1960	28.1	9.0	4.8	1.2	14.3	6.7	19.1	4.5	12.4
1961	27.5	8.7	4.7	1.1	14.9	6.6	19.1	4.6	12.8
1962	27.8	8.1	4.8	1.1	14.7	6.5	19.2	4.6	13.2
1963	27.8	7.5	4.9	1.0	15.0	6.4	19.3	4.7	13.4
1964	27.6	7.1	5.0	1.0	15.2	6.3	19.5	4.7	13.6
B. Percentage changes in civilian employment[b]									
1948–49	(7.3)	(0.8)	(0.2)	(6.4)	3.6	(4.5)	0.1	1.5	1.1
1949–50	5.5	(5.3)	7.8	(3.1)	2.9	0.8	1.3	3.3	2.2
1950–51	7.6	(6.9)	11.6	3.1	6.0	4.8	3.8	3.8	3.6
1951–52	1.5	(3.9)	1.2	(3.3)	3.4	0.5	2.7	3.9	2.8
1952–53	5.5	(6.2)	(0.4)	(3.6)	0.5	1.0	2.4	3.7	2.4
1953–54	(7.0)	2.0	(0.4)	(8.7)	1.6	(4.8)	(0.1)	4.1	2.3
1954–55	3.5	3.0	7.3	0.1	2.4	1.4	2.9	4.5	4.5
1955–56	2.1	0.1	7.0	3.8	5.3	2.5	3.1	4.0	4.2
1956–57	(0.4)	(7.4)	(2.5)	0.7	4.8	(0.1)	0.3	2.0	3.3
1957–58	(7.2)	(7.7)	(5.0)	(9.3)	3.5	(6.2)	(1.3)	1.7	0.9
1958–59	4.6	(0.2)	6.6	(2.5)	3.8	0.9	3.5	3.0	4.5
1959–60	0.7	(3.4)	(2.5)	(2.7)	4.0	(0.2)	2.4	2.9	3.9
1960–61	(2.8)	(4.2)	(2.4)	(5.6)	3.6	(2.5)	(0.5)	2.3	2.9
1961–62	3.2	(5.9)	3.1	(3.3)	0.7	0.1	2.0	2.5	4.4
1962–63	0.9	(5.2)	2.8	(2.3)	3.5	0.2	2.0	2.6	3.6
1963–64	1.8	(3.7)	4.1	0.0	3.3	1.6	3.3	2.5	3.7

[a] Government wage and salary civilian employment.
[b] Nonfarm, payroll employment based on establishment data. Alaska and Hawaii included from 1959. Farm occupations from the Household Survey; not strictly additive with establishment data. Prior to 1957, farm data do not reflect new definition of employment, and prior to 1958 averages are based on January, April, July, and October of each year. Parentheses indicate negative figures.

SOURCE: Derived from *Manpower Report of the President, 1965*, pp. 202, 233; and *Employment and Earnings*, Sept., 1965.

Construction and trade are both industries in which unit job require-ments have either risen or remained the same over time. Employment gains have not been the result of increasing shares of total real output. In contrast to this, the place where productivity growth has been the most rapid in the last two cycles has been in utilities. Its output gains have

TABLE 10: Distribution and Percentage Change of Real Output[a] by Industry, 1948–63

Year	Manu-fac-turing	Agri-cul-ture	Contr. con-struc-tion	Mining	Gov-ern-ment	Utili-ties	Trade	Fi-nance	Serv-ice indus-tries
A. Percentage distribution of real gross product[a]									
1948	28.9	6.8	4.5	3.0	8.9	8.9	18.3	10.8	9.9
1949	27.8	6.5	4.7	2.7	9.5	8.6	18.6	11.7	10.0
1950	28.7	6.3	4.6	2.7	8.9	8.9	19.0	11.4	9.6
1951	29.5	5.5	4.9	2.8	10.1	9.3	17.7	11.2	9.0
1952	29.6	5.5	4.8	2.7	10.5	9.0	17.8	11.1	9.0
1953	30.4	5.5	4.7	2.7	10.0	8.9	17.8	10.9	9.0
1954	28.7	5.9	4.8	2.7	10.1	9.1	18.0	11.4	9.4
1955	29.7	5.7	4.7	2.7	9.3	9.4	18.0	11.2	9.1
1956	29.0	5.4	4.9	2.8	9.3	9.8	18.0	11.4	9.5
1957	28.9	5.3	4.7	2.7	9.3	9.8	17.8	11.9	9.7
1958	27.5	5.5	4.6	2.6	9.5	9.9	17.9	12.5	10.1
1959	28.5	5.1	4.6	2.5	9.0	10.1	18.0	12.2	10.0
1960	27.9	5.2	4.4	2.5	9.1	10.4	17.8	12.5	10.2
1961	27.6	5.1	4.2	2.5	9.2	10.5	17.6	12.8	10.5
1962	28.6	4.9	3.9	2.4	9.1	10.5	17.6	12.7	10.3
1963	28.4	4.8	3.9	2.4	9.0	10.7	17.6	12.8	10.3
B. Percentage changes in real gross product[a]									
1948–49	(4.8)	(4.5)	2.2	(11.2)	4.9	(4.5)	0.4	6.8	0.3
1949–50	13.1	5.2	8.8	11.4	3.2	13.8	12.1	6.4	5.1
1950–51	10.2	(6.4)	14.1	10.2	20.8	11.8	0.2	5.7	1.0
1951–52	2.9	4.2	0.6	(1.0)	6.9	(0.6)	2.9	1.8	2.2
1952–53	6.6	3.6	0.6	(3.1)	(0.5)	2.2	4.0	1.5	4.1
1953–54	(7.2)	4.4	0.6	(3.0)	(1.1)	0.3	(1.1)	3.0	1.8
1954–55	12.4	4.7	7.5	10.4	0.0	12.8	8.9	6.3	5.6
1955–56	0.3	(1.8)	4.8	5.7	1.6	6.2	2.4	4.1	6.7
1956–57	1.2	(1.8)	(1.5)	0.0	1.9	2.3	0.0	5.9	3.4
1957–58	(6.9)	1.4	(4.2)	(8.9)	0.3	(1.7)	(1.7)	3.3	2.3
1958–59	11.0	(0.5)	6.0	3.9	1.6	9.4	8.1	4.4	5.4
1959–60	0.2	5.1	(2.6)	1.9	2.8	4.6	0.6	4.8	4.9
1960–61	0.0	0.0	(2.1)	1.9	2.5	2.4	0.5	3.8	3.8
1961–62	9.9	0.0	0.5	1.8	4.9	6.2	5.9	4.8	4.5
1962–63	3.3	3.5	1.6	2.7	2.3	6.3	4.1	5.2	3.7

[a] Based on constant 1954 dollars (value added). See Chapter 4, n. 21–23. Parentheses indicate negative figures.

SOURCE: Derived from *Manpower Report of the President, 1965*, p. 258.

been among the highest. Technological change unrelated to demand problems is clearly the cause of its employment declines except in railroads. (Note that the figures for the entire industry group include railroads.)

Table 11 presents arithmetic averages of year-to-year changes over each cycle for unit job requirements, output, and employment. The definitions used by Clague and Greenberg are applied to these data. Employment declines appeared in two industries over the first cycle, agriculture and mining, while output increased for all industries. The employment declines in both cases were attributable in the framework being used to technological change. In the second cycle four industries show employment declines, as does the total of goods producers. Again, output rose in all industries, and, though the rates of employment decline in agriculture and mining were lower than in 1948–53, the influence of technology had spread to manufacturing and utilities.

The third cycle shows the influence of both technological displacement and a demand decline in some industries. Five industries show employment declines as construction is added to the previous four. Technological change affects these four. The rate of decline of unit job requirements in agriculture is higher in the 1957–60 cycle despite a faster output rate than either of the two other cycles. In manufacturing and utilities the rate of decline in unit job requirements was about the same in the third cycle and in the second. In the third cycle the decline in mining is attributable both to demand and technology. The 3.7 percent decline in unit job requirements was exceeded by the 4.8 percent average annual drop in employment, as output fell 1 percent per annum. Contract construction is the sole case in which the employment drop is clearly a result of a fall in output.

These figures suggest that the positive aggregate relationship between productivity, output, and employment are not valid on a disaggregative level. There is also evidence of an increase in the range of technological displacement since the first cycle. The clearest danger from technological displacement appears to be in agriculture, mining, and utilities, since, particularly in the first two instances, the skills involved would not appear to be easily transferred. This does not deny the effects of demand inadequacies. The figures for output growth by industry indicate a decided slowdown in the 1957–60 period. However, it is possible that an increase in over-all demand would not have solved the unemployment problems created by technological change. In those industries where productivity continues to outpace output, workers will have to find sufficient and suitable jobs in industries where output outpaces productivity. Only government seems to have performed strongly as a consistent source of new employment.

TABLE 11: Average Annual Rates of Change in Three Postwar Cyclcs:ᵃ Real Output, Employment, and Unit Job Requirements by Industry, 1948–53, 1953–57, 1957–60

Industry and period	Real gross product	Employment	Unit job requirements
1948–53			
Manufacturing	5.6%	2.6%	(2.8)%
Agriculture	0.4	(4.6)	(4.7)
Contract construction	5.3	4.0	(1.1)
Mining	2.5	(2.7)	(4.7)
Government[b]	7.1	3.3	0.6
Utilities	4.5	0.5	(3.6)
Trade	3.9	2.1	(1.6)
Finance	4.4	3.2	(1.0)
Service industries	2.5	2.4	(0.1)
Total goods-producers	4.6	0.5	(3.8)
Total service-producers[b]	4.3	2.2	(2.0)
1953–57			
Manufacturing	1.7	(0.4)	(1.7)
Agriculture	1.4	(0.6)	(1.9)
Contract construction	2.8	2.8	(0.2)
Mining	3.3	(1.0)	(3.9)
Government[b]	0.6	3.5	0.2
Utilities	5.4	(0.2)	(5.4)
Trade	2.6	1.6	(1.0)
Finance	4.8	3.6	(1.4)
Service industries	4.4	3.6	(0.7)
Total goods-producers	1.8	(0.2)	(1.8)
Total service-producers[b]	3.4	2.3	(1.0)
1957–60			
Manufacturing	1.4	(0.6)	(1.8)
Agriculture	2.0	(3.8)	(5.5)
Contract construction	(0.3)	(0.3)	0.0
Mining	(1.0)	(4.8)	(3.7)
Government[b]	1.6	3.8	0.4
Utilities	4.1	(1.8)	(5.3)
Trade	2.3	1.5	(0.6)
Finance	4.2	2.5	(1.3)
Service industries	4.2	3.1	(1.2)
Total goods-producers	1.1	(1.4)	(2.4)
Total service-producers[b]	3.2	2.0	(1.1)

ᵃ Average annual rates based on arithmetic averages of year-to-year percentage changes.
[b] Employment based on civilians only. Unit job requirements calculated from civilian plus military employees.
Parentheses indicate negative figures.

SOURCE: Tables 8, 9, and 10. See Chapter 4, n. 21–24.

The Evidence in Manufacturing

The effect of technological change in manufacturing over the three cycles can be explored further, since additional data are available. These are presented in Table 12. It appears that the capacity utilization rate in manufacturing was the same, on the average, in the first two cycles and lower in the third. However, output growth was more rapid in the first cycle than in the second. This suggests a greater expansion of capacity in the earlier period and the employment figures support this conjecture. Unit job requirements declined much more slowly in the second cycle than in the first. In the second cycle, however, productivity seems more responsive to output increases. The decline in unit job requirements was 100 percent of the output rise in 1953–57, while it was only 50 percent in 1948–53, despite faster output growth in the earlier cycle.

TABLE 12: Production, Productivity, and Capacity Utilization in Manufacturing, Average Annual Rates for Three Postwar Business Cycles

Average annual rates	1948–53	1953–57	1957–60
(1)–(6) percentages			
(1) Capacity utilization rate[a]	88.0	88.0	82.0
(2) Changes in real gross product	5.6	1.7	1.4
(3) Total employment changes	2.6	(0.4)	(0.6)
(4) Changes in unit job requirements	(2.8)	(1.7)	(1.8)
(5) Changes in unit total manhour requirements	(3.5)	(3.2)	(3.7)
(6) Changes in unit production manhour requirements	(4.1)	(4.4)	(4.6)
(7) Peak-to-peak point change in average annual ratio of nonproduction workers to total employees	2.8	3.3	1.9

[a] Federal Reserve Board Estimates. The data are based on an average of two series which utilize Federal Reserve Board output indexes, McGraw-Hill capacity and utilization rate figures, and Department of Commerce capital stock estimates.
Parentheses indicate negative figures.

SOURCE: (1) U.S. Congress, Joint Economic Committee, Subcommittee on Economic Statistics, *Measures of Productive Capacity, Report*, 87th Cong., 2nd Sess. (Washington: U.S. Government Printing Office, July 24, 1962), p. 16. (2), (3), (4) from Table 11. (5), (6) derived from *Higher Unemployment Rates*, p. 31. (7) from *Manpower Report of the President, 1964*, p. 228.

Unit job requirements were even more responsive to output growth in 1957–60. We look to 1953–57 for the reason. The ratio of nonproduction workers to total employees increased more in 1953–57 than in the other two cycles. [27] Even if we pro-rate for the lengths of the cycles there is no

[27] Measured from peak to peak, as in Table 12. This is also true measured from trough to trough; the figures are: 3.0, 3.4, and 1.2, respectively. Within the cycle the ratio is higher at troughs than at peaks.

denying that the shift to overhead labor accelerated in 1953–57. In one specific year the most dramatic change appeared. The year 1955–56 shows practically no growth in gross production, yet there was a 2-percent rise in employment. Unit job requirements increased by that 2 percent. The 1955–56 change was the second time in the postwar period when more nonproduction workers were hired than production workers (213,000 compared with 148,000). In 1951–52, 248,000 overhead workers were hired and there was a loss of 9,000 production worker jobs, probably due to mobilization. In that earlier year output, employment and productivity all increased, and the year was a prelude to the following year's spurt in all three categories. Not so in 1955–56. The following year saw production worker employment actually dropping in a peak output year.

With the rise in overhead labor, output per worker became more sensitive to changes in output. This suggests technological changes which permit greater output at the same level of capacity use, but rapidly rising worker productivity with increases in output. In the second cycle an average output gain of 1.7 percent was accomplished with a small loss in employment. In the 1948–53 cycle, with the same level of capacity use, employment had to be increased to raise output. Thus the lower rate of productivity growth in the second cycle was strictly a function of the rate of growth of output. The technological base for faster productivity gains was there. In the second and third cycles there is almost the same rate of decline in unit job requirements, but at a lower level of capacity use. Worker productivity grew faster relative to output increases.

Further evidence of a change in the skill composition of employment comes from manhour productivity data. Averaged over the three cycles, total unit manhour requirements fell by 3.5, 3.2, and 3.7 percent per year. In contrast, an accelerated fall is apparent in production worker manhour requirements: 4.1, 4.4, and 4.6 percent per year. Production worker employment fell not only in recession years, but in 1956–57 and in 1959–60. In 1959–60 output grew by 0.2 percent; 138,000 nonproduction workers were hired, but 17,000 production workers lost their jobs. In 1962–63 output grew by 3 percent, but of the 1 percent rise in employment, almost half went to nonproduction workers.

Conclusions

Technological change is evident in the postwar period and shows signs of having provided conditions for a rise in structural unemployment; it also seems to have affected the level of over-all demand through a reduction in unit capital requirements.

THE GOODS-TO-SERVICES SHIFT

Have there been changes in the composition of final demand such that structural dislocations in labor could have been a by-product? What is the relationship between demand shifts and the rate of output growth? This section attempts to find answers to these questions.

Structural shifts in the composition of output can give rise to structural unemployment when skill requirements and the location of the contracting industries are markedly different from those of the expanding industries. If the shift between industrial sectors is gradual, with time for natural attrition and for new labor force entrants to smooth the way, structural unemployment need not result. The problem arises when rapid changes in the labor requirements of the sectors do not allow for a smooth adjustment. The analysis here is directed to the shift from goods-producing industries to service-producing industries—already suggested by the data in Tables 9 and 10.[28]

After World War II and the depression that predated it consumers' hunger for durable goods was unfulfilled, first because of depression incomes and second because of material scarcities. Not until the mid-1950's was the predepression level of the ratio of goods to services in output restored. The increase in the service producers' share of output and employment since then is the really new development.

The goods-to-services ratio in both industrial gross product and employment are presented in Table 13, with annual rates of change. As is evident from the table, the goods-to-services ratio in employment has been declining throughout the postwar period, rising only in the recovery years 1949–50 and 1954–55.[29] In the 1958–59 recovery the ratio held steady and in 1961–62 the ratio declined, but at a decelerated rate. On the other hand, the goods-to-services ratio in production was already lower than in employment in 1948 but shows many more years of positive change than does the employment ratio.[30]

Averaged over the cycle, the declines in the ratios appear to have accelerated. This supports the argument that the shift in the composition

[28] W. G. Bowen and S. H. Masters show that shifts in demand within manufacturing were accelerated in the 1955–57 period, but not thereafter. Concern here is with shifts among the nine broad industry groups. ("Shifts in Demand and Inflation," *American Economic Review*, Dec., 1964, pp. 975–84.)

[29] These were cyclical phenomena, reflecting the cyclical vulnerability of goods-producing industries such as producers' and consumers' durables and of production workers generally, who are concentrated in goods production.

[30] The higher employment ratio reflected the low labor content in the service-producing sector, suggested in Table 8.

60   STRUCTURAL UNEMPLOYMENT AND AGGREGATE DEMAND

TABLE 13: Ratio of Goods to Services by Industry Output and Employment, 1947-64

Year	Goods industries as percentage of service industries		Year	Percentage change in G/S ratios	
	Gross product[a]	Employ-ment[b]		Gross product[a]	Employ-ment[b]
1947	73.8	104.7	—	—	—
1948	75.8	101.8	1947–48	2.7	(2.8)
1949	71.4	96.6	1948–49	(5.8)	(5.1)
1950	73.2	96.8	1949–50	2.5	0.2
1951	74.4	96.1	1950–51	1.6	(0.7)
1952	74.3	93.5	1951–52	(0.1)	(2.7)
1953	76.3	93.4	1952–53	2.7	(0.1)
1954	72.5	88.9	1953–54	(5.0)	(4.8)
1955	75.1	89.4	1954–55	3.6	0.6
1956	72.6	88.1	1955–56	(3.3)	(1.5)
1957	71.2	84.4	1956–57	(1.9)	(4.2)
1958	66.9	78.5	1957–58	(6.0)	(7.0)
1959	68.4	78.5	1958–59	2.2	0.0
1960	66.7	75.9	1959–60	(2.5)	(3.3)
1961	65.0	72.6	1960–61	(2.5)	(4.3)
1962	66.2	72.0	1961–62	1.7	(0.8)
1963	65.3	70.1	1962–63	(1.2)	(2.6)
1964	—	68.6	1963–64	—	(2.1)
	Average annual rates:[c]		1948–53	0.2	(1.7)
			1953–57	(1.6)	(2.5)
			1957–60	(2.1)	(3.4)

NOTE: See Chapter 4, n. 21–24.
[a] Gross product by industry in constant 1954 dollars (value added).
[b] Wage and salary workers in nonagricultural establishments by industry plus employed farm workers by occupation; only civilian government employment included in services.
[c] Arithmetic averages of year-to-year changes.
Parentheses indicate negative figures.

SOURCE: Derived from *Manpower Report of the President, 1965*, pp. 202, 233, 258; and *Employment and Earnings*, Sept., 1965.

of output was one of the preconditions which may have caused a rise in structural unemployment. In a BLS study for the Joint Economic Committee, this point is made as follows:

. . . a fundamental transformation such as is involved in the goods to services shifts poses many obstacles to smooth adjustments. Differences in skills, rates of pay, and hiring systems as between workers in goods-producing industries and the service rendering activities reduce the mobility of displaced workers and impede their desire and ability to find equivalent places for themselves in faster expanding alternatives.[31]

[31] *The Extent and Nature of Frictional Unemployment*, p. 69.

The BLS found that from 1948 to 1956 the unemployment rate in the goods-producing sector rose from 4 to 5 percent and was somewhat offset by the decline in the rate of the service-producing sector: ". . . workers in goods-producing industries experienced a relatively large increase in structural unemployment as compared to a reduction for the faster growing service industries." [32]

The data for the 1957–60 period show continued high unemployment among wage and salary workers in the goods-producing industries along with increased rates for all sectors. The long-term rates of unemployment continue to be highest in the goods industries. The greatest absolute point rise over the 1957–60 period came in agriculture, forestry, and mining (taken as a unit), followed by construction, trade, and manufacturing.

The reader will note that the shift from goods to services is more rapid in employment than in output. For 1947–48 to 1962–63 the regression of percentage changes in the goods-to-services ratio in employment (X_e) against the ratio changes in output (X_o) in Table 13 is $X_e = -2.02 + 0.60\ X_o$ $(r = 0.87)$. Thus, when the output ratio is constant, the employment ratio falls by about 2 percent. The explanation comes from the fact that a large part of productivity increases have come in precisely those goods sectors which are experiencing relative or absolute declines in demand, so that the employment shift out of goods has been accelerated.

The faster decline in the employment ratio relative to the output ratio is apparently due to the differential rates of productivity in the two sectors. Both the employment ratio changes and the output ratio changes are highly correlated with output changes, the coefficients of correlation being 0.89 and 0.91 respectively. However, the employment ratio equation is $X_e = -4.69 + 0.61\ X_2$, while the output ratio equation is $X_o = -3.96 + 0.91\ X_2$. [33] Thus, at zero output change, the employment ratio falls about 5 percent while the output ratio falls 4 percent. It takes an output increase of about 8 percent to hold the employment ratio steady, but only 4 percent to hold the output ratio steady.

The observations that deviate 2 standard errors or more are 1952–53 and 1955–56 for the employment ratio (both declined less than expected),

[32] *Ibid.*, p. 65; and *Unemployment: Terminology Measurement and Analysis*, p. 70. The studies define structural unemployment as "that which arises from the permanent disappearance of existing jobs because of important changes in an entire industry" (*ibid.*, p. 69).

[33] For the industry employment ratio the 1963–64 prediction is accurate within half a standard error. The real GNP series used for regression is based on the older NID series in the case of the industry output ratio and the revised series in the case of the industry employment ratio. The latter regression gives similar results with the older NID series.

and 1947–48 and 1952–53 for the output ratio (both rose more than expected). In the case of output, the two changes reflect the backed-up desire for goods after wartime. In the case of employment, the 1952–53 rise in favor of goods is a reflection of the behavior of the output ratio. But the 1955–56 deviation in the employment ratio is not echoed by a similar deviation in the output ratio. On the contrary, the latter was below its expected value by 1 standard error, while the employment ratio was above by 2 standard errors. The employment ratio change reflected an increase in employment in goods industries unrelated to output in the goods sector. As suggested earlier, this marked the influx of overhead labor attached to the new capital equipment.

The high correlations of the ratio changes with output changes suggest that the very slackness in the growth of demand which is used to expain high unemployment rates worked to accelerate one of the structural changes which, in turn, helps to explain the higher rates. The slower the rate of growth, the faster the shift to services. It is clear that investment demand, which is a goods demand, would be higher in more rapid output years. In addition, it appears that the very occupations associated with greater proportionate expenditures on goods are the ones being displaced.

Table 14 supports this point. It presents data on proportionate purchases of goods (actually, a rough equivalent) out of total consumer expenditures by occupation of the family's chief wage earner. In 1950 and 1960 skilled, semi-skilled, and unskilled wage earners made the highest proportionate goods expenditures. The proportion of expenditures on goods items fell in all occupations over the decade; but the share of these particular occupation groups in the population had fallen by 1960 so that the shift away from goods was intensified.

The shift from goods to services has some additional links with over-all demand. Part of the investment boom of 1955–56 was a result of the shift from less capital-using industries such as agriculture and manufacturing toward more capital intensive industries such as communications and public utilities. Hickman suggests that the shift in the composition of output continues to be in the direction of capital intensive industries. This should have worked toward lowering the aggregate output to capital ratio.[34] The fact that the ratio has nevertheless moved in the other direction gives added strength to the argument that recent technological changes have been capital-saving in nature. But the capital-saving character of the technological changes have themselves helped to accelerate the shift from goods to services.

It is possible that the shift from goods to services is partly due to inadequate demand, but the shift itself may be holding back demand. A

[34] Hickman, *Growth and Stability*, p. 287.

TABLE 14: Goods as a Percentage of Consumption Expenditures for Selected Urban Consumer Units, 1950 and 1960

Classification of group	Expenditure on goods[a] as percentage of consumption		Percentage of all units	
	1950	1960	1950	1960
Total all consumer units	**62.8**	**56.2**	**100.0**	**100.0**
Occupation of family head			100.0	98.8
Self-employed	61.3	53.8	9.8	6.5
Salaried prof., mgr., of.	60.0	55.4	13.6	17.3
Skilled wage earners	67.3	60.2	17.8	16.4
Clerical and sales	60.3	54.7	13.1	13.9
Semi-skilled wage earners	66.4	60.3	17.1	14.2
Unskilled wage earners	63.2	56.4	14.9	13.0
Not gainfully employed	56.9	—	13.7	—
Retired	—	48.8	—	12.3
Other reasons	—	49.7	—	5.2

NOTE: Consumer units include families in household units and persons living alone. Occupation of family head represents major activity of year.

[a] Includes food prepared at home, beverages, tobacco, furnishings and equipment, clothing and clothing services, recreation, reading matter, automobile purchase and expenses; excludes toilet articles. Thus the measure is a very rough approximation of the goods share of expenditures.

SOURCE: Derived from U.S., Bureau of Labor Statistics, "Consumer Expenditures and Income, Urban United States, 1960–61," Report No. 237–38, (Washington: U.S. Government Printing Office, April, 1964); and U.S., Bureau of Labor Statistics and the Wharton School, *Study of Consumer Expenditures, Incomes and Savings–1950*, Vol. XVIII, Univ. of Pa., 1957.

study done at Cornell University concludes that the goods-to-services shift in employment cost average employee compensation in 1960 about $75 (real) and total output about $4 billion. This is because each of the industries in which employment declined between 1953 and 1960 had average earnings substantially above the aggregate average. [35]

Conclusions

The shift from goods to services production gives evidence of having accelerated since the mid-1950's, partly as a result of technological changes. Not only was this a precondition which could have induced structural unemployment, but sluggish demand reinforced the shift, which in turn reinforced the drag on demand.

[35] Michael E. Bradley, "Effects on Economic Growth of the Employment Shift to Service Industries," *ILR Research*, IX, 3 (1964), pp. 3–6. The study uses a standardization procedure with the 1953 industrial distribution as a base. It uses 1960 total employment and average annual compensation per equivalent full-time employee. The assumptions that total employment and average wages are unaffected by the distribution of employment are questionable, however.

DISTRESSED AREAS

According to the definition of structural unemployment used here, structural unemployment in distressed areas is based on the concentrated regional effects of structural changes and must be analyzed in a similar manner. However, this does not discount the fact that specific areas of the country have suffered persistent hardship and poverty equal to the depression years of the thirties, while aggregate structural effects have clearly not been as severe.[36] This section does not offer a full-blown analysis of area unemployment, but merely examines evidence to show that area distress is structural in origin and may negatively affect over-all demand.

The nature of distressed area unemployment may be clarified by examining the histories of sixteen major distressed areas so listed in May, 1963. It is possible to find data on these areas' unemployment classification back to September, 1951, ignoring minor changes in area definition. A total of eighteen major areas was listed in May, 1963, two in Puerto Rico. Of the sixteen in the United States, nine had been continuously classified as areas of surplus labor or substantial unemployment since 1951. An additional one was absent from the roster only for 1956 and 1957. Table 15 presents the summary history of the sixteen areas and their industrial profiles in 1950 and 1960. Of the sixteen, thirteen were still listed in October of 1964. Those which recovered were Detroit, Erie, and Pittsburgh.

The causes of localized high unemployment can be traced to particular characteristics of the areas: first, the inherited weaknesses—concentrated industrial employment and thus vulnerability—and second, the infecting germ—structural change. The changes abolished jobs in the areas on a permanent and mass scale. There are a few areas where persistent high unemployment is caused by excessive seasonality of employment patterns or marked cyclical vulnerability, but, in the main, we are dealing with permanent losses. Within the context of broad movements of industry and people across the country and broad changes in demand and technology, certain areas have been dealt staggering blows.

---

[36] A "distressed area" for the purposes of this study is an area of persistent and substantial unemployment. The Bureau of Employment Security uses a rate of over 6 percent as substantial unemployment. An area which suffers this rate, discounting seasonal factors, and has had a rate at least 50 percent above the national average for three of four preceding years (or 75 percent above the average for two of three preceding years, or 100 percent above for one of two preceding years) is a distressed area. The major areas are roughly the same as standard metropolitan statistical areas. The BES recognizes 150 in the country. It breaks down other regions into "smaller areas" and "very small areas."

The major characteristic of these areas is that they were heavily dependent on one or two industries for their economic life, with few alternative sources of employment. The working population of these areas were more heavily distributed in wage and salary occupations than the average and were employed by industries that experienced major structural changes in the postwar period.

TABLE 15: Selected Major Areas of Substantial and Persistent Unemployment as of May, 1963, by Duration and Major Industries

State and standard metropolitan area		Percentage of total Census employment			Percentage change 1950–60
		Industry	1950	1960	
Substantial unemployment continuously since September, 1951					
Mass.-R.I.	Fall River	Textiles	25	14	(43)
Mass.	Lowell	Textiles	24	7	(65)
N.J.	Atlantic City	Other personal services (incl. hotels)	15	11	(9)
Pa.	Altoona	RR & R'way express	32	19	(44)
	Johnstown	Mining	23	8	(69)
	Scranton	Mining	13	4	(76)
		Apparel	10	11	(4)
R.I.	Providence-Pawtucket	Textiles	18	9	(49)
W.Va.	Charleston	Mining	20	4	(83)
	Huntington-Ashland	RR & R'way express	8	6	(33)
Substantial unemployment continuously since September, 1951, excluding 1956 and 1957					
Minn.-Wisc.	Duluth-Superior	RR & R'way express	9	6	(34)
Substantial unemployment continuously for at least 6 years after 1956					
Mass.	New Bedford	Textiles	20	8	(58)
Mich.	Detroit[a]	Motor Vehicles	28	19	(26)
Pa.	Erie[a]	Nonelectric machinery	11	5	(56)
	Wilkes-Barre–Hazleton	Mining	23	5	(81)
Substantial unemployment at least throughout 1962					
Pa.	Pittsburgh[a]	Primary metals	18	16	(9)
W.Va.-Ohio	Wheeling[b]	Primary metals	22	10	b
		Mining	9	5	b

[a] Not listed as of Oct., 1964. The areas listed do not include all those listed at dates given.
[b] In 1950: Wheeling-Steubenville.
Parentheses indicate negative figures.

SOURCE: Derived from various issues of *The Labor Market and Employment Security*, (BES), and Bureau of the Census, 1960 and 1950 *Census of Population*, General Characteristics of the Population (Area Reports).

Of the sixteen areas listed in Table 15, nine had at least one-fifth of total employment in a single two-digit SIC industry in 1950. Most of the other seven were concentrated in two industries. This concentration was not serious in itself. [37] It was a problem because the concentrated industries moved away, were affected by technological change, or were hurt by changes in demand and/or exhaustion of raw materials. Among the sixteen areas, eight industries are involved. Textiles appears three times, mining five, railroads three, and primary metals twice, as industries whose declines were primarily responsible for the areas' distress. Shifts in location, declines in industry demand, exhaustion of raw materials, and technological change are all represented.

A major cause of unemployment in distressed areas is the migration of industry. This occurs when obsolete or unprofitable plants are closed. Often the managements reopen elsewhere, as in textiles. Loss of local industry is also caused by decentralization policies, as in automobiles. The migration of industry, in Lubin's opinion, has been accelerating in recent decades. [38] Killingsworth points out that automation, which often makes it profitable to build completely new plants, "tends to increase the geographical mobility of industry." [39] Stella Manor comments that the growing durable goods industries such as transportation equipment, electrical machinery, and fabricated metal products are moving to the South and West, while the service industries are following population movements in the same direction. [40]

Another major cause of area job loss is a decline in the demand for specific industry products. When the industry is at all regionally concentrated, the result is geographically concentrated distress. Foreign competition, changes in consumer taste, changes in competitive market positions, and competition from new products all are possible causes. The coal areas are affected by a complex of these causes and by exhaustion of

[37] Lowell Gallaway attempted to show that depressed areas are not "one-industry towns," and that they are not nondiversified, but in the writer's opinion he has not succeeded. He compared the averages of 1950 area concentrations of employment in depressed areas with those of nondepressed areas, and the depressed areas came out with only a slightly higher average. But there is no reason to believe that nondepressed areas are not highly concentrated, only that they have not been concentrated in declining or migrating industries. See Lowell Gallaway, "Some Aspects of the Economic Structure of Depressed Industrial Areas," *Land Economics*, XXXV, 4 (Nov., 1959), pp. 337–46.

[38] Isador Lubin, "Reducing Unemployment in Depressed Areas," *American Economic Review*, L, 2 (May, 1960), p. 166.

[39] Charles C. Killingsworth, "Automation in Manufacturing," *Proceedings of the Eleventh Annual Meeting*, Industrial Relations Research Association, Chicago, Dec. 1958, p. 27, n. 25.

[40] Stella P. Manor, "Geographic Changes in U.S. Employment from 1950 to 1960," *Monthly Labor Review*, Vol. 86, No. 1 (Jan., 1963), pp. 1–10.

raw materials. Additional causes are shifts in government procurement and military needs, and changes in tariff or support policies. [41]

Not only are the distressed areas vulnerable to structural changes, but they are also more prone to cyclical distress in greater degree and longer duration. Lubin writes:

> There was a tendency for [transportation equipment, primary metals (steel), and electrical and non-electrical machinery] . . . to lay off proportionately more people in the chronic surplus areas than in other areas during the 1957–1958 recession. In many instances, also, their rate of reemployment did not rise as fast as in other areas. [42]

The industries mentioned by Lubin represented (in 1959) "significant sources of employment in more than half of the 17 major chronic labor surplus areas." [43]

The effects of structural change in a basic industry is transmitted in the locality much as it is in the nation, but it is more evident on a local scale. The secondary effects can be classed as direct and indirect. The direct effects of a decline in a major industry come as cutbacks in its supplying, distributing, and auxiliary industries. The indirect effects are felt among those industries that depend on local demand and respond to income changes in the area. Thus the distressed areas are a kind of microcosm of structural distress. In 1959, while hard goods unemployment rates were higher in distressed areas, the rates in such "secondary" industries as construction, transportation, and trade were higher, too. [44]

Structural unemployment in distressed areas affects the level of demand in those areas. There is an out-migration of younger workers and workers with more transferable skills. [45] Those who remain face reduced incomes.

[41] U.S., Bureau of Employment Security, *Chronic Labor Surplus Areas* (Washington: U.S. Government Printing Office, July, 1959), p. 1; and National Planning Association, *The Rise of Chronic Unemployment*.

[42] Lubin, "Reducing Unemployment in Depressed Areas," p. 163.

[43] *Chronic Labor Surplus Areas*, p. 18.

[44] U.S., Bureau of Labor Statistics, *The Structure of Unemployment in Areas of Substantial Labor Surplus*, Study Paper No. 23, Study of Employment, Growth, and Price Levels, Joint Economic Committee, 86th Cong., 2nd Session (Washington: U.S. Government Printing Office, Jan. 30, 1960), p. 4.

[45] The Area Redevelopment Administration reports that "the relative aging of the population . . . [of distressed areas came in the 1950–60 decade] apparently because of out-migration of younger people. The population of the areas had also grown at rates much lower than in other urban areas." *Population, Labor Force and Unemployment in Chronically Depressed Areas*, (Washington: U.S. Government Printing Office, Oct., 1964), p. 5.

As a result there is a loss of local purchasing power. Other problems include the loss of tax revenues and a deterioration of social capital and public services. Secondary unemployment, lowered property values, and a tightness in local credit are further consequences. Thus the community finds itself in a vicious circle such that it is unattractive to the new enterprises it must attract to overcome its problems. These are aspects of demand declines directly traceable to structural change.

The approach taken by Knowles and Kalacheck is that when modernization of industry is a cause of plant shifts and close-downs, the incidence of unemployment is all that is shifted:

> . . . after allowing some period of time for necessary adjustments, the major impact of a geographic change will be on the incidence of unemployment, rather than on its level. This is true even if the plant shutdown in the original location leads to induced declines in service or trade activities, since these should be compensated for by induced increases in the new location. Some of the secondary effects may lead, however, to more protracted unemployment. The average age of the discharged work force at the old location will probably be higher than the average age of the newly engaged work force. Consequently, the category of unemployed persons will now contain a higher proportion of less mobile and less reemployable individuals.[46]

It may be an error to expect a symmetry in the secondary effects. Can we expect that the effects on spending patterns and quantities due to prolonged unemployment in the old location will be offset by new employment for others in the industries' new locations? If the newly employed have been formerly short-term unemployed or are new entrants, or are simply workers removed from less productive occupations, then the positive increment in spending will be less than the decrement where the decline is of long duration, and the income involved is more likely of a family head.[47] This is especially true after the exhaustion of unemployment benefits. The authors' description of the workers in the old location is precisely a description of structurally unemployed workers. This is a logical explanation of how structural unemployment can rise or fall independent of the level of demand.

Where areas face the effects of shut-down of obsolete facilities, the authors suggest that these plants can be kept ready to meet cyclical peaks in demand. Where this occurs, "the area will enter the depressed category

---

[46] *Higher Unemployment Rates*, p. 46.

[47] The positive multiplier effects of investment and government spending are also not likely to be as high as the negative effects in the old industry locations.

early in the recession and emerge only when the recovery is well under way." [48] The authors seem to imply that the length of the recovery period is important. If, indeed, old jobs would be available with an increase in demand of reasonable proportions, the problem is not a structural one. However, the distressed areas face, for the most part, the disappearance of jobs, not their temporary obliteration. Having studied the behavior of unemployment in distressed areas, Berman and Kaun conclude:

> It appears that for most of the communities with continued high unemployment as of May 1964, the unemployment problem will not show dramatic improvement with a more rapid cyclical recovery for the nation as a whole. In general the mix of basic industries in these areas is such that somewhat better than average response to increases in aggregate demand might be expected. However, in most cases the actual employment growth thus far in the recovery has been considerably less than might be expected for the existing industry mix. [49]

CONCLUSION

The period after 1954 shows evidence of structural shifts in technology and in the composition of final demand and probably in the location of industry such that structural unemployment could have resulted. In the case of technology there is evidence of a substitution of direct for indirect labor. In the case of demand there is evidence of substitution of services for goods. Concentrations of these changes geographically could have added to over-all unemployment rates. Technological and locational changes may have helped to lower the level of over-all demand, while the small increases in demand since 1956 may have accelerated the structural shift from goods- to service-producing industries.

This chapter has established that there were conditions after 1955 that could have resulted in an increase in structural unemployment through a reordering of labor skills requirements. These were compatible with and related to a decrease in the adequacy of over-all demand.

[48] *Ibid.*, p. 47. Use of obsolete facilities at the peaks is one reason why productivity decelerates at that stage of the cycle.

[49] Barbara Berman and David E. Kaun, *Characteristics of Cyclical Recovery and the Measurement of Structural Unemployment*, (Washington: The Brookings Institution [mimeo., probably May–June, 1964]), p. 27.

CHAPTER 5

CHANGES IN
EMPLOYMENT REQUIREMENTS

As evidence in Chapter 4 showed, structural changes in employment can be caused by technology, modifications in the composition of demand, and shifts in the location of industry. If these elements altered employment requirements in terms of skill or location, a basic precondition for structural unemployment was created. This is the next subject of inquiry.

Skill requirements here are identified with employment categories listed by industry and by occupation; locational requirements are identified by broad regional groupings. The changing proportions of employment and the concentration of employment changes are explored by industry, occupation, and area. Voluntary part-time work is assumed to involve skills different from full-time work, and changes in part-time work are considered. Changes in the occupational content of industry employment are then investigated. The question raised is this: Do the postwar years show evidence of such marked changes in labor requirements that dislocations and structural unemployment could have resulted?

CHANGES IN EMPLOYMENT PROPORTIONS

Table 9, in Chapter 4, showed changes in employment proportions among nine broad industries. Manufacturing rose to a high of 31 percent of the total in 1953 and declined thereafter. The decline in agriculture was even more dramatic, from 15 percent in 1949 to 7.5 percent in 1963. Mining and utilities displayed less pronounced but steadily declining employment shares. The industries showing dramatic share increases were civilian government employment and "service industries"; trade and finance also displayed growth in their share of employment. The construction share has fluctuated without any pronounced trend, rising slightly to 1956 and declining slightly thereafter.

Technology calls for particular skills and training and occupational titles reflect these requirements. It is generally agreed that the skills identified by occupation are probably less easy to transfer than those identified by industry. For example, production workers in manufacturing may find it easier to perform in trade or service industries than to switch to nonproduction jobs within manufacturing.[1] We therefore expect the impact of technological change to be more clearly reflected in the changing occupational composition of the labor force.

Data on employment by occupation are presented in Table 16. A serious difficulty with the data is that the eleven broad occupational groups represented are so vaguely constructed and titled as to mask the underlying technical requirements, and thus they mask changes.[2] The category of "professional and technical" includes highly trained scientists and laboratory assistants; "managers, officials, and proprietors" includes both the salaried president of a corporation, the department store buyer, and the candy store owner who is self-employed. "Clerical" covers secretaries and file clerks but also mail carriers and telephone operators. "Sales workers" covers clerks in retail trade, real estate brokers, and computer salesmen. The blue-collar category of "craftsmen" includes foremen, workers in construction, mechanics, repairmen, metal craftsmen, and railroad engineers and firemen.

"Operatives" is the least precise category since it is the largest. It includes semi-skilled workers in manufacturing, but also workers in mining and service industries as well as drivers and deliverymen. The auto attendant, dressmaker, laundry worker, and factory examiner are all operatives. This makes the category of "service workers" difficult to comprehend because repairmen are craftsmen and deliverymen are operatives. "Service workers" (except household) includes those holding protective jobs, attendants, waiters, cooks, bartenders, and those performing personal services.

The "laborers" category excludes farm and mine workers and covers workers doing unskilled work in most industries including construction and manufacturing. "Private household workers" includes the baby sitter

---

[1] On the other hand, industries such as mining and construction are very much identified with specialities which cannot be transferred. The mining operative finds it as hard to leave the mining industry as to leave the occupational group of operatives, but his problem is locational as well.

[2] See the paper presented by John T. Dunlop at the Research Conference on the Measurement and Interpretation of Job Vacancies, Feb. 11–13, 1965, to be published by the National Bureau of Economic Research, Inc., in 1966.

TABLE 16: Distribution and Percentage Changes of Employment by Occupation, 1948–64

Year*	Prof., tech.	Mgrs., of., prop.	Cleri-cal	Sales	Pr. house-hold	Other service	Crafts men	Op-era-tives	Labor-ers	Farm-ers	Farm labor
A. Percentage distribution of employment											
1948	6.7	10.7	12.5	6.1	3.0	7.2	13.7	20.9	5.9	7.9	5.4
1949	6.9	11.0	12.7	6.4	3.0	7.7	13.0	20.1	5.8	8.0	5.3
1950	7.5	10.8	12.8	6.4	3.2	7.8	12.9	20.3	5.9	7.4	5.1
1951	7.9	10.2	12.6	6.2	3.1	7.7	13.9	20.7	6.5	6.6	4.7
1952	8.3	10.1	13.3	6.0	3.0	7.7	14.3	20.3	6.1	6.5	4.4
1953	8.8	10.4	12.9	6.1	3.0	8.3	13.9	20.6	5.9	6.2	3.9
1954	9.1	10.1	13.4	6.4	2.9	8.2	13.6	20.0	5.9	6.3	4.1
1955	9.2	10.2	13.3	6.3	3.1	8.2	13.2	20.2	5.8	6.0	4.5
1956	9.4	10.1	13.6	6.3	3.3	8.4	13.4	19.7	5.7	5.6	4.5
1957	9.9	10.3	14.1	6.3	3.2	8.5	13.3	19.3	5.7	5.1	4.2
1958	10.9	10.6	14.3	6.5	3.4	8.8	13.2	17.9	5.6	4.8	3.9
1959	10.9	10.6	14.2	6.7	3.4	8.9	13.1	18.1	5.7	4.6	3.9
1960	11.2	10.6	14.7	6.6	3.3	9.2	12.8	18.0	5.5	4.2	3.9
1961	11.5	10.7	14.8	6.6	3.5	9.5	12.9	17.6	5.2	4.1	3.7
1962	11.9	10.9	14.9	6.4	3.5	9.5	12.8	17.7	5.2	3.8	3.3
1963	12.0	10.6	14.9	6.3	3.4	9.8	13.0	18.2	5.2	3.5	3.2
1964	12.2	10.6	15.2	6.3	3.3	9.9	12.8	18.4	5.2	3.3	3.0
B. Percentage change in civilian employment											
1948–49	1.3	1.4	0.0	2.6	0.2	5.2	(6.1)	(5.0)	(3.1)	0.7	(3.0)
1949–50	11.5	(0.1)	2.6	2.3	7.2	3.2	0.6	3.1	4.6	(6.6)	(3.2)
1950–51	6.6	(3.3)	0.3	(1.9)	(0.7)	0.3	10.0	3.9	12.3	(8.4)	(4.6)
1951–52	6.3	(0.6)	6.1	(2.0)	(3.4)	0.4	3.7	(2.1)	(6.2)	(1.5)	(7.2)
1952–53	7.0	3.5	(1.6)	2.9	2.5	8.9	(1.8)	3.2	(1.4)	(3.0)	(10.8)
1953–54	2.6	(3.0)	2.2	4.1	(4.9)	(2.0)	(3.2)	(3.9)	(1.5)	0.3	4.7
1954–55	3.7	4.0	2.4	1.1	10.6	3.3	0.2	4.2	2.2	(3.0)	12.1
1955–56	5.2	1.6	5.6	3.4	9.1	6.3	4.4	0.4	(0.3)	(2.2)	3.3
1956–57*	6.1	2.3	3.6	0.4	(1.2)	0.9	(0.3)	(2.2)	0.3	(8.9)	(5.5)
1957–58	7.6	1.2	(0.2)	1.1	5.1	1.3	(2.3)	(8.7)	(2.2)	(7.4)	(8.1)
1958–59	2.6	2.2	2.1	5.3	(0.3)	4.2	1.1	3.6	4.0	(2.1)	2.2
1959–60	4.6	1.9	4.9	0.2	0.9	5.0	0.0	1.1	(2.1)	(7.9)	2.0
1960–61	3.1	0.7	0.8	0.9	4.6	3.1	0.7	(1.9)	(5.1)	(2.5)	(6.0)
1961–62	4.3	4.1	2.5	(2.1)	1.0	2.2	0.6	2.4	2.4	(4.3)	(7.6)
1962–63	2.8	(1.6)	1.6	0.2	(1.4)	4.1	2.8	3.9	(0.2)	(7.7)	(2.3)
1963–64	3.5	2.2	3.9	2.3	0.7	3.1	0.7	3.3	2.1	(3.2)	(4.3)

* Figures prior to 1957 not adjusted to the definitions of employment and unemployment adopted in 1957.
Data are based on the Household Survey.
Data prior to 1958 are based on figures for January, April, July, and October of each year.
Parentheses indicate negative figures.

SOURCE: Derived from *Manpower Report of the President, 1965*, pp. 202–3.

and the domestic servant. "Farm workers" are divided into "farmers and farm managers" and "farm laborers." The latter group includes hired hands, migratory workers, and unpaid family workers. These are the categories with which the analyst must work, because the data are generally available only for the eleven broad groupings.

The most dramatic change occurred in the growth of the professionals' share, from 6.7 to 12.2 percent in the years 1948 to 1964. Also dramatic was the decline in the two farm occupations. Other growth occupations are clerical and nonhousehold service workers, while occupational declines occurred for operatives, laborers, and craftsmen. Laborers reached their peak share in 1951 and declined thereafter, while craftsmen declined from their 1952 peak share. Managers and proprietors have been fairly stable, although the "self-employed" portion of this category has declined. Sales workers and private household workers have fluctuated within rather narrow bounds.

The declining industries encompass skills that are not easily transferred, especially in agriculture, which requires low skills and little training, and in mining. The growing industries such as government and services include jobs requiring high skills or different skills in the main, although some service industries have unskilled jobs. The occupational shifts show manual labor replaced by highly trained professional labor or indirect clerical labor.[3] Both the industrial and the occupational shifts suggest possible structural dislocations. Moreover, the shift was more rapid from 1955 to 1963 than in the period 1948 to 1955—away from manufacturing and utilities and toward government, trade, and service industries. By occupation the later period also shows an acceleration of shift. Losses in shares were greater from 1955 to 1963 than from 1948 to 1955 for operatives, laborers, and both farm occupations. Gains were more rapid for professionals, managers, clericals, and both service categories.

If employment changes by occupation or industry were not accompanied by dislocations, marked shifts in the location of employment might still provide a precondition for structural unemployment. Table 17 presents nonfarm wage and salary employment by area. The data are

[3] The Knowles-Kalacheck Report suggests that one structuralist argument is that a major cause of structural unemployment is the "imbalance between the skills and attainments of unemployed blue-collar workers and the requirements of employers ..." (p. 11). The authors ask how significant the downtrend in blue-collar occupations and goods-producing industries has been. However, the test offered is a decade-to-decade tabulation of the percentage changes in the labor force for the eleven occupational groups from 1900 to 1960. The labor force total for each includes the unemployed along with the employed. The authors assert without evidence that "changes in the size of the blue-collar labor force were strongly influenced by the availability of job opportunities" (p. 38), but the effect on unemployment was not presented in that section of the report.

TABLE 17: Distribution and Percentage Changes in Nonfarm Wage and Salary Employment by Area, 1948–63

Year	New Eng.	Mid. Atl.	E-N Cent.	W-N Cent.	South Atl.	E-S Cent.	W-S Cent.	Mount.	Pacif.[a]
	A. Percentage distribution of employment[a]								
1948	7.6	24.6	23.2	7.9	12.2	5.0	7.2	2.7	9.6
1949	7.5	24.5	22.9	8.0	12.3	5.0	7.4	2.8	9.6
1950	7.4	24.3	23.1	8.0	12.4	5.0	7.4	2.8	9.6
1951	7.4	23.7	23.0	8.0	12.5	5.0	7.5	2.9	10.0
1952	7.2	23.5	22.7	8.0	12.6	5.1	7.7	3.0	10.2
1953	7.2	23.4	23.2	7.9	12.5	5.0	7.6	3.0	10.2
1954	7.2	23.3	22.7	8.0	12.6	5.1	7.7	3.0	10.4
1955	7.1	22.9	22.9	7.8	12.7	5.1	7.8	3.1	10.6
1956	7.0	22.8	22.6	7.7	12.9	5.1	7.9	3.1	10.8
1957	6.9	22.8	22.3	7.7	13.0	5.1	7.9	3.2	11.1
1958	6.9	22.7	21.6[b]	7.8	13.2	5.1	8.1[b]	3.3	11.3
1959	6.9	22.3	21.7[c]	7.8	13.3	5.1	8.0	3.4	11.5
1960	6.9	22.2	21.6	7.8	13.4	5.1	7.9	3.5	11.6
1961	6.9	22.0	21.2	7.8	13.6	5.1	8.0	3.6	11.8
1962	6.9	21.8	21.1	7.7	13.7	5.2	8.0	3.6	12.0
1963	6.8	21.5	21.1	7.7	13.9	5.2	8.0	3.7	12.1
	B. Percentage change in civilian employment								
1948–49	(4.1)	(3.2)	(3.8)	(0.9)	(1.8)	(3.7)	(0.1)	0.0	(2.4)
1949–50	3.4	2.4	4.3	3.3	4.5	4.0	3.5	4.6	3.6
1950–51	4.8	4.5	5.5	5.3	7.2	6.9	8.1	7.7	8.9
1951–52	0.2	0.8	1.2	2.1	3.2	2.7	4.0	4.9	5.0
1952–53	2.1	2.1	4.5	1.7	1.3	2.2	1.6	2.3	3.0
1953–54	(2.6)	(3.0)	(4.4)	(1.7)	(1.8)	(2.5)	(1.0)	(0.9)	(0.7)
1954–55	1.6	1.7	4.1	1.6	4.4	3.5	3.8	5.2	5.2
1955–56	2.8	2.8	2.1	2.2	4.7	3.5	4.6	5.6	5.7
1956–57	0.0	1.2	(0.2)	0.6	2.1	1.2	2.4	3.7	3.2
1957–58	(3.1)	(3.3)	(5.6)[b]	(1.1)	(0.6)	(1.2)	(1.2)[b]	1.5	(0.8)
1958–59	3.3	1.5	3.6[c]	3.1	4.0	3.1	2.7	5.1	5.6
1959–60	1.5	1.2	1.5	1.5	2.3	1.6	0.8	4.2	2.2
1960–61	0.5	(0.7)	(2.4)	(0.2)	0.9	0.2	0.4	2.9	1.7
1961–62	1.9	1.9	2.6	2.0	3.9	3.4	3.0	4.0	4.4
1962–63	0.4	0.2	1.7	1.5	3.4	3.1	2.4	3.0	3.0

[a] Pacific States and total exclude Alaska and Hawaii.
[b] Continuity affected by conversion to 1957 SIC classifications in 1958.
[c] Break in series in 1959.
Parentheses indicate negative figures.

SOURCE: Derived from Manpower Report of the President, 1965, p. 239.

such that acceptable series are available only on a broad, nine-area basis; they exclude Alaska and Hawaii for the sake of continuity.[4] This table shows that changes in the distribution of nonfarm employment by area have been almost as dramatic as those by occupation or industry. The Pacific states have increased their share rapidly since 1951. The South Atlantic, Mountain, and West South Central states also have shown growing shares. In contrast, the Middle Atlantic and New England states have fallen steadily in their shares, while the East North Central states have declined except for cyclical, peak-year gains. Two regions with fairly stable shares are the West North Central and the East South Central.

CONCENTRATION OF EMPLOYMENT CHANGES

Knowles and Kalacheck reason that concentration of employment changes should provide a measure of structural shifts due to technological and demand changes.[5] They reason that if the standard deviation of employment changes is accounted for by the absolute size of aggregate employment changes, a structural problem is not involved. There are two errors implicit in the approach used. First, Knowles and Kalacheck limit the analysis to production workers within manufacturing industries (because of lack of detailed data). This ignores the fundamental shift from manufacturing and other goods-producing industries to service-producing industries. It overlooks the shift from production worker employment to

---

[4] The data are supplied by state employment services and therefore exclude the self-employed and agricultural employment. The Census Household Survey is not designed for regional analysis and cannot be used to estimate regional employment. The nine regions are divided as follows:

New England: Maine, New Hampshire, Vermont, Massachusetts, Rhode Island, and Connecticut.
Middle Atlantic: New York, New Jersey, and Pennsylvania.
East North Central: Ohio, Indiana, Illinois, Michigan, and Wisconsin.
West North Central: Minnesota, Iowa, Missouri, North Dakota, South Dakota, Nebraska, and Kansas.
South Atlantic: Delaware, Maryland, District of Columbia, Virginia, West Virginia, North Carolina, South Carolina, Georgia, and Florida.
East South Central: Kentucky, Tennessee, Alabama, and Mississippi.
West South Central: Arkansas, Louisiana, Oklahoma, and Texas.
Mountain: Montana, Idaho, Wyoming, Colorado, New Mexico, Arizona, Utah, and Nevada.
Pacific: Washington, Oregon, California, (Alaska, and Hawaii).

[5] See *Higher Unemployment Rates*, pp. 18–19, 35–37. The authors seek an autonomous shift in the deviations of employment changes from the average. They seem to imply that shifts in technology and demand would produce more structural unemployment if they were concentrated.

nonproduction worker employment and ignores the location of employment changes.[6] Second, concentrated employment shifts need not result in unemployment. This result would be expected only if the displaced workers (or new entrants) could not be absorbed into expanding sectors because of lack of qualifications. The incidence of change is therefore important.[7]

The Knowles-Kalacheck standard deviation essentially is a weighted standard deviation based on differences between component percentage employment changes and a weighted average change.[8] It neither represents concentrated differences in percentage changes nor concentrated differences in absolute figures, but rather a concentration measure of weighted differences of percentage changes. The approach taken in this section is that the numerical distribution of employment change among sectors is significant; therefore, the size of the sectors as well as their percentage employment changes is equally important. A slightly different measure was devised to reflect both, as follows.

The three subject areas are employment changes by industry, occupation, and area. Within each, the standard deviation is expressed as follows:

$$ SD = \sqrt{\frac{\sum\left[W_i\,E_i{}^* - \dfrac{\overline{E}^*}{N}\right]^2}{N}} $$

[6] The authors do raise the possibility that changes in the industrial distribution of the labor force may affect its occupational composition. After presenting annual employment changes by industry averaged for three postwar cycles, the authors conclude: "Changes in employment in goods-producing industries and in other activities have been sharply divergent in recent years, but this is not an unprecedented phenomenon" (p. 39). One is moved to ask why divergence must be unique to the recent period to have helped promote unemployment increases.

[7] Knowles and Kalacheck found that their weighted standard deviation of employment changes in manufacturing was determined primarily by the absolute value of the employment change and could point to no autonomous shift since 1957 (pp. 35–36). However, the Korean years of 1950–51 and 1951–52 show standard deviations so high they cannot be explained by the change in manufacturing employment. Thus, the Korean period shows evidence of a structural shift in manufacturing employment. The authors do not comment on the fact that unemployment declined in both 1950–51 and in 1951–52.

[8] The actual computation of the standard deviation is described as ". . . the antilogarithm minus 100 of the weighted standard deviation of the logarithm of the indexes of the annual rate of change in employment among 3-digit manufacturing industries." "The indexes are weighted by employment in the base year" (p. 37). This method might also be expressed as follows:

$$ \sqrt{\sum W_i\,[E_i{}^* - \overline{E}^*]^2} $$

where $E_i{}^*$ is the component percentage change of year two over year one, $\overline{E}^*$ is the aggregate percentage change, and W_i is the component share of employment in year one. The sum of the weights is 1.

where W_i is component i's share of total employment in the base year of each year-to-year change, E_i^* is the percentage year-to-year change for a component, $\bar{E}^*$ is the aggregate percentage change, and N is the total number of components (nine by industry and area, eleven by occupation). This method provides a standard deviation of the weighted employment change and is similar to a standard deviation of numerical employment changes, except expressed in percentage form (and limited by the usual weighting problem encountered with index numbers).

Year-to-year changes in aggregate employment and the standard deviation (SD) of weighted employment changes by industry, occupation, and area, using the data in Tables 9, 16, and 17, are shown in Table 18. The SD for the nine industries is positively correlated with aggregate employment changes (when it is used without regard to sign); r is 0.76, significant at the 0.01 probability level. Major deviations greater than two standard errors of estimate include 1954–55, 1955–56, and 1958–59, when the standard deviation was lower than expected from the aggregate employment change (unemployment fell in each year), and in 1956–57,

TABLE 18: Employment Changes and Variability by Industry, Occupation, and Area, 1948–49 to 1962–63

(percentages)

Year	Wage and salary workers (by industry)[a]		Civilian employment (by occupation)		Nonfarm wage and salary workers (by area)	
	Aggregate change	Standard deviation[b]	Aggregate change	Standard deviation[b]	Aggregate change	Standard deviation[b]
1948–49	(2.2)	6.3	(1.4)	4.5	(2.7)	2.7
1949–50	2.0	5.1	2.0	3.8	3.6	2.3
1950–51	4.0	7.0	2.0	6.0	6.0	3.1
1951–52	1.3	2.6	0.2	4.2	2.1	1.3
1952–53	1.8	5.4	1.3	4.2	2.6	2.6
1953–54	(1.9)	6.5	(1.0)	3.5	(2.6)	2.9
1954–55	3.3	2.6	3.0	2.8	3.3	2.3
1955–56	3.0	2.1	3.1	2.8	3.4	2.0
1956–57	0.03	3.3	0.1	3.5	1.2	1.1
1957–58	(3.3)	6.2	(1.6)	6.3	(2.6)	3.6
1958–59	3.5	3.6	2.5	2.1	3.3	1.9
1959–60	1.3	2.5	1.7	3.2	1.6	0.9
1960–61	(0.6)	3.3	0.2	2.4	(0.2)	1.8
1961–62	1.6	3.3	1.6	2.8	2.9	1.6
1962–63	1.4	2.5	1.4	3.1	1.8	1.3

[a] Plus farm occupations.
[b] Standard deviation of weighted percentage change in employment. See text.
Parentheses indicate negative figures.

SOURCE: Derived from Tables 9, 16, and 17.

when the standard deviation was higher than expected (unemployment rose). Thus 1956–57 suggests a concentrated structural shift.

For the eleven occupations the standard deviation and the unsigned aggregate employment change are not correlated ($r = -0.11$, not significant at the 0.05 level). The SD is highest, relative to the absolute value of the aggregate change in 1951–52, 1956–57, and 1960–61, when the employment change is close to zero. The unemployment rate fell in the first case and rose in the second two periods. In 1951–52, when employment changes by occupation were highly concentrated, over-all employment by broad industry was not much concentrated. The occupational shift was centered within manufacturing. Since 1953 shifts in the concentration of employment by occupation appear to have reflected broad shifts in industry employment. In 1956–57, however, industry concentration predominates, while in 1960–61 the concentration reflects a shift in occupations more than industries.

There is a positive but low correlation between standard deviations taken by area and unsigned aggregate employment changes ($r = 0.52$, significant at the 0.05 level). The regression equation provides two observations which deviate beyond two standard errors. These are in 1950–51, when the standard deviation is lower than expected and the unemployment rate fell, and in 1960–61, when the standard deviation was higher than expected and the unemployment rate rose. The ratio of the SD to absolute values of the employment change is highest at cyclical troughs but has increased from trough to trough, seemingly independent of the employment change.

On balance, the concentration measures suggest that 1956–57 and 1960–61 were years of employment changes involving structural shifts aside from demand considerations which supported unemployment increases; however, the results are ambiguous.

THE INCIDENCE OF EMPLOYMENT CHANGES

Study of the incidence of employment shifts is important for the understanding of structural change. This section examines the incidence and the concentration of positive and negative deviations from the average employment change. This is done by using the deviation of individual components' changes from the average and expressing each as a percentage of the standard deviation. The resulting figures are comparable over time and are called the standard variation (SV).

To explain more fully, $W_i E_i^* - \overline{E}^*/N$ approximates the component's numerical employment deviation from the average. This is expressed as a percentage of SD and is the standard variation. The standard variation is zero if the component's change equals the average change. It is 100 if the component's change equals the value of the standard deviation. The individual deviation and SV will be positive if they are above average, regardless of the actual direction of change, and negative if below average, regardless of the actual direction of change. An SV can therefore be negative even when all employment rises simply because a component is small in size or because its increment is low.

Concentration measures for above (below) average employment changes were constructed to express the greatest positive (negative) standard variation as a percentage of the sum of all other SV's of the same sign for any given year-to-year change. It can be written as $X_i/(\Sigma X - X_i)$ where X_i is the largest positive (negative) SV, and ΣX is the sum of all SV's of the same sign. The sum of all standard variations regardless of sign, just as the sum of all deviations from the average, is zero. A high value for $X_i/(\Sigma X - X_i)$ means that the deviations of components having that particular sign are concentrated, in numerical terms, in one component and not evenly spread out.

The investigation is conducted because it seems logical, a priori, that when deviations from the average change (especially below-average deviations) are concentrated in one sector, structural difficulties will occur. This would seem to be most probable when over-all employment declines. It makes sense that if large displacements occur in one industry, occupation, or area, it will be more difficult to find alternative working places than if declines are more evenly distributed.

The measure of above- and below-average concentration of employment changes are presented in Figures 2 and 3. The measures may validly be compared over time since they are independent of the value of the average change. Table 19 presents the standard variations on which they are based. The above- and below-average concentration measures were correlated with point changes in the unemployment rate; the results are listed in Table 20.

Concentration of above-average employment changes by industry are negatively related to changes in the unemployment rate, although the correlation is low and not significant at the 0.05 level. Figure 2 shows a clear pattern, however, with highest concentration in peak years of employment change and lowest concentration in recession years. The years 1951–52, 1955–56, 1959–60, and 1962–63 also show low concentration in above-average variations. Of the four years just mentioned, the unemployment rate fell in 1951–52 and 1955–56; in these years manufacturing employment was among the high gainers. In 1959–60 and 1962–63, the unemployment rate rose; in these years manufacturing employment grew only slightly above average.

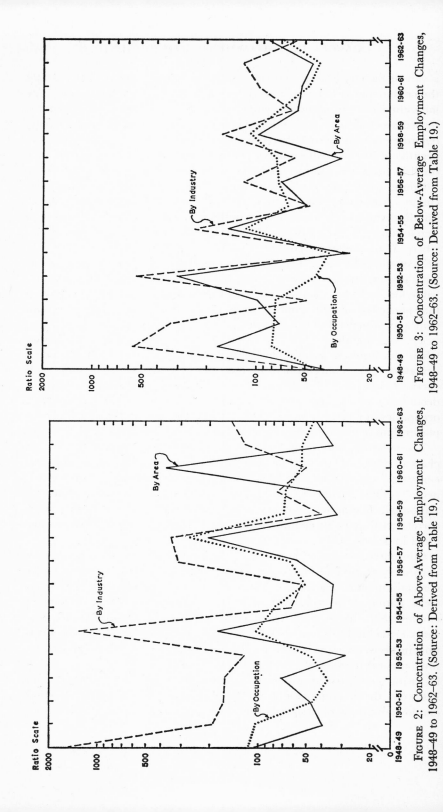

FIGURE 2: Concentration of Above-Average Employment Changes, 1948–49 to 1962–63. (Source: Derived from Table 19.)

FIGURE 3: Concentration of Below-Average Employment Changes, 1948–49 to 1962–63. (Source: Derived from Table 19.)

The correlation coefficient of -0.53 for above-average concentration by occupation is significant at the 0.05 level. This suggests that the more concentrated the above-average changes (in absolute numbers) by occupation, the more the fall in the unemployment rate. The explanation seems clear. The years of highest above-average concentration, 1954–55 and 1958–59, show the highest standard variations for operatives. The unemployment rate fell 1.2 points in the former year and 1.3 points in the latter. A greater drop appeared in 1950–51 (2.0 points); in that year the operatives also have a high SV but are joined by craftsmen with a higher SV, and laborers. In years when operatives and professionals both show positive and high SV's, 1940–50, 1952–53, and 1961–62, the unemployment rate fell.

Above-average concentration by area is also negatively but not significantly correlated with the unemployment rate. From 1951–52 to 1958–59 the movement of above-average concentration by area echoes that of above-average concentration by industry; thereafter it follows above-average concentration by occupation. As in industry, the highest concentration comes in 1952–53. The East North Central states show the highest SV in that year. In other high-concentration years, 1949–50 and 1954–55, the same area predominates. Unemployment also declined in these years. The falling trend in above-average concentration seems to reflect the inability of these states to recapture their formerly dominant role in employment gains.

Concentration of above-average employment changes by industry has fallen from peak to peak and has dampened in its fluctuation by area since 1953–54. This may account for the lack of significance in the two correlation coefficients. There is no discernible trend by occupation, which has a significant correlation. On balance, it appears that the inability of manufacturing, operatives, and the East North Central states to grow numerically as rapidly as in earlier years, relative to the average, may have contributed to unemployment.

All three categories of below-average concentration are significantly and positively related to changes in the unemployment rate. The higher the concentration among numerically below-average components, the greater the rise in the unemployment rate. In this sphere the industry concentration series is most highly correlated, with an r of 0.70, followed by the area series (0.65) and then by occupation (0.61). The average of the three series is still more highly correlated (0.80), and this suggests that the three series have a cumulative effect.

Below-average concentration by industry (Figure 3) has fallen from recession to recession as it has from peak to peak. On the other hand, below-average concentration by area has offset this by rising from recession to recession, but it has been stable from peak to peak. The movement of below-average concentration by occupation is not regular. It shows relatively high nonrecession levels from 1955–56 to 1962–63, and is high in each recession except in 1960–61. The movements of industry and area below-average concentration are most clearly related from

TABLE 19: Standard Variations of Employment Change by Industry, Occupation, and Area, 1948–49 to 1962–63

(percentages)

A. Nonfarm wage and salary workers by industry plus farm workers

Year	Manu-fac-turing	Agricul-ture	Contr. con-struc-tion	Mining	Govern-ment[a]	Utilities	Trade	Finance	Service indus.
1948–49	(272)	18	34	17	90	(16)	37	42	50
1949–50	232	(180)	19	(48)	19	(28)	3	(18)	1
1950–51	225	(182)	8	(51)	31	(10)	29	(40)	(10)
1951–52	105	(220)	(30)	(70)	88	(37)	116	(2)	49
1952–53	243	(158)	(36)	(43)	(23)	(20)	40	(10)	8
1953–54	(273)	60	27	11	56	(21)	27	51	63
1954–55	233	(8)	9	(129)	27	(93)	59	(66)	41
1955–56	121	(142)	2	(123)	131	(68)	100	(75)	53
1956–57	(33)	(226)	(36)	2	161	(3)	14	22	100
1957–58	(248)	(61)	17	34	118	(11)	19	64	68
1958–59	225	(101)	(16)	(105)	35	(81)	69	(64)	37
1959–60	15	(165)	(96)	(63)	145	(56)	109	(6)	115
1960–61	(198)	(85)	(12)	1	162	(27)	(7)	18	102
1961–62	187	(187)	(10)	(59)	(21)	(47)	53	(33)	82
1962–63	27	(202)	2	(75)	124	(59)	86	(28)	125

B. Nonfarm wage and salary employment by area

Year	New Eng.	Mid. Atl.	E-N Cent.	W-N Cent.	South Atl.	E-S Cent.	W-S Cent.	Mount.	Pacif.
1948–49	(4)	(161)	(192)	75	26	38	96	99	23
1949–50	(56)	75	232	(53)	62	(78)	(55)	(106)	(21)
1950–51	(91)	120	171	(71)	63	(94)	(21)	(131)	52
1951–52	(158)	(33)	28	(49)	117	(72)	46	(67)	188
1952–53	(48)	79	253	(53)	(43)	(61)	(57)	(76)	6
1953–54	30	(129)	(221)	47	19	50	65	80	66
1954–55	(98)	12	222	(93)	74	(72)	(29)	(82)	68
1955–56	(79)	116	45	(91)	96	(88)	(9)	(90)	100
1956–57	(109)	90	(144)	(72)	106	(60)	42	(18)	165
1957–58	18	(115)	(238)[b]	50	52	56	47[b]	83	49
1958–59	(65)	(12)	194[c]	(62)	76	(97)	(69)	(92)	126
1959–60	(83)	67	151	(69)	130	(106)	(124)	(42)	75
1960–61	28	(67)	(250)	3	72	14	27	62	100
1961–62	(108)	58	135	(94)	123	(84)	(45)	(101)	117
1962–63	(120)	(109)	106	(60)	179	(29)	(8)	(65)	107

C. Civilian employment by occupation

Year[d]	Prof., tech.	Mgrs., of., prop.	Cleri- cal	Sales	Pr. house- hold	Other serv- ice	Crafts- men	Op- era- tives	Labor- ers	Farm- ers	Farm labor
1948–49	52	67	31	69	32	122	(172)	(223)	(14)	44	(9)
1949–50	180	(56)	44	(10)	10	19	(31)	130	25	(208)	(103)
1950–51	57	(99)	(26)	(56)	(38)	(29)	203	112	99	(147)	(76)
1951–52	124	(22)	196	(38)	(34)	2	129	(120)	(111)	(32)	(94)
1952–53	121	62	(86)	15	(11)	148	(98)	139	(53)	(81)	(154)
1953–54	99	(69)	116	106	(18)	(23)	(110)	(222)	1	34	85
1954–55	24	50	18	(79)	13	(1)	(96)	219	(56)	(179)	86
1955–56	78	(44)	181	(25)	2	92	117	(76)	(114)	(159)	(50)
1956–57	175	68	149	4	(17)	19	(17)	(140)	1	(160)	(82)
1957–58	158	48	21	38	55	46	(28)	(269)	4	(40)	(34)
1958–59	28	2	37	60	(124)	73	(44)	216	(3)	(171)	(74)
1959–60	121	17	189	(49)	(42)	102	(53)	16	(95)	(180)	(26)
1960–61	154	27	48	20	63	125	34	(165)	(137)	(55)	(115)
1961–62	137	115	88	(110)	(42)	26	(26)	109	(7)	(125)	(166)
1962–63	73	(108)	39	(41)	(64)	93	82	200	(50)	(150)	(73)

[a] Civilian employment.
[b] Continuity affected by conversion to 1957 SIC classifications in 1958.
[c] Break in series in 1959.
[d] Definition of employment 1948–56 not adjusted to that adopted in 1957.
Parentheses indicate below-average deviations.

SOURCE: Derived from Tables 9, 16, and 17.

TABLE 20: Concentration Measures Correlated with Point Changes in the Unemployment Rate, 1948–49 to 1962–63

Concentration measure	Coefficient of correlation	Significance at 0.05 or 0.01 level
Above-average by:		
Industry	−0.44	none
Occupation	−0.53	0.05
Area	−0.39	none
Average of three series	−0.51	0.05
Below-average by:		
Industry	0.70	0.01
Occupation	0.61	0.05
Area	0.65	0.01
Average of three series	0.80	0.01

1951–52 to 1955–56. From 1955–56 to 1958–59 the three series move together, and thereafter they diverge. The years of high below-average concentration are the recession years—except for 1960–61, when concentration is high only by area. In addition 1959–60 is high by industry and occupation; industry concentration is also high in 1956–57, 1961–62, and 1962–63.

By industry, the manufacturing SV is the chief negative component in recession years. The negative value of its SV has declined since 1954 as the size of the industry has declined. On the other hand, its high positive SV has also declined in employment growth years. The incidence of below-average SV's shifted from two components in the first two recessions to three in 1957–58 and five in 1960–61. But in nonrecession years, especially 1956–57, agriculture carries the chief negative SV. Taken by area, the negative SV of the East North Central states is of major importance. Unlike manufacturing, its negative deviations have increased from trough to trough; by contrast, its compensating positive SV's in good years have diminished from peak to peak since 1952–53. Below-average concentration by occupation is centered among operatives in 1948–49, 1953–54, and 1957–58. In 1960–61 concentration is low, negative SV's having spread to all blue-collar and agricultural jobs except craftsmen. No distinct occupational pattern of concentration has emerged.

When the regression equation using the average value of all three below-average concentration measures (1948–49 to 1962–63) is used to compute expected changes in the unemployment rate, the decline in the rate is under-stated by 2 standard errors in 1950–51, when the Korean mobilization mopped up much unemployment. The rise in the rate is under-stated by an equal amount in 1957–58, when below-average concentration by occupation provides a more accurate measure. Aside from these two points, the regression equation using average below-average concentration deviates by no more than 1 percentage point in predicting unemployment rate changes. The standard error is 0.8.

This section has established a tie between the incidence of below-average employment changes and changes in the unemployment rate. It therefore lends support to the argument that the skill and locational content of employment changes may have been a cause of the rise in unemployment and that some of the increase was structural. This is not conclusive evidence because the contents of the below-average changes involve the very areas, industries, and occupations that are cyclically sensitive. Beyond this, correlation does not discriminate between the dog and the tail; it does not specify which causes the wag.

PART-TIME WORK

Changed labor requirements may be reflected in changes in normal hours of work within industry. That is, part-time work is not just a shorter period of regular employment; it reflects different production requirements.[9] Thus changes in the proportions of part-time work for noneconomic reasons can reflect shifts in employment requirements.[10] "More than half the employment increase between 1947 and 1962 was in part-time jobs," according to the Labor Department.[11] Voluntary part-time employment grew more than 100 percent between 1950 and 1964; it grew by only 20 percent for nonfarm workers on full-time schedules.[12] Involuntary part-time work is cyclically sensitive, while voluntary part-time work has been increasing steadily.

Full-time work is most common for high skill occupations, those requiring a good deal of educational preparation, among white-collar workers and among the self-employed. Involuntary part-time work is a major problem among service workers and laborers. The manufacturing work week falls below a full week only in recession periods. Along with mining and construction, part-time work in these latter industries is more likely to be for economic reasons.

Voluntary part-time work is most concentrated in finance, service industries, and trade.[13] All three industries are increasing in their share of total employment.[14] The changes by occupation and industry therefore largely account for the observed trend, but increases have appeared in almost every occupation and industry.

THE OCCUPATIONAL CONTENT OF INDUSTRIAL EMPLOYMENT

The eleven-title classification system for which most occupational data are collected can be misleading unless the occupations are broken down at least by broad industry groupings as well. This kind of breakdown,

[9] Other evidence of marked changes in labor requirements comes from the sex content of employment changes; however, this will be discussed in Chapter 6.

[10] Part-time for noneconomic reasons excludes those working part-time because of short demand. It is called voluntary part-time work.

[11] *Manpower Report of the President, 1963*, p. 41.

[12] Robert L. Stein and Jane L. Meredith (BLS) "Unemployment Among Full-time and Part-Time Workers," *Special Labor Force Report*, No. 45, Sept., 1964, p. 1009.

[13] Robert L. Stein and Jane L. Meredith (BLS), "Growth and Characteristics of the Part-Time Work Force," *Special Labor Force Report*, No. 10, Nov., 1960.

[14] Rapid as the growth in part-time jobs has been, it is being outpaced by the demand for them; thus the unemployment rate for the part-time labor force has been rising. See Jane L. Meredith, "Persons Seeking Part-Time Jobs," *Employment and Earnings*, Vol. 9, No. 12 (June, 1963), p. iv.

however, currently exists in only two places—the 1950 and 1960 *Census of Population* and annually in the BLS's *Special Labor Force Reports*, taken from the Household Survey. The latter data are available only from 1958, however, and therefore cannot illuminate prior structural change.

The Census data give actual numbers, while the Household Survey data only give percentage distributions. When the Census data are converted to comparable distributions, however, the overlap year of 1960 shows some unexplained differences. For example, professionals are 7.7 percent of manufacturing employment according to Census data and 8.5 percent according to the Survey. Managers, officials, and proprietors are 9.8 percent of contract construction employment in the Census and 12.2 percent in the Survey.[15]

Both sets of data are presented in Tables 21 and 22 to indicate trends (the percentages total to 100 percent by industry). It is likely that the direction of change and general magnitudes are more comparable than the absolute levels. The advantage of the Census data is that they cover a fairly long period, so that cyclical variations can be somewhat ignored; however, only changes in proportions between 1950 and 1960 of more than one percentage point will be considered. A drawback is that there is a loss of detail in the terminal-year, decade comparison. The major structural shift toward blue-collar employment that accompanied the Korean War is hidden since it was later reversed. The annual Survey data reveal strong cyclical fluctuations among occupational shares within industries. The changes from 1959 to 1963 are therefore more indicative than those from 1958 to 1963.

Examination of changes in the occupational distribution of industries is a complex problem. An occupation can gain in its share of employment because the demand for other occupations has declined or because its own demand has increased. In the first case its total numbers need not increase. In the second its numbers do increase. In addition, the proportion for an occupation may decline, but if it is in a growing industry its actual numbers may increase. Tables 21 and 22 suggest that changing aggregate proportions among occupations from 1950 to 1963 are the result both of changing skill requirements within industries and of the changing rates of growth among industries. Structural dislocations are therefore somewhat masked when aggregate occupational data are used alone.

Professionals have substantially increased their employment shares over the entire period 1950–60 in mining, manufacturing, utilities, services,

---

[15] A possible explanation comes from the fact that there are nonreporting problems with Census data. Since the Survey is done from a sample, nonreporting problems are minimized. In addition, the Census data rely on a single point in time; the Survey data are twelve-month averages.

TABLE 21: Percentage Distribution of Employment in Industries by Occupation, 1950 and 1960[a]

Occupation and year	Manu-fac-turing	Agricul-ture	Contr. constr.	Min-ing	Public admn.	Utilities	Trade	Finance	Serv-ice indus.
Prof., tech.									
1950	4.9	0.7	3.8	3.6	11.8	3.5	2.1	3.3	32.1
1960	7.7	1.3	4.6	7.5	14.0	5.2	2.0	3.4	34.3
Mgrs., props.[b]									
1950	4.9	61.6	8.6	4.1	9.3	7.1	23.5	17.1	6.1
1960	5.2	58.1	9.8	6.1	10.2	7.7	19.2	17.7	5.1
Clerical									
1950	10.9	0.3	3.1	4.6	44.2	23.5	11.4	42.1	9.5
1960	12.2	0.7	4.6	7.6	42.8	24.3	13.9	47.0	12.2
Sales									
1950	2.9	0.1	0.3	0.2	0.2	0.5	27.5	23.6	0.9
1960	3.8	0.2	0.4	0.5	0.1	1.0	27.4	22.3	1.0
Service[c]									
1950	1.9	0.2	0.5	0.8	16.5	3.3	13.6	9.0	31.7
1960	1.7	0.3	0.5	1.0	17.2	2.8	14.0	5.8	32.5
Craftsmen									
1950	19.6	0.3	56.8	17.3	8.5	21.4	6.2	2.4	9.3
1960	20.0	0.7	54.1	22.5	8.6	21.6	7.5	1.9	6.9
Operatives									
1950	46.0	0.8	7.6	69.3	4.7	27.8	12.5	0.7	8.1
1960	43.4	2.4	8.8	54.8	3.6	28.2	12.2	0.5	6.1
Laborers[d]									
1950	8.8	36.0	19.3	0.1	4.8	12.9	3.2	1.8	2.3
1960	6.0	36.3	17.2	0.0	3.5	9.2	3.8	1.4	1.9

[a] Totals are all those reporting industry and occupation. Percentages total by industries.
[b] Includes farmers and farm managers.
[c] Includes private household workers.
[d] Includes farm laborers and unpaid family workers.

SOURCE: Derived from U.S., Bureau of the Census, *Census of Population, 1950 and 1960, Detailed Characteristics of the Population, U.S. Summary Volume.*

and public administration. More important, these include two growing industries. At the same time there was no loss in shares in any other industry. Services, a growing industry, is where professionals are most concentrated. The over-all share going to nonagricultural managers, officials, and proprietors has remained fairly stable over time. They have experienced a large gain in construction, an industry with a stable share of employment. Managers and proprietors are most concentrated in agriculture and trade. In the first they are declining in a declining industry; in the second they are declining in a growing industry. They show

TABLE 22: Percentage Distribution of Employment in Industries by Occupation, 1958–63

Occupation	Year	Manu-fac-turing	Agri-cul-ture	Contr. constr.	For., fish., mining	Public admn.	Utili-ties	Trade	Serv. & fi-nance
Prof., tech.	1958	8.4	0.6	4.5	n.a.	n.a.	5.0	1.9	26.5
	1959	8.4	0.5	4.4	10.2	14.6	5.1	1.9	26.2
	1960	8.5	0.7	4.7	10.2	14.7	6.2	1.8	26.4
	1961	8.8	0.7	4.9	12.1	15.3	5.6	1.8	26.3
	1962	9.2	0.7	4.4	10.6	15.8	5.6	2.0	26.6
	1963	9.1	0.8	4.5	12.0	16.5	5.7	1.9	26.7
Mgrs., props.	1958	6.0	0.3	12.1	n.a.	n.a.	8.3	24.5	8.8
	1959	5.5	0.0	11.9	7.7	9.3	8.5	24.3	8.8
	1960	6.1	0.5	12.2	8.3	9.2	8.3	24.3	8.8
	1961	6.5	0.6	12.3	7.7	9.7	8.6	23.8	8.7
	1962	6.6	0.7	13.2	8.1	10.3	8.6	23.9	9.2
	1963	6.2	0.6	12.9	7.0	9.7	9.0	23.0	9.0
Clerical	1958	12.7	0.3	4.3	n.a.	n.a.	25.3	13.2	16.2
	1959	12.6	0.0	4.5	6.9	42.0	24.8	12.9	16.3
	1960	12.6	0.5	4.6	8.5	42.0	24.3	13.3	17.5
	1961	12.4	0.6	4.7	6.7	41.4	24.0	13.8	17.3
	1962	12.4	0.7	5.3	8.8	39.9	24.6	13.9	17.2
	1963	12.2	0.6	4.9	8.5	38.6	23.7	14.3	17.5
Sales	1958	3.1	0.1	0.3	n.a.	n.a.	0.6	23.3	3.9
	1959	3.1	0.0	0.4	0.4	0.2	0.5	23.8	4.2
	1960	3.3	0.1	0.3	0.3	0.1	0.7	23.7	3.8
	1961	3.7	0.1	0.2	0.4	0.1	0.9	24.0	3.5
	1962	3.7	0.2	0.2	0.3	0.1	0.7	23.1	3.4
	1963	3.4	0.1	0.2	0.6	0.1	0.8	23.1	3.4
Service[a]	1958	2.0	0.1	0.5	n.a.	n.a.	2.8	13.0	30.7
	1959	1.8	0.0	0.4	1.1	18.8	2.7	13.1	31.1
	1960	1.9	0.2	0.5	1.6	18.8	2.7	13.5	31.0
	1961	1.8	0.2	0.4	1.4	18.8	3.2	13.6	31.1
	1962	1.8	0.2	0.5	1.3	18.3	2.8	13.8	30.9
	1963	1.7	0.3	0.5	1.0	19.4	2.6	14.1	31.0
Craftsmen	1958	19.6	0.2	49.8	n.a.	n.a.	22.0	6.3	5.6
	1959	19.2	0.0	50.3	20.4	8.1	22.2	5.9	5.5
	1960	18.6	0.5	50.4	20.6	8.6	21.8	6.0	5.2
	1961	18.8	0.6	51.0	20.3	8.5	22.6	6.3	5.2
	1962	18.3	0.8	49.7	20.7	9.0	21.9	6.8	5.0
	1963	18.4	0.7	50.8	20.5	8.9	21.6	6.9	5.1
Operatives	1958	41.6	1.3	8.9	n.a.	n.a.	25.1	13.8	5.4
	1959	41.9	0.0	8.7	41.8	3.5	26.0	13.9	5.3
	1960	42.4	1.8	8.7	40.9	3.1	25.9	13.2	4.9
	1961	42.2	1.3	8.5	42.2	2.9	25.7	12.5	5.1
	1962	42.4	1.5	9.2	42.1	2.9	26.4	12.2	4.9
	1963	43.4	1.8	9.3	40.5	2.9	26.9	12.3	4.6

Occupation	Year	Manu-fac-turing	Agri-cul-ture	Contr. constr.	For., fish., mining	Public admn.	Utili-ties	Trade	Serv. & fi-nance
Laborers	1958	6.7	1.2	19.4	n.a.	n.a.	10.8	4.0	2.8
	1959	7.0	1.3	19.4	11.3	3.6	10.1	4.1	2.7
	1960	6.6	1.5	18.7	9.6	3.5	10.1	4.2	2.5
	1961	5.8	1.3	17.9	9.2	3.3	9.5	4.3	2.7
	1962	5.8	1.5	17.4	7.9	3.7	9.5	4.4	2.8
	1963	5.5	1.7	16.9	9.9	3.9	9.7	4.3	2.7
Farmers	1958		52.3						
	1959		51.6						
	1960		48.6						
	1961		49.6						
	1962		50.0						
	1963		48.4						
Farm labor	1958		43.5						
	1959		46.5						
	1960		45.7						
	1961		45.0						
	1962		43.8						
	1963		44.9						

NOTE: Percentages total within industries, not across occupations.
n.a.: not available.
ª Includes private household workers.
SOURCE: U.S., Bureau of the Census, "Annual Report on the Labor Force," *Current Population Reports*, Series P-50, No. 89, 1958, p. 39; and BLS, *Special Labor Force Reports*, No. 4, p. A-24; No. 14, p. A-26; No. 23, p. A-25; No. 31, p. A-23; and No. 43, p. A-23.

some gain in manufacturing between 1959 and 1963, but the year 1962–63 shows a major loss in total nonagricultural managers and proprietors; but this was recouped in 1963–64. The 1962–63 loss reflects the share losses in every industry listed in Table 22 except utilities, which is a declining employment industry.

Clericals are an occupational group whose over-all share has risen over the 1948–1963 period. This change, however, masks certain differences on an industry level which may indicate structural problems.[16] Clericals have increased their shares in mining, a declining industry, and in construction, a stable industry, as well as in trade, finance, and services, all growth industries. However, they lost in public administration over the 1950–63 period and in utilities in the 1959–63 period. They increased in manufacturing from 1950 to 1960 but began to lose ground from 1959 to 1963. Clericals are most concentrated in public administration, where their declining share has been offset by rapid growth. They are also

[16] Of course, clerical skills are expected to be transferable among industries.

concentrated and losing in utilities, a declining employment industry. The kinds of clerical work associated with the transportation, communications, and public utilities group may not be as easily transferred as those in other industries since they include other than normal office skills. It would also not be surprising if more and more losses began to appear among other clericals as new technology becomes more widely applied to office work and as large office operations force them into the expendable roles of proletarianized white-collar workers. That is, they should be expected more and more to have the employment characteristics of direct labor.

Sales workers in finance have shown declines over the 1950–60 period. Declines appeared in trade in 1950–60 and more strongly over the 1959–63 period. Sales workers' over-all share has remained fairly stable over the years 1948 to 1963; no industry outside of manufacturing shows them with a marked share increase. They are most concentrated in trade and finance, and both these industries have been growing, which has compensated for reduced sales proportions in some industries. Future declines in sales are quite likely if technological inroads continue in selling techniques.

Service workers are an occupational group which appears to have grown more through association with growing industries than with major share increases. Their share actually declined in finance between 1950 and 1960, although it increased in trade from 1959 to 1963. But service workers are concentrated in the service industries, in public administration, and in trade. In each industry there was only a tiny rise in their share from 1950 to 1960, but these are rising employment industries. In 1959–63 there was no rise in their share in services and finance combined; there was a small rise in public administration but a sizable gain in trade.

The pattern for craftsmen is extremely complex, as the category covers both the blacksmith, the repairman, and the maintenance mechanic. Craftsmen have kept a fluctuating but fairly stable share of over-all employment from 1948 to 1963. They have gained ground in mining and trade in the periods 1950–60 and 1959–63, while they also increased in agriculture and public administration; on the other hand, their 1959–63 share declined in manufacturing. Craftsmen are most concentrated in construction, followed by utilities and manufacturing. None of these is a growing industry, and the skill of the craftsman is a very specific one. From 1950 to 1960 craftsmen lost ground to operatives and managers in construction, held steady in utilities, and gained slightly in manufacturing. In 1959–63 they gained only slightly in construction, lost slightly in utilities, and lost considerable ground in manufacturing. The outlook for the future, therefore, is of continued differences among industries. It is likely that technological change begins by changing the artisan to a craftsman as mass production is introduced. It then eliminates the craftsman in favor of the operative as automation introduces self-correcting, self-repairing machines and less manual complexity.

Operatives have lost considerable ground largely because they have been concentrated in declining industries—manufacturing, mining, and utilities. In 1950–60 and 1959–63 operatives lost shares in mining, services, and public administration and gained in agriculture and construction. They lost in addition in finance and in trade, even while they gained shares in manufacturing and utilities. The 1962–63 increase of 465,000 operatives was almost as large as that of 1950–51; however, the entire increase in manufacturing production employment in 1962–63 was only 70,000 while it was 845,000 in 1950–51. Even if one answers that some operatives hold nonproduction jobs, one cannot assume that the total manufacturing rise of 152,000 went to operatives in 1962–63. From 1962 to 1963 operatives increased their employment share in agriculture, construction, utilities, and trade, as well as in manufacturing. Employment grew by 2.8 and 2.0 percent in construction and trade, but only 0.9 percent in manufacturing and 0.2 percent in utilities.

In other words, operatives gained more proportionately than absolutely in 1962–63 in their traditional industries. Absolute gains went to those with a similar title in other industries. The question remains whether operatives in mining, who are still being displaced, and those in manufacturing and utilities, who were displaced in many postwar years, can find alternative work in other industries, even if the operative title appears there. Apparently the alternatives are in services, public administration, and trade. The openings are there not because of growing shares in these industries but because of industry growth.

Although nonfarm laborers have shown employment declines in nine out of fifteen postwar observations, the over-all share going to laborers has not changed very much between the terminal years 1948 and 1963. Laborers' shares have declined in construction, manufacturing, utilities, and public administration from 1950 to 1960. The terminal year comparison masks the high employment growth years for laborers during the Korean period and so the decline from 1951 to 1963 is minimized. Laborers, however, face continued losses as their share in construction and utilities falls since they have negligible shares in other industries. The decline of the laborers' share is most significant because it means the decline of an occupation for which minimal training requirements are necessary.

The other category requiring minimal skills is that of agricultural laborers. Farmers and managers had declined in agriculture from 1950 to 1960, leaving a slightly larger share to farm laborers. This echoes the move to corporate farming as well as the loss of marginal farms. The increased farm laborers' share did not mean farm job increases, however, since the entire industry was declining. On the other hand, professionals, clericals, craftsmen, and particularly operatives have experienced increased agricultural shares, indicating inroads of modern technology.

CONCLUSION

The evidence presented in this chapter indicates that there were marked shifts in the occupational, locational, and industrial composition of employment in the postwar period. Analysis of the occupational content of industrial employment also shows marked shifts in skill proportions among some industries. The existence of the same occupational title within several industries is no guarantee of easy transference from declining to growing industries; thus the evidence by industry reinforces the suggestion of dislocations. Structural problems appear to have developed for those workers whose skills are both in declining industries and declining occupations, and possibly also in declining regions. The continuing shifts among occupations within industries suggest that the problem still persists.

There is a relationship between concentration of below-average employment changes by occupation, industry, and area and changes in the unemployment rate. This relationship better explains recession, rather than nonrecession, behavior; however, shifts in the incidence of below- and above-average concentration since the early 1950's, as well as several highly concentrated nonrecession years for below-average deviations by industry and occupation, suggest structural difficulties. And these difficulties, which create preconditions for a rise in structural unemployment, have been evident since the mid-1950's.

CHAPTER 6

LABOR FORCE ADJUSTMENTS TO CHANGING EMPLOYMENT REQUIREMENTS
Labor Force Participation and Job Mobility

The viability of an economic system depends partly on its flexibility; in this respect labor has proved itself amazingly adaptive. In the space of three generations it has shifted its composition and skill mix and accommodated itself to new kinds of capital equipment so that it could turn out products as different as the horse and buggy, the space vehicle, and the computer. The rapid changes in the postwar period have called for major labor force adjustments. The purpose of this and the next chapter is to examine the adequacy of those adjustments and to glean what they imply with respect to recent unemployment rates.

This chapter deals with two of four varieties of labor force adjustments. The first is the response of the population through labor force participation rates. Participation rates by sex are used as proxy representations of different skill endowments. Second is the response through job shifting by occupation, where the occupations are proxy representations of skill requirements. The third, spatial adjustment through geographic migration, and the fourth, response to new skill requirements through education and training, are dealt with in Chapter 7.

THE LABOR FORCE PARTICIPATION RATE

The labor force participation rate is the percentage of a population category that is in the labor force. Demographic factors determine the composition of the population and social and economic factors determine the participation rates. The demographic factors affecting the age, sex, and racial composition of the population are birth rates, death rates, and immigration. Custom and institutions set the normal age for starting work and for retirement. They affect the normal time spent in school and the availability of schooling, funds available for the retirement of the aged, and attitudes toward working women, particularly married women and women with preschool children. The general health of the population is another factor, and participation rates are also very much affected by national emergencies such as war and by economic factors. There are large seasonal shifts in labor force participation rates due to mobility in and out of the labor force of young people (students on vacation), housewives (looking for holiday and part-time jobs), older people (supplementing pensions), and seasonal and casual workers.

There is general agreement that the participation rates of women, younger workers, nonwhites, and older workers rise in periods of expanding production and employment in response to increased job opportunities, wage increases, and less rigid hiring policies. There is a debate, however, concerning whether these secondary income earners enter the labor force in depression periods when the primary wage earner becomes unemployed.[1] If they do, this would increase the size of the labor force and raise unemployment rates. But it is also argued that this is balanced or more than offset by the withdrawal of discouraged, unemployed wage earners from the labor force. Discouragement is said to have the same effect on new workers who do not enter in prolonged periods of depression.[2]

The questions raised here are, first, to what extent do labor force participation rates show adaptive behavior? The participation rates would be considered adaptive if they displayed a strong relationship to employment changes. The reasoning is that a decline in labor force participation, in the face of declining employment, reduces pressures on the unemployment rate. The second question is, if the answer to the first question is affirmative, are there indications of structural shifts in employment requirements that may have produced structural unemployment despite

[1] The term "secondary workers" refers to workers who are not the main source of income either for themselves or for their families. In this sense a divorced woman raising a child and working and a teen-ager supporting himself are not secondary wage earners.

[2] A recent discussion of this question asserts with evidence that "an initial decline in employment from a cyclical peak results in large-scale discouragement and withdrawal from the labor force. Subsequent declines in employment are met by a smaller decline in labor force participation. As the period of economic slack grows longer, pressure on additional workers to enter the labor force builds up and this tends partially to offset the discouragement effect." From Kenneth Strand and Thomas Dernburg, "Cyclical Variation in Civilian Labor Force Participation," *The Review of Economics and Statistics*, XLVI, 4 (Nov., 1964), p. 378.

the behavior of participation rates? The approach taken here is that differences in skills and training by sex are reflected in different occupational distributions by sex. That is, particular occupations attract one sex more than another. Thus, when there is a shift in skill requirements that are related to sex, persons outside the labor force with required skills may be attracted while those in the labor force with redundant skills may leave. If the newly required skills are scarce, however, both among those outside as well as inside the labor force, withdrawal is possible and structural unemployment is possible. If it can be determined that labor force behavior follows distinct patterns with respect to selective employment conditions, then it may be possible to diagnose the postwar years by an appropriate set of "profiles."[3]

Are Participation Rates Adaptive?

The first question raised is, have postwar participation rates shown adaptive responses to the market? If they have been responsive to employment changes, even structural changes might not result in pressure on unemployment rates because the disemployed would leave the labor force. Table 23 presents civilian labor force participation rates for the aggregate, for males, and for females, together with the respective percentage changes in employment. Female participation rates have been rising secularly while male rates have declined. The net effect has been a fairly stable aggregate labor force rate, except that the trend from 1948 to 1956 was upwards, while it declined somewhat from 1956 to 1964. The decline in the male rate has accelerated since 1956, while the female labor force rate reached its highest acceleration in the 1954–56 period.

There is no doubt that institutional factors are involved in the trends. The most dramatic aspect of women's participation in the labor force has been the rate of increase of older and married women's participation,

[3] Knowles and Kalacheck use labor force participation rates in a slightly different manner. Since they assume that structural unemployment cannot exist except in the presence of "adequate" demand, the changes in labor force rates are used as one of a series of tests for labor scarcities in the presence of adequate demand (pp. 12–13, 22–23, 75–76, 78). The authors' reasoning apparently is as follows: First, they assume that the definition of structural unemployment implies the existence of demand adequate to achieve full employment. The unemployed workers must therefore be matched by unfilled needs for which they are not suited by reasons of skill or location. Thus, in the presence of unemployment rates above the frictional minimum, they would expect to find one or a combination of three adjustments. These are (1) more job vacancies, (2) longer hours of work, or (3) an increased labor force participation rate—presumably drawing on workers who are qualified to fill the unmatched jobs but who would have remained out of the labor force in normal circumstances. We would add the possibility of selective wage and salary increases in the areas of skill scarcities if (3) were not marked. If (3) did not draw on a surplus labor reserve, higher wages might be expected to be one of the inducements to a higher labor force rate.

TABLE 23: Civilian Labor Force Participation Rates and Percentage Changes in Employment, Aggregate and by Sex, 1947–64

	Civilian labor force participation rate[a]				Percentage change in employment[b]		
Year	Total	Male	Female	Year	Total	Male	Female
1947	56.8	84.0	31.0	—	—	—	—
1948	57.3	84.2	31.9	1947–48	2.3	1.4	3.1
1949	57.4	84.1	32.4	1948–49	(1.2)	(1.9)	0.6
1950	57.7	84.0	33.1	1949–50	2.3	1.7	3.8
1951	57.7	84.0	33.8	1950–51	1.7	0.5	4.8
1952	57.4	83.6	33.8	1951–52	0.4	(0.3)	2.0
1953	57.2	83.3	33.5	1952–53	1.5	1.7	1.0
1954	57.1	82.9	33.7	1953–54	(1.7)	(1.9)	(1.3)
1955	57.6	82.7	34.8	1954–55	3.4	2.3	5.7
1956	58.3	82.9	35.9	1955–56	2.8	2.0	4.6
1957	57.8	81.9	35.8	1956–57	0.5	0.0	1.5
1958	57.5	81.2	36.0	1957–58	(1.6)	(2.2)	(0.5)
1959	57.4	80.9	36.1	1958–59	2.5	2.4	2.7
1960	57.5	80.4	36.7	1959–60	1.8	0.9	3.3
1961	57.2	79.5	36.9	1960–61	0.2	(0.4)	1.3
1962	56.5	78.4	36.6	1961–62	1.6	1.3	2.1
1963	56.4	77.9	37.0	1962–63	1.4	1.0	2.3
1964	56.5	77.6	37.4	1963–64	2.2	1.8	3.1

[a] The civilian labor force participation rate is the percentage of the noninstitutional population fourteen years or older not in the Armed Forces who are employed or unemployed.

[b] Employment data are based on definitions adopted in 1957. Parentheses indicate negative figures.

SOURCE: Derived from *Manpower Report of the President, 1965*, p. 193.

indicating permissive social conditions. Only girls between the ages of sixteen and nineteen decreased their participation rates between 1947 and 1963. The largest rise came in the group forty-five to fifty-four years old, women who have drawn on war work experience. Married women played a dominant role in the increase. Nearly half of the nation's labor force growth between 1951 and 1962 was accounted for by married women.[4] The increase in labor force participation among women has come mostly from white women, since Negro women were already in the labor force in large numbers; on the other hand, Negro men have left in greater proportions than white.

In contrast to women, the most significant development among men is their declining labor force participation. The decline has been marked for teen-age boys and older men. The movement from farm to town areas explains part of the drop; teen-age boys have fewer job opportunities off

[4] Jacob Schiffman (BLS), "Marital and Family Characteristics of Workers, March 1962," *Special Labor Force Report*, No. 26, Jan., 1963, p. 29.

the farm and are more likely to be in school. Declining male youth participation also reflects the greater period and pressure of time spent at school. The prime work years show little change in the male participation rate, while the older age groups among men reflect the increasing availability of pension incomes, both under social security and private sources. Voluntary and enforced retirements have also been part of the pattern.

Sex characteristics seem to be associated in society with different training and skills; in fact, women have gained most in absolute numbers chiefly in occupations which have been theirs traditionally. Women filled most of the clerical jobs added since the 1950's while men filled most of the professional and technical openings. Thus, the differential behavior in the two sets of participation rates by sex should reflect occupational changes in employment requirements. To test the adaptiveness of the participation rate, point changes in the aggregate participation rate from 1947–48 to 1962–63 were regressed against percentage changes in total employment.[5] The correlation is very low, not significant at the 0.05 level; however, the scatter of points shows that the recession years 1948–49, 1953–54, and 1957–58 mark a separate group and there does seem to be a relationship for the other points. The last recession year, 1960–61, seems to lie with the nonrecession points and not with the three recession years; nevertheless, all four recession observations were eliminated and the correlation was run for twelve observations. The value of r rose to 0.77 (0.74 adjusted), significant at the 0.01 level.

When the regression values of the point changes are computed, three things become apparent. First, the only deviation beyond two standard errors comes in 1961–62, when the decline in the labor force rate was under-estimated. Second, the change in 1963–64 is correctly predicted. Third, when the same equation is used to predict the recession points, each one shows less of a decline than expected. Only the 1960–61 point deviates less than two standard errors. The other three are four or more standard errors above the nonrecession year expected values; thus, the secondary

[5] Support for the adaptation hypothesis is offered by Jacob Schiffman, describing conditions in 1950 and 1960:

The fact that fewer married women worked in . . . areas of high unemployment, despite the tendency for wives of unemployed men in general to have high participation rates, underscores the extent to which the types of industries and the economic conditions of an area determine suitable job opportunities and worker rates for married women [ibid., p. 36].

[In 1960] . . . areas with high [married women] participation rates generally had a greater concentration of employment in service industries and nondurable goods manufacturing than other areas. Relatively little employment was in durable goods manufacturing, particularly in the steel producing and using industries. In 7 of the 8 areas with the highest participation rates, textile and apparel manufacturing accounted for anywhere from 10 to 33 percent of total employment . . . [in 1960], [ibid., p. 31].

worker effect does overcome the discouragement effect, at least for yearly data. This does not necessarily mean positive increases in the participation rate, but it does indicate changes not as negative or more positive than would otherwise be expected. The 1960–61 recession possibly was too mild to display this secondary response behavior or indicates a rise in structural rather than demand unemployment (Table 24 summarizes these and other results). The first indication, then, is that the participation rate is largely adaptive in nonrecession years.

The regression of point changes in the female labor force rate against female employment changes was calculated from twelve observations. In the recession years 1953–54, 1957–58, and 1960–61 the female rate rose by 0.2 points and in 1948–49 by 0.5 points. Without these observations r is 0.88, significant at the 0.01 level. In this case none of the twelve predicted values is above two standard errors; in 1961–62 the female rate increase is almost two standard errors below expectations. The prediction for 1963–64 is correct. The regression equation under-estimates the rise

TABLE 24: Regression of Point Changes in Labor Force Participation Rates against Percentage Changes in Employment, 1947–48 to 1962–63

Population group	r	No. of obs.	Regression coefficients		Level of significance of r at 0.01 and 0.05	Recession behavior compared to normal[d]
			a	b		
Civilian labor force						
Total	0.77	12[a]	−0.67	0.37	0.01	higher
Female	0.88	12[a]	−0.57	0.32	0.01	higher
Male	0.39	12[a]	−0.57	0.19	none	was higher, declining
Male noninstitutional labor force						
14–19	0.57	16[b]	−0.77	0.14	0.05	no difference, declining
20–24	−0.84	8[c]	0.05	−0.08	0.01	no difference, higher in 1948–49
25–34	0.42	16[b]	0.08	0.04	none[e]	no difference
35–44	0.57	12[a]	−0.18	0.09	none[e]	no difference, higher in 1957–58
45–54	0.49	16[b]	−0.10	0.09	0.05	no difference
55–64	0.96	16[b]	−0.45	0.25	0.01	somewhat higher except 1948–49
65 and over	0.72	12[a]	−1.26	0.17	0.01	somewhat higher

[a] Excludes the recession years 1948–49, 1953–54, 1957–58, and 1960–61.
[b] Includes entire period 1947–48 to 1962–63.
[c] Excludes 1947–48 to 1951–52 and recession years.
[d] Normal refers to predicted values based on regression coefficients.
[e] Almost significant at 0.05 level.

SOURCE: Derived from Tables 23, 25, and 26.

in the female rate for recession years by almost four standard errors in 1948–49 and 1957–58 and by over four standard errors in 1953–54; in 1960–61 it is off by almost two standard errors. Thus the female rate undoubtedly shows secondary entrance in recession years. In all other years changes in employment account for 77 percent of the variation in the participation rate.

The question of male participation is more ambiguous. The correlation for twelve observations is only 0.39, not significant at the 0.05 level. The regression line, though of dubious validity, was calculated. The predicted changes show a deviation of more than two standard errors only in 1961–62, when the male participation rate declined more than expected. For 1963–64 the predicted decline under-states the actual by only 0.1 point; on the other hand, the regression equation over-estimates declines in the male labor force rate for the three earlier recessions. The size of the error at recessions has diminished over time, suggesting a falling secondary worker trend. Changes in the male labor force rate evidently are not as adaptive as those of the female rate. However, the actual values for changes in male participation in nonrecession years from 1956–57 to 1963–64 have all been below the predicted values, so that trend declines are evident. In recession years, female more than male participation rates appear to contribute to higher unemployment rates through secondary responses, but males contribute by their stronger labor force attachments.[6]

[6] This approach is in contrast to that of Knowles and Kalacheck, who state that they are looking for "larger than normal gains in the size of the labor force" (p. 13). This could mean an increase in the labor force participation rate or an increase in the rate greater than expected in relation to aggregate employment changes. Presumably, smaller than "normal" gains would show inadequacy of demand. Knowles-Kalacheck find that "the overall labor force participation rate declined between 1957 and 1960" (p. 78). This is the support for their position, so we assume that the authors chose a rate decline as a less than "normal" gain in the labor force. They offer this as proof of the inadequacy of demand. The assumption must be that the labor force participation rate responds positively to any unfilled labor demand, no matter how selective; but, in fact, the lower rates could equally show the inability of the population to supply needed skills. If some of the structurally displaced left the labor force and were replaced by those with appropriate skills, the over-all rate could remain the same or even decline. In other words, if the rate response shows qualitative as well as quantitative reactions, changes in the labor force rate might not by themselves differentiate between inadequate demand and an inappropriate skill composition in the population.

If there is a secondary worker response during recessions, more than "normal" increases in labor force rates could be symptomatic of (1) inadequate demand as easily as of (2) structural unemployment. It could also occur with (3) an inflationary excess demand for labor without structural change. In (1) and (2) there could be an increase in the aggregate unemployment rate, while in (2) and (3) there could be a decline in the unemployment rate. It is all a matter of what happens to the new entrants and the structurally displaced.

If one drops the adequate demand condition set by Knowles-Kalacheck and accepts the possibility of structural unemployment existing together with inadequate demand, a decreased labor force rate with an increase in structural unemployment is entirely possible.

Male participation rates were broken down into six age categories for further clarification (see Tables 25 and 26).[7] Male teen-agers fourteen to nineteen years of age show a steadily declining labor force rate although their employment declined only in the first two recessions, during the Korean mobilization and in 1956–57. The correlation coefficient is 0.57, significant at the 0.05 level.[8] The 1963–64 figure is predicted within 0.1 point.

In the case of teen-age males the last three recession years have shown increasingly greater-than-expected declines in the labor force rate. By 1960–61 the decline is one and one-half standard errors below expectations. In 1948–49, however, the teen-age response was much greater than expected, by one and one-half standard errors; thus, not only is there no secondary worker effect since 1948–49, but there is indication of a "discouraged worker effect," probably combined with school pressures.

An occupational breakdown of male employment by age groups is available for March, 1957.[9] Among fourteen- to nineteen-year-old males the greatest numbers were among operatives, farm laborers, and farmers—in that order. The behavior of this group's recession year participation rate reflects the cyclical vulnerability and declining trend in these occupations. The 1948–49 behavior echoes the fact that agricultural employment was countercyclical that year, but not thereafter; thus, secondary worker responses were more possible earlier.

Males twenty to twenty-four years old show a net gain in their participation rate over the 1947–63 period, but the chief increases came prior to 1954. The employed in this group in 1957 were largely concentrated in operative and craftsmen jobs, which are cyclically sensitive. This is the only age group whose participation rates move inversely with employment. This phenomenon, however, is most apparent after 1953. Accordingly, the regression was based on eight observations, including the nonrecession years from 1952–53 to 1962–63; the results produce an r of -0.84, significant at the 0.01 level. None of the predicted values including 1963–64 is beyond two standard errors. When the regression equation is applied to the earlier excluded years, the labor force participation rate is strongly

---

[7] Tables 25 and 26 present point changes in the noninstitutional labor force participation rates and percentage point changes in employment for males by age groups. Since the Armed Forces are included both in the labor force and in the population, these series are not exactly comparable with aggregate male data. The results give a higher participation rate when the Armed Forces are included because the numerator is proportionately more affected than the denominator.

[8] It is hard to say whether there would be any significant difference in the correlation coefficients if civilian data were used.

[9] U.S., Bureau of the Census, "Marital Status, Economic Status, and Family Status, March 1957," *Current Population Reports, Population Characteristics*, Series P-20, No. 81, p. 11.

TABLE 25: Point Changes in Male Labor Force Participation Rates[a] by Age, 1947–48 to 1963–64

Year	14–19	20–24	25–34	35–44	45–54	55–64	65 & over
1947–48	0.1	0.8	0.2	0.0	0.3	(0.1)	(1.0)
1948–49	(0.7)	2.1	(0.1)	0.0	(0.2)	(2.0)	0.1
1949–50	(0.4)	1.3	0.3	(0.4)	0.2	(0.5)	(1.1)
1950–51	0.5	2.0	0.9	0.0	0.2	0.2	(0.9)
1951–52	(1.8)	1.0	0.6	0.3	0.2	0.3	(2.3)
1952–53	(1.0)	0.2	(0.1)	0.3	0.4	0.4	(1.0)
1953–54	(1.6)	(0.7)	(0.1)	(0.1)	(0.1)	0.8	(1.1)
1954–55	0.2	(0.7)	0.2	0.0	0.0	(0.8)	(0.9)
1955–56	1.9	0.0	(0.3)	(0.1)	0.1	0.6	0.4
1956–57	(1.7)	(1.0)	(0.1)	(0.1)	(0.2)	(1.0)	(2.5)
1957–58	(2.3)	(0.3)	0.0	0.1	(0.1)	0.3	(1.9)
1958–59	(0.2)	0.6	0.2	(0.2)	(0.3)	(0.4)	(1.4)
1959–60	(0.7)	0.1	0.2	(0.1)	(0.2)	(0.6)	(1.1)
1960–61	(1.9)	(0.4)	(0.1)	0.0	(0.2)	0.5	(1.4)
1961–62	(1.0)	(0.7)	(0.2)	0.0	0.0	(1.1)	(1.4)
1962–63	(0.1)	(0.8)	(0.1)	(0.1)	0.2	0.0	(1.9)
1963–64	0.1	(0.1)	0.2	(0.2)	0.0	(0.6)	(0.4)

[a] Labor force including Armed Forces as percentage of noninstitutional population.
Parentheses indicate negative figures.

SOURCE: Derived from *Manpower Report of the President*, 1965, p. 194.

TABLE 26: Percentage Changes in Male Employment[a] by Age, 1947–48 to 1963–64

Year	14–19	20–24	25–34	35–44	45–54	55–64	65 & over
1947–48	4.2	2.8	1.9	1.4	1.3	1.9	(0.2)
1948–49	(7.7)	(3.6)	(1.5)	(0.5)	(0.9)	(2.5)	1.0
1949–50	3.7	1.2	11.0	1.3	1.5	1.0	0.3
1950–51	(1.2)	(11.2)	0.7	1.7	2.9	3.7	2.0
1951–52	(2.9)	(15.6)	2.2	1.5	1.7	1.7	(1.5)
1952–53	0.4	(8.8)	1.4	4.9	2.8	0.1	6.0
1953–54	(5.1)	(5.8)	(2.2)	(1.3)	(0.4)	0.5	(2.8)
1954–55	3.6	8.9	1.7	1.7	2.5	0.2	0.3
1955–56	6.1	9.0	(1.0)	1.2	2.1	2.5	3.7
1956–57	(1.9)	2.4	(1.4)	0.1	1.1	(0.3)	(5.0)
1957–58	(4.3)	(1.5)	(4.2)	(1.3)	(0.3)	(0.8)	(5.8)
1958–59	7.2	9.2	0.7	2.0	2.5	1.7	(2.0)
1959–60	4.3	4.4	(1.1)	0.6	1.5	0.8	(0.9)
1960–61	1.2	1.2	(1.7)	(0.4)	0.1	0.8	(4.2)
1961–62	3.4	2.6	(1.2)	2.5	1.5	1.7	1.9
1962–63	0.1	5.6	(0.5)	0.8	1.6	2.0	(4.6)
1963–64	5.7	6.1	1.1	0.3	1.7	1.4	0.0

[a] Civilian employment.
Data for 1947–56 not adjusted to employment definitions adopted in 1957.
Parentheses indicate negative figures.

SOURCE: Derived from *Manpower Report of the President*, 1965, p. 201.

under-estimated in 1948–49 (more than two standard errors) and 1949–50 (almost two standard errors). In the remaining three recession years the decline in the labor force rate is under-predicted by less than two standard errors, but with a declining margin. A possible interpretation is that earlier decreases in employment and increases in the participation rate were associated both with the Korean mobilization and secondary worker responses; more recently, job requirements have not encouraged secondary entry. The inverse nature of the nonrecession relationship suggests that a favorable economic climate increases employment but produces conditions that permit the potential college and graduate student to stay out of the labor force and study.

The group twenty-five to thirty-four years of age is of prime work age. This was the largest age group among labor force males from 1947 to 1957 but dropped to second place thereafter; it shows a net increase in its participation rate between 1947 and 1963. The gains, however, were primarily in the Korean period. The largest single subsequent fluctuation was a decline of only 0.3 point in 1955–56, indicating this as a group whose attachment to the labor force is strong and stable. The correlation coefficient with employment changes is the lowest of any group, 0.42, almost significant at the 0.05 level (for sixteen observations). The 1963–64 prediction has an error of 0.1 point. Recession years show neither more nor less response than other years. The greatest deviation from expected changes in the participation rate occurs in 1950–51, when the participation rate rose well beyond expectations and was probably related to mobilization.

Employment declined for males twenty-five to thirty-four years of age in every year between 1953–54 and 1962–63 except two (1954–55 and 1958–59). The only other male group to experience such consistent employment losses is males sixty-five years and over; however, employment losses were not completely economic. The noninstitutional male population twenty-five to thirty-four, including the Armed Forces, declined in every year from 1955–56 to 1962–63;[10] thus, even with a constant labor force participation rate, employment would have declined. On the other hand, the years of employment declines show somewhat larger percentage employment losses than percentage population losses. These males are most concentrated in operative jobs, followed by craftsmen jobs.

Another prime working age group is between thirty-five and forty-four years. Its 1957 employment was most concentrated in the craftsmen category, followed by operatives. This group displays a net loss in partici-

[10] U.S., Bureau of the Census, "Estimates of the Population of the United States by Age, Color, and Sex," *Current Population Reports*, Series P-25, various numbers.

pation rates from 1947 to 1963, apparently related to slow employment gains and deep recession losses. The coefficient of correlation for twelve observations is 0.57, almost significant at the 0.05 level; the prediction for 1963–64 is accurate. Recession years show a resistance to departure from the labor force despite large losses in employment. The declines in participation rates in recession years are not as large as predicted and deviate beyond two standard errors in only one year. In 1957–58 the rate actually increased 0.1 point, whereas the regression expectation was a decline of 0.3 points. After 1953 the range of fluctuation was no greater than 0.2 point. This group, despite a decline in its participation rate, has taken over from the group twenty-five to thirty-four years old since 1957 in being the largest age group in the male labor force.

The group forty-five to fifty-four years of age also includes men with strong labor force ties and little fluctuation in participation rate. The net change in 1947–63 was a slight increase, mainly in the 1950–53 period. Employment for this group declined only slightly in the first three recession years and was almost steady in 1960–61. The labor force rate is not highly correlated with employment changes since this group is strongly tied to the labor force ($r = 0.49$ for sixteen observations, significant at the 0.05 level), but the 1963–64 prediction is accurate within 0.1 point. Recession behavior is not distinctive. The only major deviation came in 1958–59, when the labor force rate declined more than expected by two standard errors. The stability of this group's employment, aside from its higher seniority, is probably due to its occupational composition. The available occupational breakdown combines this group with those fifty-five to sixty-four years of age. For the combined age category craftsmen are most important, followed by managers and proprietors, and then operatives.

Men fifty-five to sixty-four years of age represent a group who are moving into the category of secondary income earners. They are officially of preretirement age but feel structural and institutional pressures to leave the labor force. This group's participation rate from 1947 to 1963 shows a net decline, with the major losses concentrated after 1954. Its participation rates are highly correlated with employment changes. The coefficient of correlation for sixteen observations is 0.96, significant at the 0.01 level. Every nonrecession year from 1956–57 to 1963–64 shows a greater decline in participation than expected; on the other hand, the labor force rate in the three most recent recessions is under-estimated by at least one standard error. This is just the reverse of the pattern of males fourteen to nineteen years old. The older workers perhaps have replaced the younger workers as secondary labor force entrants. Another interpretation is that this older age group is still tied to the labor force and perseveres in the hunt for work in recession years, while it responds to retirement pressures in other years. There is a good possibility that the secondary recession response of this group's labor force rate is related to its high concentration in the crafts and the manager-proprietor category, occupations of most importance for the group forty-five to sixty-four; self-employment provides an outlet in recessions.

The greatest participation rate declines have come among males sixty-five years or over. The decline has been strong and steady over time but was strongest in 1951–52 and 1956–57. For twelve observations the coefficient of correlation is 0.72, significant at the 0.01 level; however, the 1963–64 prediction over-states the decline by almost two standard errors. Recession year responses predicted by the regression equation suggest a secondary worker response since declines are over-predicted. This was strongest in 1948–49. The subsequent decline in this group's secondary worker response is quite probably related to its occupational breakdown. The largest category in 1957 was that of farmers, followed by managers-proprietors, craftsmen, and service workers. In other words, after sixty-five, employment is largely self-employment, but the important outlets are declining.

The implications of these findings for labor force behavior is that the secondary worker effect is produced mainly by females, primarily married women, and to a much lesser extent by older male workers. Younger male workers do not contribute to it. The behavior of male labor force rates is less explainable by changes in employment than female rates, partly because there are divergent responses in different age groups, notably the inverse relationship among those twenty to twenty-four, and partly because the ties to the labor force predominate in the prime work years regardless of employment changes. The downtrend in male participation rates is partly due to more education and earlier retirement, but it is also explainable in terms of declining opportunities in traditionally male occupations.

A fuller answer to the question regarding the adaptive nature of participation rates requires an investigation of the behavior of unemployment rates by sex. This would be particularly significant with respect to (1) recession years when there is a secondary worker effect and (2) the period after 1955–56, when male withdrawal from the labor force is most pronounced. This is especially important in light of the fact that prime working age males do not respond to employment changes.

Unemployment rates by sex are presented in Table 27. Male and female rates are closely related to the aggregate rate; however, the institutional factors that affect female participation rates are also reflected in female unemployment rates. While women generally have higher unemployment

TABLE 27: Aggregate, Male, and Female Unemployment Rates, 1947–64

Year	Aggregate	Male	Female
1947	3.9	3.7	3.2
1948	3.8	3.6	4.1
1949	5.9	5.9	6.0
1950	5.3	5.1	5.8
1951	3.3	2.9	4.4
1952	3.1	2.8	3.7
1953	2.9	2.8	3.3
1954	5.6	5.3	6.1
1955	4.4	4.2	4.9
1956	4.2	3.8	4.9
1957	4.3	4.1	4.7
1958	6.8	6.8	6.8
1959	5.5	5.3	5.9
1960	5.6	5.4	5.9
1961	6.7	6.5	7.2
1962	5.6	5.3	6.2
1963	5.7	5.3	6.5
1964	5.2	4.7	6.2

NOTE: All figures adjusted to reflect current definitions.

SOURCE: *Manpower Report of the President, 1965*, p. 193.

rates than men, their behavior in response to cyclical downturns mini-
mizes the differences in recession years. Because of the part-time and
temporary nature of much female employment (due to their home
responsibilities), women more often than men leave the labor force when
they become unemployed; but, as their labor attachment grows, this
source of unemployment rate reduction declines. For example, in May,
1963, 80 percent of unemployed women were looking for full-time work—
despite the fact that the major rise in voluntary part-time work has come
from women's entry into the labor force.[11]

Both male and female unemployment rates move with the aggregate.[12]
A major deviation from the aggregate came in 1950–51 when the male
rate declined more than two standard errors as predicted from the
aggregate rate. In that year mobilization of unemployed and employed
youth and expanded employment opportunities for other men account for
the deviation. For females the 1947–48 unemployment rate rose three
standard errors above expectations; in 1951–52 it fell below expectation

[11] Meredith, "Persons Seeking Part-Time Jobs," p. v.

[12] For sixteen observations, changes in the male unemployment rate have a correlation of 0.98 with aggregate changes, while the changes in female unemployment rates
have a correlation of 0.96. The 1963–64 male and female rate changes are correctly
predicted by the regression equations.

by two standard errors. The latter decline was probably connected with employment requirements such that women came from outside the labor force directly to employment. The single largest occupational gain in numbers was among clericals in 1951–52. The participation rate change was in line with the employment change. The unexpected rise in female unemployment in 1947–48 is apparently related to the unwarranted increase in the female participation rate. It exceeded the value predicted by employment changes by two standard errors. In other words, the female labor force participation rate has been adaptive in all but one year.

Further investigation of the adaptive role of participation rates comes from regressing changes in unemployment rates against changes in employment. Deviations from expected patterns are examined with reference to labor force participation rates. The sixteen observations of changes in unemployment rates and changes in employment by sex show correlation coefficients of -0.75 for males and -0.78 for females. The regression equations are $U_f = 1.35 - 0.50E_f$, and $U_m = 0.56 - 0.76E_m$, in which the left-hand term is the respective unemployment rate change and the right-hand variable is the percentage change in employment by sex. The 1963–64 predictions are within 0.2 point of the actual. The estimated values show that secondary worker responses and male labor force attachment may raise unemployment rates in recession years. Recession years all show higher-than-expected rises in unemployment rates; however, the under-estimation of rises in the unemployment rates in these years are all within one standard error.

The female unemployment rate fell by almost two standard errors more than expected in 1952–53 and 1961–62. In the earlier year, 1952–53, the labor force rate is as expected, so the reduction was attributable to a decline in frictional unemployment. In 1961–62 the female labor force withdrawal is almost two standard errors beyond the predicted value. Male unemployment rate changes deviate markedly from predicted values only in 1950–51, falling almost four standard errors beyond expectations. Here the Korean mobilization, not the participation rate, is the explanation. In addition to the draft and the obvious need for prime-age males, the major numerical increase by occupation in 1950–51 was among craftsmen and drew on older workers. The regression equation under-states increases in the male unemployment rate in each of the years from 1959–60 to 1963–64. Added to the fact that declines from 1956–57 to 1963–64 in the male participation rate are under-estimated by regression against employment, there is evidence of structural problems with respect to male unemployment. This evidence leads to the conclusion that labor force participation rates of both males and females have not contributed to higher unemployment rates in nonrecession years but have largely been adaptive;[13] they probably added little to unemployment levels in recession years.

With respect to the Knowles-Kalacheck work, it is pertinent to note that greater-than-"normal" increases in the aggregate participation rate come in recession years if "normal" is equated with the usual behavior of participation rates relative to employment changes. Increases in the participation rate, therefore, cannot be used as a test for structural unemployment; on the contrary, structural unemployment is more aptly tested by differential declines in participation rates taken in conjunction with movements of employment and unemployment. Although the categories used here are quite gross, logic suggests that larger-than-"normal" increases in the labor force would have to draw on housewives, youth, retired workers, and those who previously left the labor force for lack of opportunity or some other reason. It is hardly likely that many high skills would be found in these groups.

If the structural transformation of labor demand is toward higher skills such as professionals, why should one expect an increased labor force rate when the existing labor force cannot supply them? Only if the shift were toward manual or female-linked skills would one expect an increased labor force rate to be brought out by structural skills shortages. But even in this case one cannot be sure that structural shifts would induce *aggregate* labor force rate increases. If the structurally unemployed or potential entrants were discouraged, the aggregate labor force rate could decline. Yet demand could be potentially "adequate."

An increase in the labor force rate would be more likely if the structurally unemployed did not withdraw from the labor force and if additional labor demand could draw on skills existing among groups outside the labor force. An example might be the clerical boom of 1951–52 and 1955–56 and the sharp rise in the employment of craftsmen and laborers in 1950–51, rather than the 1956–57, 1957–58, and 1961–62 high demand years for professionals. Nevertheless, without recourse to movements of unemployment rates and employment, little can be said of a diagnostic nature.

Structural Employment Shifts by Sex

To investigate whether structural shifts in employment are linked with occupational differences by sex, percentage increments in male and female employment from 1947–48 to 1962–63 were regressed against the aggregate increment. The results show that increments by sex were highly

[13] The correlations between changes in participation rates and changes in unemployment rates by sex are close to zero and not statistically significant.

correlated with the aggregate. For sixteen observations, r was 0.89 for females and 0.97 for males, both significant at the 0.01 level. The regression equations are:

$$X_f = 1.09 + 1.09 \, X_t, \text{ and}$$

$$X_m = -0.52 + 0.94 \, X_t,$$

where X_f and X_m represent percentage changes in female and male employment and X_t represents the aggregate percentage change. Females gain about 1 percent in employment even when the aggregate change is zero, because at that level male employment declines about 0.5 percent. The percentage change in male employment is generally less than female percentage increases but the numerical relationship is the reverse. The 1963–64 predictions were off by less than 0.5 percent. The general trend shows a normally larger percentage increase in female rather than male employment. The result has been a secular rise in female employment as a percentage of total employment, from 29 percent in 1948 to 34 percent in 1963. Roughly the same rise has occurred in the female share of the civilian labor force.[14]

Three observations deviated markedly from the pattern. One came in 1952–53, when the male employment gain was greater and the female gain was less than expected by over two standard errors. The same direction of error but somewhat under two standard errors occurred in 1958–59. In 1950–51, by contrast, females gained more than two standard errors beyond expectations. The employment change in 1952–53 was marked by substantial increases for professionals, service workers, and operatives, largely male occupations. There were declines for clericals. A similar phenomenon appeared in 1958–59, when operatives and service workers led the numerical increases by occupation. By contrast, 1950–51 shows a marked shift toward female employment, due more to the absence of civilian males than to an increased need for female skills. The numerical increase for females was four times the male increase but was not the result of a shift toward "female" occupations. There was a net employment gain of 386,000 female clericals; this little more than offset the 362,000 decline among male clericals. The employment increments that year show the largest numerical increases for craftsmen, followed by operatives. The increase in craftsmen probably was filled by the decline among male proprietors and managers, since there are few female craftsmen. But there was a rise of 332,000 female operatives. Clericals and operatives accounted for 75 percent of the female employment increase.

[14] As indicated in Chapter 3, this change in proportions has not in itself been responsible for a rise in unemployment rates.

The mid-1950's seemed to be a period of "stocking up" in female occupations. For example in 1955–56 clericals were the group with the largest numerical increase. And clerical, sales, and the two service occupations accounted for 87 percent of the female employment increase. As overhead labor costs rose in relation to total costs, these traditionally female jobs might have later become more expendable. The newer shifts in requirements have been more related to educational differences than sex differences.

Returning to Table 24, one finds that in nonrecession years it takes a rise in female employment above 1.8 percent to increase the female participation rate. This requires an aggregate employment rise of at least 0.7 percent. Aggregate employment changes at this level or below, however, would probably be of a recession character and would call forth a female labor force rate increase anyway; in each of the four recession years the female rate rose slightly. The conclusion, therefore, is that the female participation rate is expected to increase except in nonrecession years of slow growth. A decline should suggest a nonrecession structural shift away from female-linked skills.

If the male coefficients of Table 24 are accepted for the sake of discussion, a rise of 3.0 percent would be needed in male employment to keep the male labor force rate from declining. This implies an aggregate rise of 3.7 percent. Short of this, the male labor force rate can be expected to decline. It does not rise even in recessions since the vanishing secondary worker response merely keeps the rate from falling as much as expected. Both structural and demand conditions seem to have combined with institutional factors to accelerate the decline in the male participation rate.

Diagnosis of the Postwar Period

Broad profiles based on the direction of change of the labor force rate, the unemployment rate, and employment for the aggregate and by sex may be interpreted in terms of what has been learned thus far. For example, in recession years aggregate and male employment can be expected to fall but may rise for females; each unemployment rate will rise and the labor force rate will fall for males but rise for females. Thus the direction of change for the aggregate labor force rate may be positive or negative. This is the first profile presented in Table 28, and it corresponds with three of four recessions.[15]

In good demand years the total and female labor force rates will rise but the male rate will fall except in years of exceptional demand increases. Unemployment rates will fall except where female labor force entry is too

[15] In 1960–61 the employment rise for the aggregate excludes it from the "profile."

TABLE 28: Classification of Years by Direction of Change in Labor Force Activity, 1947–48 to 1963–64

Classification and year	Aggregate profile			Male profile			Female profile		
	LF	Un.	Emp.	LF	Un.	Emp.	LF	Un.	Emp.
Recession									
1948–49	+	+	−	−	+	−	+	+	+
1953–54	−	+	−	−	+	−	+	+	−
1957–58	−	+	−	−	+	−	+	+	−
Good demand									
1947–48	+	−	+	+	−	+	+	+	+
1949–50	+	−	+	−	−	+	+	−	+
1954–55	+	−	+	−	−	+	+	−	+
1955–56	+	−	+	+	−	+	+	0	+
1963–64	+	−	+	−	−	+	+	−	+
Skill shortage									
1950–51	0	−	+	0	−	+	+	−	+
1951–52	−	−	+	−	−	−	0	−	+
1952–53	−	−	+	−	0	+	−	−	+
1958–59	−	−	+	−	−	+	+	−	+
1961–62	−	−	+	−	−	+	−	−	+
Weak demand and/or structural unemployment									
1956–57	−	+	+	−	+	0	−	−	+
1959–60	+	+	+	−	+	+	+	0	+
1960–61	−	+	+	−	+	−	+	+	+
1962–63	−	+	+	−	0	+	+	+	+

LF: Labor force participation rate; Un.: Unemployment rate; Emp.: Percentage change in employment.

SOURCE: Tables 23 and 27.

ambitious, as in 1947–48, when the female labor force rate showed an excessively large rise. Employment will rise for each group. This profile is represented by the second group of Table 28, namely, 1947–48, 1949–50, 1954–55, 1955–56, and 1963–64.

If there is a shortage of skills not associated with females that cannot be met from outside the labor force and a redundancy of skills within the labor force, the aggregate and each labor force rate by sex would probably fall since the male rate falls in any but high growth years. It can rise for females if there is a rise in female employment. An adjustment involving an exit of redundant workers from the labor force should produce a decline in unemployment rates. Since demand would be above recession levels, there would be some rise in aggregate employment and, therefore, rising female employment, while male employment would rise or fall. The years 1950–51, 1951–52, 1952–53, 1958–59, and 1961–62 fit this description and are the third group in Table 28.

The 1950–51 change is clearly one of short male skills due to mobilization. The male unemployment rate was below expectations while male entry was greater than predicted by civilian employment changes. Female entry was not as great as expected, but females were used as substitutes for males. The entry of males beyond usual expectations centered among those fourteen to thirty-four years old. In 1951–52 males were still in short supply and the female unemployment rate was lower than expected. In 1952–53 there was a continued shortage of males since the Armed Forces declined by only 1.3 percent and the changeover to peacetime production unleashed pent-up consumer demand. There was a stronger employment increase for men than women but the female unemployment rates were lower than expected. In 1958–59 the female participation rate increased but the incremental employment balance was more strongly in favor of males. However, the participation rates of males forty-five to fifty-four and twenty to twenty-four years of age were less than expected, as was the total labor force rate, in view of the employment increases. In 1961–62 all three participation rates not only declined, but the loss was much more than expected from the changes in employment; thus in all five years there is evidence of structural strains, and the labor force rate seems to play an adaptive role in reducing unemployment. In the Korean period, unlike the other years, it is a passive adaptation. It appears that these were years of structural skill shortages.

The years listed in the last group of Table 28 are not easily diagnosed. The aggregate unemployment rate rose in each case but, unlike recession years, it did not always rise for both components. (It did so in 1960–61, which is officially classed as a recession year.) Aggregate employment increased in each year. The year 1960–61 is grouped here because it shows a numerical employment increase of 115,000, which is greater than the numerical increase in 1956–57. Nonrecession behavior is suggested since the female labor force rate actually declined in 1956–57 and in none of the four years did it display a secondary worker response; the same is true for males. The over-all labor force rate declined in each year except 1959–60. The choices of diagnosis are (1) chronic, slack demand at above-recession levels, (2) structural unemployment, or (3) both. The last verdict is most plausible.

The male unemployment rate rose in 1956–57 despite a decline in the labor force rate, while male employment was steady. The numerical employment increase was highest for professionals and clericals. In 1959–60 the male unemployment rate increased, even with an increase in male employment. Gains appeared in clerical, professional, and service occupations. In 1960–61 male and female unemployment rates both rose while female employment rose and male employment declined. The most numerical growth was in professional and service occupations. Among fourteen- to nineteen-year-old males there was a strong withdrawal. In 1962–63, despite the strength of employment increases among operatives, service workers, craftsmen, and professionals, all the component groups' labor force rates responded to employment as predicted. The result was a decline in over-all labor force participation and a rise in each unemployment rate.

Conclusion

Of the seven observations from 1956–57 to 1962–63, two are recession years; nevertheless, some structural dislocations appear to be evident in six of the cases, with signs of structural unemployment in four. The four profiles suggest diagnoses regarding *changes* in unemployment rates; however, the absolute level is also involved in the problem under study. The level of unemployment is thus still undiagnosed. Nevertheless, if the skill shortages suggested in 1959 and 1962 are added to the low level of demand from 1957 to 1963, the combination suggests that structural as well as demand unemployment were at high levels. The changes in 1963–64 due to tax cuts, private investment, and United States involvement in a "conventional" war in Vietnam ameliorated both the demand and the structural problems.

The conclusion reached, therefore, is that the labor force participation rate has largely played an adaptive role but in recent postwar years was unable to adjust fully to skill shortages that the labor force reserve could not fill. It also could not lower unemployment through exits from the labor force since males of prime labor force age were involved. Structural changes during the Korean period did not create higher unemployment, but structural changes after 1956 may have contributed to higher unemployment levels.

JOB MOBILITY BY OCCUPATION

This section examines the mobility patterns between occupations displayed by labor force members who are able to change jobs. Shifts of workers between jobs is significant, not only because it smooths the transition from one set of labor coefficients to another, but because it also determines which jobs remain available to new entrants.[16]

Job Mobility of the Unemployed

There are several sources of public data that touch on job shifts and refer to recent years; however, these are not in continuous series and can be considered only indicative. One such source indicates that there is a shift in the incidence of unemployment as a result of worker mobility from contracting to expanding sectors. Jane Meredith writes:

> The effects of structural change or a business down-turn on long-term unemployment rates in a particular industry may in some cases be obscured by job mobility, i.e., a few unemployed workers from one industry may subsequently find temporary jobs in other industries. Upon losing this latter job, they would be counted as unemployed from the industry of the temporary job. Comparison of data on industry [and occupation] of longest job held during the year with the monthly data lends moderate support to this hypothesis, since the average of the monthly data shows a slightly larger concentration of the unemployed in trade and services—industries where temporary work is often available—and a slightly smaller proportion in manu-facturing.[17]

The data just discussed are presented in Table 29. They show a higher concentration in the "last job" category than in the "longest job" category among service workers and laborers as well as professionals and clericals. The "longest job" category is higher for craftsmen, operatives, and farm occupations. Since the respondents were unemployed in 1959, a recovery year, the data suggest that the shifts have been to temporary employment even in expanding occupations. Further support for the view that job shifts may involve temporary work comes from interviews in April, 1963,

[16] In the Knowles-Kalacheck Report some attention is given to job mobility; however, the authors rely on case studies for their conclusions since very limited data exist on the subject. The authors state, "Independent investigations indicate the existence of an extraordinary amount of interindustry mobility" (p. 78). Aside from the questionable validity of using case studies for broad generalizations, one wonders how the authors are able to come to conclusions about behavior between 1957 and 1960 when the data in the studies do not extend beyond 1953. The areas and years covered are as follows: ". . . two medium-sized Massachusetts cities during the late 1930's" (p. 68); ". . . a New England town in the 1940's" (p. 69); and ". . . gross change data from the household survey of the Bureau of the Census for selected months in the 1949–53 period" (p. 69).

[17] Meredith, "Long-Term Unemployment in the United States," pp. 607, 609.

TABLE 29: Industrial and Occupational Distribution of Experienced Unemployed by Last Job and Longest Job Held, 1959

(percentages)

Major industry or occupation	(1) Average of experienced unemployed each month, by last job held	(2) Total unemployed sometime during year but who had some work, by longest job held
Industry (wage and salary workers)	100.0	100.0
Agriculture, forests, and fisheries	6.9	7.4
Contract construction	14.7	15.0
Manufacturing	32.4	35.5
Utilities	5.8	5.8
Trade	19.1	17.3
Services and finance	18.8	17.3
Government	2.2	1.8
Occupations	100.0	100.0
Prof., tech.; mgr., offic., propr.	6.3	5.5
Clerical; sales	15.5	14.7
Craftsmen, foremen	14.1	17.1
Operatives	28.8	31.7
Private household workers	3.3	2.9
Other service workers	11.9	9.5
Laborers	15.7	13.1
Farm occupations	4.4	5.4

NOTE: Sums do not total 100.0 because of rounding.

SOURCE: Jane L. Meredith (BLS), "Long-Term Unemployment in the United States," *Special Labor Force Report*, No. 17, June, 1961, p. 609.

with respondents who had been unemployed five weeks or more in 1961 (a recession year).[18]

Those interviewed answered questions about their first job, their "best" job, and their current or last job (if currently unemployed). White-collar occupations were 22 percent of best jobs, but 20 percent of current or last jobs, possibly reflecting the movement of automation into offices. Blue-collar jobs rated 64 percent as best and 62 percent as last or current job. Service jobs were rated best by 11.5 percent and current or last by 14 percent. Persons who were unemployed at the time of the interview (April, 1963) were asked if they expected recall to their last job. The highest proportions of workers not expecting recall were operatives,

[18] The interviews were conducted in conjunction with the annual Census review of the work history of the labor force. The supplementary interviews covered only persons over eighteen years. Robert L. Stein (BLS), "Work History, Attitudes, and Income of the Unemployed," *Special Labor Force Report*, No. 37, Dec., 1963.

clerical workers, nonhousehold service workers, and craftsmen, in that order. This indicates something of the temporary nature of the white-collar and service jobs and of the displacement of blue-collar workers. It also indicates that job mobility was utilized as an adjustment to changing labor demand.

Job Mobility, 1955 and 1961

When workers move from one job to another they often are trying to better their position or have been forced to leave their last employment. In the latter case the reason may be lack of work, although, of course, there are other personal, noneconomic reasons such as health. A move to improve job status involves a change of occupation more often than does a move resulting from job loss. In recession years moves for improvement (voluntary shifts) usually decline in relation to moves because of job loss. The discussion that follows examines and compares the mobility patterns of a boom employment year, 1955, and a later recession year, 1961.

The best available data on job shifts by occupation were collected in connection with the Household Survey. Two major limitations in a comparison of the data must be borne in mind. First, 1955 was a year when technological changes may have been underway and there are no earlier years for comparison. Second, and most important, 1955 and 1961 represent very different phases of the business cycle. No major shifts in behavior can thus be ascribed solely to structural causes unless obvious inadequacies in demand in 1961 are accounted for. On the other hand, even though there were fewer job shifts in 1961 than in 1955, and proportionately fewer due to voluntary reasons, there was a net increase in employment both between 1955 and 1961 and between 1960 and 1961.

By way of background, the reader may recall that 1954–55 showed a higher concentration of below-average employment change by occupation than by industry or area. These were centered in the farm occupations. The chief above-average gains were among operatives. In 1960–61 the concentration among below-average occupations was not as high as it was for industries and areas, or as in previous recessions. It declined as it would in a high-employment year. The concentration of above-average gains by occupation fell as expected but rose by industry. The gains by occupation were strongest in professional and service occupations. Farm workers and laborers shared the below-average change with operatives.

Table 30 presents the basic data. It is a ten-by-ten matrix of job shifts by occupation for 1955 and for 1961. A job shift is defined as a change in employer (or to or from self-employment). It does not include a change of occupation without a change of employer; it thus excludes promotions or demotions within a firm. In the case of private household workers, a change in the household worked for does not constitute a job shift; only a change of occupation would be registered. Since individuals may switch jobs more than once within the year, job shifts number more than the total number of job changers in any year. Job shifts are used exclusively in studying the direction of job changes by occupation because the data for shifts are more detailed and job changers can be classed by only one occupation.

The movements of female craftsmen and laborers are not represented in Table 30 and female managers are grouped with professionals (all the

TABLE 30: Direction of Job Shifts by Occupation, 1955 and 1961

(thousands)

Job shifts from:				Job shifts to:						
	Total	Prof.ᵃ	Mgrs.ᵇ	Cleri-cals	Sales	Crafts-menᶜ	Oper-atives	Labor-ersᵈ	Pr. house.ᵉ	Serv-iceᶠ	Farm occup.
1955											
Prof.ᵃ	638	390	24	80	45	24	29	18	2	21	5
Mgrs.ᵇ	358	28	95	39	33	51	65	22	—	7	18
Clericals	1,134	82	20	639	116	23	111	38	14	82	9
Sales	907	27	61	176	336	42	127	32	28	64	14
Craftsmenᶜ	1,525	22	72	31	29	941	236	84	—	43	67
Operatives	2,617	39	75	140	124	205	1,363	342	35	152	142
Laborersᵈ	1,654	18	20	83	119	109	380	662	—	68	195
Pr. house.ᵉ	264	8	—	38	19	—	36	—	44	61	58
Serviceᶠ	1,170	47	22	77	95	34	175	79	50	534	57
Farm occup.	1,159	6	24	17	40	76	231	194	51	84	436
Total	11,426	667	413	1,320	956	1,505	2,753	1,471	224	1,116	1,001
1961											
Prof.ᵃ	886	580	23	99	57	21	47	12	2	34	11
Mgrs.ᵇ	360	20	138	25	51	41	49	20	—	5	11
Clericals	1,444	102	17	887	112	30	130	47	7	103	9
Sales	857	46	65	172	351	21	86	36	8	67	5
Craftsmenᶜ	1,654	46	46	31	27	1,126	200	88	—	45	46
Operatives	2,226	68	49	113	80	212	1,175	263	23	136	107
Laborersᵈ	1,184	24	16	52	31	96	285	486	1	84	99
Pr. house.ᵉ	176	4	—	16	17	—	24	—	9	78	28
Serviceᶠ	1,299	56	14	93	87	30	193	84	52	661	29
Farm occup.	690	12	10	3	5	35	101	135	20	39	330
Total	10,776	957	378	1,491	818	1,612	2,290	1,181	122	1,252	675

NOTE: Categories are abbreviations of those used previously except: (ᵃ) professionals include female managers; (ᵇ) managers are male only; (ᶜ) craftsmen are male only; (ᵈ) laborers are male only; (ᵉ) private household workers are female only; and (ᶠ) service workers include male private household workers. In 1955 total shifts were 11,495,000. Excluded were 64,000 shifts. In 1961 excluded were 92,000 in a total of 10,868,000 shifts. In 1955 figures for farm occupations were partly derived as remainders.

All figures except totals reconstructed from percentage data in sources. Job shifts are changes of employers (or self-employment) in calendar year. The data come from single interviews in the years 1956 and 1962.

SOURCE: U.S., Bureau of the Census, "Job Mobility of Workers in 1955," *Current Population Reports*, Series P-50, No. 70, 1957; and Gertrude Bancroft and Stuart Garfinkle (BLS), "Job Mobility in 1961," *Special Labor Force Report*, No. 35, Aug., 1963.

titles used here are abbreviations of the usual longer ones). Male household workers are grouped with other service workers. This was necessary in order to keep the two years exactly comparable and to adjust for differences in the way the data were reported in the sources. Job shifts to occupations sum vertically and tell what occupations were left behind by the new transfers into another job. Jobs shifts from occupations sum horizontally and tell where those who left jobs found new employment. All the figures except the original totals were derived by working back from the percentage distributions reported in the sources. Analysis would be impossible without absolute numbers, but the numbers are not as statistically reliable as the percentages because the data come from a probability sample later blown up. This entire section must be interpreted with this reservation in mind.

The most important thing to remember about job shifts is that they represent successful completion of a transfer within a year—even though unemployment may have intervened; each shift has employment at either end within the year. Loss of a job without re-employment in the year provides a drop in employment but no job shift. Employment from outside the labor force or from unemployment provides a rise in employment but no job shift. Unemployment may or may not intervene and the unemployment rate may or may not be affected. We thus focus on those workers who were qualified for another job after leaving employment to find out about the adaptiveness of workers to jobs.

Whether demand is high affects the number of available jobs, but the skills required and the characteristics of the disemployed also determine whether they are job changers or just unemployed. A decline in job shifts from 1955 to 1961 could come because fewer of the disemployed found jobs open due to the decline in demand, or it could come because employment was more stable; on the other hand, there was a net increase in employment between 1960 and 1961 and 1955 and 1961. The decline in job shifts could also show dislocations in skill requirements and availabilities.

The bulk of job shifts usually take place within the same occupation group, mainly because persons are best able to qualify in an occupation they already know. This is also the usual response to a job loss—the most usual cause of a shift. A voluntary change to improve status or income more often involves a change of occupation. At any point in time, therefore, the amount of shifting *within* an occupation reflects the degree of stability of employment and transferability of skills (both inversely related to shifts). Changes over time reflect changes in these two qualities and in the economic climate.

Craftsmen and professionals, whose jobs require a high degree of training, show the highest proportion of internal shifts.[19] Professionals and managers have the lowest shift rates;[20] their employment is more stable and they are less able to accommodate or be accommodated by other occupations. Household workers have the highest proportions of shifts to and from other occupations, but a fairly low shift rate. This is less a matter of stability and transferability than the difficulty with the way shifts to other households are handled in the enumeration, as already noted. Male laborers' proportion of internal shifts is higher than expected due to the unstable nature of employment and the difficulties in shifting out of or into an occupation that is at the bottom rung in skills and income. The rate of total shifts, however, is the highest of all, as expected.

The rank order of occupations by their proportions of internal shifts is stable between 1955 and 1961. In going from a boom year to a recession year, the internal-shift proportions would be expected to increase for each occupation as voluntary moves decline. This was not true among operatives, farm workers, laborers and household workers, where proportions declined; thus, where these occupations had members who were displaced and who could find new work, they more often had to find work in other occupations in 1961 than in 1955. At the same time, new jobs were more often filled from outside the occupation. Aside from household workers, these are the groups in which employment declines were concentrated in 1960–61. In the case of laborers there is some possibility that greater stability among the employed workers may have occurred. While unemployment rose 3.9 points for operatives between 1955 and 1961, and 2.0 points for farm workers, it actually fell by 1.8 points for laborers.

Table 31 presents job shift rates—shifts to an occupation, shifts from, and the total shifts, each as a percentage of employment in the occupation group. Their rough, inverse correspondence with the special training needs for each is evident. Managers, officials, and proprietors, however, show a surprisingly low rate, but here the requirement of experience in operating a specific business or for a particular firm serves in lieu of special training.

Between 1955 and 1961 all the total job shift rates decreased except for professionals, clericals, and craftsmen; these groups all had employment increases, but so had four other occupations. These three may have suffered skill shortages as well as unemployment. Craftsmen had a net movement out of the occupation in both years, and here one suspects that

---

[19] The number in the ith row and ith column as a percentage of shifts to and shifts from the ith occupation.

[20] The number of shifts to plus the number of shifts from the ith occupation as a percentage of employment in the ith occupation.

displacement was increasing even while placement was good and new skill needs opened up. Clericals and professionals had a net movement in, in both years. This seems to be evidence that standards for entry had been lowered in response to labor demand.

The relative mobility to and from occupations can be further examined by adjusting for shares in employment and job shift shares. This is done in Table 31 by presenting the ratios of shares of shifts to shares of employment. The ratios are obviously varied within the year, but changes in the ratios between 1955 and 1961 indicate the relative increase of shift shares to employment shares. Professionals, clericals, craftsmen, operatives, and service workers all increased the value of shift shares relative to employment shares. Operatives were the only group of the five to have an employment decline at the same time; the rise in its ratio indicates that the drop in total shifts was not as great as the drop in employment. For service workers, the number of shifts increased and the rise in the share of shifts was greater than the rise in the employment share. This could mean greater instability of employment, but, even so, there was a decline in the shift rate. This again leaves professionals, clericals, and craftsmen as the increasingly mobile occupations.

The total job shift rate by occupation, when plotted against the appropriate unemployment rate by occupation, shows a clear positive relationship. Private household workers show a higher unemployment rate than would be expected, while sales workers show a much lower unemployment rate than expected. Household workers were eliminated from the regression analysis because it is clear that the exclusion of shifts between households from the definition of shifts in this category accounts for the low shift rate.

A cross-section correlation for each year was run with nine observations. In 1955, r is 0.94, significant at the 0.01 level. In 1961, r is 0.87, also significant at the 0.01 level.[21] The change in the regression lines is very interesting. In 1955, where U is the component unemployment rate and J is the component job shift rate, $U_{55} = -1.905 + 0.158J$. But in the next equation, $U_{61} = 0.139 + 0.164J$. Notice that the slopes are very similar. The difference in the two intercept terms is significantly different from zero at the 0.01 level. There was an autonomous rise in unemployment rates relative to job shift rates from 1955 to 1961.

Operatives increased their job shift share relative to their employment share, as observed earlier. This, combined with an unusually large upward shift in unemployment with respect to job shift rates, suggests internal

[21] As expected, sales workers are below in unemployment more than two standard errors in 1955, but only a little over one standard error in 1961. In 1961, operatives are above in unemployment by more than two standard errors.

dislocations involving unemployment, not only more often in connection with a job change, but more often with no relocation. Duration of unemployment also probably increased, adding to the unemployment rate. In addition to this, since there is a net shift into operative jobs, operative displacement was from existing jobs while gross new jobs were often taken by those formerly in other occupations.

The paradox of less job shifting and higher unemployment existing along with a positive relationship between job shift rates and unemployment rates is explained by an autonomous upward shift in the line of regression between the two. This shift may be explained by the recession

TABLE 31: Job Shifts as a Percentage of Employment, and the Distribution of Job Shifts and Employment by Occupation, 1955 and 1961

	Job shifts as percentage of employment						Change: 1955–61
	1955			1961			
	To	From	Total	To	From	Total	Total
Prof., tech.	9.8%	9.4%	19.2%	10.8%	10.0%	20.8%	1.6%
Managers	7.6	6.6	14.2	6.3	6.0	12.3	(1.9)
Clericals	15.8	13.6	29.4	15.1	14.6	29.7	0.3
Sales	24.0	22.8	46.8	18.4	19.3	37.7	(9.1)
Craftsmen	18.5	18.8	37.3	19.2	19.7	38.9	1.6
Operatives	21.6	20.5	42.1	19.5	18.9	38.4	(3.7)
Laborers	41.1	46.3	87.4	34.8	34.9	69.7	(17.7)
Pr. household	11.8	13.9	25.7	5.4	7.8	13.2	(12.5)
Service	21.5	22.5	44.0	19.6	20.3	39.9	(4.1)
Farm occup.	15.3	17.7	33.0	13.1	13.3	26.4	(6.6)
Total	18.2%	18.2%	36.4%	16.2%	16.2%	32.4%	(4.0)%

	Percentage distribution				Change: total shifts 1955–61
	Total shifts	Employment	Total shifts	Employment	
	1955	1955	1961	1961	thousands
Prof., tech.	5.7%	10.8%	8.5%	13.3%	538
Managers	3.4	8.7	3.4	9.0	(33)
Clericals	10.7	13.3	13.6	14.8	481
Sales	8.1	6.3	7.8	6.7	(188)
Craftsmen	13.3	12.9	15.1	12.6	236
Operatives	23.5	20.4	21.0	17.7	(854)
Laborers	13.7	5.7	11.0	5.1	(760)
Pr. household	2.2	3.0	1.4	3.4	(190)
Service	10.0	8.3	11.8	9.6	265
Farm occup.	9.4	10.4	6.4	7.8	(795)
Total	100.0%	100.0%	100.0%	100.0%	(1,300)

	Job shift share as percentage of employment share			Percentage change: employ- ment
	1955	1961	Change: 1955–1961	1955 to 1961
Prof., tech.	52.8%	63.9%	11.1%	29.9%
Managers	39.1	37.8	(1.3)	10.1
Clericals	80.5	91.9	11.4	17.9
Sales	128.6	116.4	(12.2)	11.6
Craftsmen	103.1	119.8	16.7	3.6
Operatives	115.2	118.6	3.4	(7.8)
Laborers	240.4	215.7	(24.7)	(5.0)
Pr. household	73.2	41.2	(32.1)	18.4
Service	120.5	122.9	2.4	22.7
Farm occup.	90.4	82.1	(8.3)	(20.9)
Total	100.0%	100.0%	0.0%	6.1%

NOTE: See notes to Table 30. Employment figures based on job shift groups. Parentheses Indicate negative figures.

SOURCE: Derived from Table 30 and *Manpower Report of the President, 1964*, p. 199.

conditions of 1961. The recession can also explain the decline in inter-occupational shifts and in the number considered to be income improvements. (This is mentioned in the 1961 study, which asked about income.) But even with this diagnosis, the direction of the shifts remains to be examined as a clue to transferability of skills and relative demand and supply conditions.

Table 32 presents the occupational directions of the twenty most numerous job shifts in each of the two years; as was indicated, most internal shifts are included. There is a decline in the absolute number of internal shifts among operatives, laborers, and farm workers, with a rise for craftsmen, clericals, service workers, professionals, and managers. The rank order in the top twenty stays the same only for craftsmen and operatives. Laborers and farm workers show a significant drop in internal shifts as the opportunities to move within the occupation disappear.

There are several important changes in shifts between occupations. The rank order of the movement from farm work to operative jobs is drastically cut from twelfth place in 1955 to twenty-fourth place in 1961. The flow from craftsmen to operatives is reversed. Laborers going to the farms falls from fourteenth to twenty-fifth place while the net flow is from farms to laborers' jobs in 1961. That flow itself falls from fifteenth to seventeenth position. It is interesting to note that though total shifts and employment fell for operatives, the movement into this occupation from certain others increased in rank position. These are service and clerical

TABLE 32: Rank Order, Number, and Percentage of Total: Top Twenty Job Shifts by Occupation, 1955 and 1961

			1955			1961		
Order	Shift from	Shift to	Thou-sands	Per-cent-age	Order	Thou-sands	Per-cent-age	Direction of numerical change 1955–61
1	Operatives	Operatives	1,363	11.9	1	1,175	10.9	−
2	Craftsmen	Craftsmen	941	8.2	2	1,126	10.4	+
3	Laborers	Laborers	662	5.8	6	496	4.6	−
4	Clericals	Clericals	639	5.6	3	887	8.2	+
5	Service	Service	534	4.7	4	661	6.1	+
6	Farm occup.	Farm occup.	436	3.8	8	330	3.1	−
7	Prof.	Prof.	390	3.4	5	580	5.4	+
8	Laborers	Operatives	380	3.3	9	285	2.6	−
9	Operatives	Laborers	342	3.0	10	263	2.4	−
10	Sales	Sales	336	2.9	7	351	3.3	+
11	Craftsmen	Operatives	236	2.1	12	200	1.9	−
12	Farm occup.	Operatives	231	2.0	24	101	—	−
13	Operatives	Craftsmen	205	1.8	11	212	2.0	+
14	Laborers	Farm occup.	195	1.7	25	99	—	−
15	Farm occup.	Laborers	194	1.7	17	135	1.3	−
16	Sales	Clericals	176	1.5	14	173	1.6	−
17	Service	Operatives	175	1.5	13	193	1.8	+
18	Operatives	Service	152	1.3	16	136	1.3	−
19	Operatives	Farm occup.	142	1.2	21	107	—	−
20	Operatives	Clerical	140	1.2	19	113	1.0	−
	Managers	Managers	95	—	15	138	1.3	+
	Clerical	Operatives	111	—	18	130	1.2	+
	Clerical	Sales	116	—	20	112	1.0	−

NOTE: See notes to Table 30.
SOURCE: Derived from Table 30.

workers and may be the result of improper labeling of new jobs opened up by technological changes or the ambiguous nature of the title system. The picture indicates an intense competition for operative jobs.

There are no data on incomes by occupations related to job shifts; therefore, we have taken each two-way combination of job shifts and called one an upgrade and one a downgrade. The determination is based on the conventional import of the title and on average annual incomes by occupation available from the Census Bureau.[22] The net change for every combination of shifts in both years is calculated. (The net changes are the shifts in one direction less the shifts in the opposite direction for each pair of occupations.) The results are presented in Table 33. At first glance it appears that the level of the employed labor force is being upgraded through shifting. It must be remembered, however, that (1) the data refer to only those who successfully completed a shift within the year, (2) inter-occupational shifts are a small part of total shifts in both years, and (3) we

[22] Herman P. Miller, U.S., Bureau of the Census, *Trends in the Income of Families and Persons in the United States: 1947 to 1960*, Technical Paper No. 8, 1963.

TABLE 33: Classification of Net Job Shifts between Occupations, 1955 and 1961

(thousands)

From	To	1955	1961	From	To	1955	1961
Net upgrading in both years				*Net downgrading in both years*			
Clerical	Prof.	2	3	Prof.	Sales	18	11
Operatives	Prof.	10	21	Managers	Clerical	19	8
Pr. house.	Prof.	6	2	Managers	Laborers	2	4
Service	Prof.	26	22	Craftsmen	Clerical	9	1
Farm	Prof.	1	1	Clerical	Service	5	10
Sales	Managers	28	14	Craftsmen	Service	9	15
Craftsmen	Managers	21	5	Pr. house.	Farm	7	8
Sales	Clerical	60	60				
Laborers	Clerical	45	5	*Net downgrading only in 1955*			
Pr. house.	Clerical	24	9	Prof.	Craftsmen	2	
Sales	Operatives	3	6	Sales	Pr. house.	9	
Service	Sales	31	10	Craftsmen	Operatives	31	
Laborers	Craftsmen	25	8	Service	Laborers	11	
Laborers	Operatives	38	22	Laborers	Farm	1	
Pr. house.	Operatives	1	1				
Service	Operatives	23	57	*Net downgrading only in 1961*			
Pr. house.	Service	11	26	Prof.	Managers		3
Farm	Service	27	10	Managers	Service		20
				Managers	Farm		1
Net upgrading only in 1955				Clerical	Operatives		17
Managers	Prof.	4		Clerical	Farm		5
Operatives	Managers	10		Craftsmen	Sales		6
Service	Managers	15		Sales	Laborers		5
Farm	Managers	6		Craftsmen	Farm		11
Operatives	Clerical	29		Operatives	Farm		6
Farm	Clerical	8					
Sales	Craftsmen	13		*Sum of net changes from occupations*			
Laborers	Sales	87		*Net upgrading*			
Farm	Sales	26		Sales		95	75
Farm	Craftsmen	9		Operatives		49	27
Farm	Operatives	89		Laborers		194	47
				Pr. house.		35	39
Net upgrading only in 1961				Service		84	89
Craftsmen	Prof.		24	Farm		166	47
Laborers	Prof.		12	Total		623	324
Pr. house.	Sales		9				
Operatives	Craftsmen		12	*Net downgrading*			
Farm	Laborers		36	Prof.		10	14
				Managers		17	33
Total net change: upgrading				Clerical		3	29
1955:			565	Craftsmen		28	4
1961:			244	Total		58	80

NOTE: Net change = shifts to, less shifts from an occupation.
SOURCE: Table 30.

only guess whether there were actual improvements, based on the titles. These are very broad and often outmoded.

Even with these words of caution one might be encouraged by the directions of change, except that an analysis of the content of the changes shows that managers and clericals have been increasingly downgraded, possibly for technological reasons. The upgrading continued for service and sales workers, but for the other occupations showing upgrading the reduction from 1955 to 1961 is of major proportions. For the top and bottom occupations the data are not analytically meaningful because any movement out of the occupation had to be down for the top and up for the bottom. Net upgrading does emerge in both years but in 1955 net upgrades across occupations were 565,000 out of 11,426,000, or 1 in 20. In 1961 it was 244,000 in 10,776,000 or 1 in 44. In 1961 the gains in upgrading indicate that the standards for professional jobs may have been lowered or retraining improved, but the movement from households to sales and from farms to laborers is no major indication of anything but increased urbanization. On the other hand, clerical workers, craftsmen, operatives, and laborers were obviously getting at the head of the line for farm, operative, and laborers' jobs, which were shrinking in supply. Besides ousting the current holders of these skills, the downgraded workers were blocking the traditional entry jobs in 1961.

The Problem of Entry Jobs

Finding scope for job changes is one problem; finding jobs for new labor force entrants is the other side of the coin. New entrants to employment are able to ease the shift from one set of job requirements to another when they enter where increases in labor demand occur. An entry job is defined here as a job which is filled by the currently unemployed or those just entering or re-entering the labor force. [23]

Table 34 presents some idea of the net jobs created for entrants after the job shifters had made their adjustments. The reasoning is as follows. In every occupation there is a net movement of job shifts in or out. When this is positive and employment has increased, there are more people in the occupation than before, but there are fewer jobs filled by new entrants than the amount of the employment increase. Subtracting the net job shift figure from the net change in employment provides an idea of how many jobs were filled by new entrants. If the employment change is positive and net shifts are negative, more jobs are filled by entrants than the employment-change figure shows.

[23] The term is usually used to mean only the jobs for brand new entrants to the labor force. The broader definition is used because it can be measured.

TABLE 34: Incremental Employment Available to Entrants after Job Shifting by Occupation, 1955 and 1961

| Selected occupations | Thousands | | | (4) Net entry jobs as percentage of employment change (3)/(1) |
	(1) Employment change 1954–55	(2) Shifts to, less shifts from	(3) Net entry jobs (1) — (2)	
1955				
Prof.	250	29	221	88.4%
Managers	204	55	149	73.0
Clericals	199	186	13	6.5
Sales	42	49	(7)	(16.7)
Craftsmen	41	(20)	61	148.8
Operatives	509	136	373	73.3
Laborers	84	(183)	267	317.9
Pr. household	186	(40)	226	121.5
Service	166	(54)	220	132.5
Farm occup.	189	(158)	347	183.6
Total	1,870	0	1,870	100.0%
1960–61				
1961				
Prof.	247	71	176	71.3%
Managers	36	18	18	50.0
Clericals	78	47	31	39.7
Sales	38	(39)	77	202.6
Craftsmen	69	(42)	111	160.9
Operatives	(224)	64	(288)	(128.6)
Laborers	(186)	(3)	(183)	(98.4)
Pr. household	84	(54)	138	164.3
Service	207	(47)	254	122.7
Farm occup.	(225)	(15)	(210)	(93.3)
Total	124	0	124	100.0%

NOTE: When net jobs gained from shifts are algebraically greater than employment change we assume that displacement leading to unemployment without a new job in the same year has occurred. This is evident in sales, 1955, and operatives in 1961. However, it should be noted that the job shifts refer to changes in jobs and can number more than job changers. The employment data refer to employed individuals. Therefore the figures should be interpreted only as rough indications of magnitudes.

Parentheses indicate negative figures.

SOURCE: Derived from Table 30 and *Manpower Report of the President, 1964*, p. 199.

If the number of new jobs is positive but smaller than the net gain by shifts, there is reason to expect displacement of employed workers into unemployment or out of the labor force and their replacement by others from different occupations. This leaves no openings for entrants, and, in fact, is like a net employment loss as far as entrants are concerned. An

employment loss accompanying a net gain in job shifts is as if the employment loss had been even greater with respect to entrants. (Of course, the
total of new entry jobs is equal to total new employment, except where
entrants displace employed workers, who then become unemployed or
leave the labor force.) The figures in Table 34 must be considered only
as broadly indicative. Job shifting can always involve double counting of
individuals, while the employment data, in principle, cannot; thus the two
sets of data are not strictly additive.

If total employment is growing and workers are moving up the occupational scale, the lowest occupations and the ones requiring fresh
education are the entry jobs. Even in 1955 when technological change was
already evident, this situation prevailed. There were more entry jobs
than shown by the employment increases for craftsmen, laborers, and
household, service, and farm workers. Except for craftsmen these were the
lowest skilled jobs. The figure for craftsmen probably reflected the scarce
supply of the newer skills, such as repair crafts. The largest absolute source
of entry jobs in 1955 was operatives, with farm and labor occupations
following. The highest ratio of entry jobs to employment change was
among laborers and farm workers. Clerical and sales jobs showed little or
no net openings for entrants.

The picture is changed in 1961. Operatives show a decline in employment. Because the net effect of job shifts is *into* the occupation the number
who were displaced from employment and unable to shift elsewhere is
assumed to have increased, with an additional number replaced by
workers with other occupational backgrounds. Sales workers, craftsmen,
household workers, and service workers were now the occupations where
a negative net shifting provided more entry jobs than the employment
changes show. But, of course, the figures are small in absolute numbers
because it is a recession year. The greatest source of entry jobs was service
occupations and professional and technical work, followed by crafts and
household work.

The situation is complicated by the fact that the household jobs are for
females and the craftsmen and professional jobs require special training.
This leaves the service occupations as the chief source of low-level entry
jobs. But its entry jobs declined as a percentage of its employment change
between 1954–55 and 1960–61. Entry jobs as a percentage of the employment change increased for clericals, sales, craftsmen, and household
workers. In the first two cases the numbers involved were small; in the
second two there is the problem of special training or strictly female
employment.

The concept of an entry job requires change. Rather than being
considered as an unskilled job, it should be seen as a job which happens

to be available to entrants. A major structural change is that the entry job now requires the most, not the least, preparation. If jobs created through current and potential expansion in demand are to offer the maximum employment for the minimum increase in demand, the programmatic task becomes one of equipping new entrants and pre-entrants with the skills to fill the new entry jobs.

Conclusion

The mobility of workers between occupations has been and continues to be an adaptive tool of adjustment to changing skill requirements. The effectiveness of the tool is naturally impaired by inadequate levels of demand. The change from 1955 to 1961 shows that a smaller proportion of all changes in jobs were across occupations. A smaller proportion involved upgrading across occupations.

There have been structurally induced shifts to occupations which require greater education and training. The skill requirements for jobs to be filled by those not presently employed have been upgraded; this may have been part of the reason for the reduced mobility across occupations. To the extent that these requirements are realistic and not just the result of a loose labor market, a new preparation for entry jobs and mobility is necessary to permit workers to move up within the various skill families. These conclusions are only tentative because the recession conditions of 1961 forbid attributing all the phenomena discussed to structural change.

CHAPTER 7

LABOR FORCE ADJUSTMENTS TO CHANGING EMPLOYMENT REQUIREMENTS
Geographic Mobility and Educational Adaptation

This chapter continues the study of labor force adjustments to changes in labor requirements. The first section deals with the spatial movement of males in the labor force. The second discusses changes in the educational attainments of the labor force. In both cases the adaptive role of the mechanism is discussed theoretically and then the adequacy of the changes displayed are assessed. Finally, implications are drawn with regard to structural unemployment.

GEOGRAPHIC MOBILITY

When there are spatial changes in the skill content of labor demand or changes in the location of industry, the labor force can adjust through the mechanism of geographic mobility. That is, workers can go to where the jobs are located. This mechanism is in operation in depressed areas and generally throughout the economy.[1] It is displayed in Table 35, which shows that, except for the East North Central states (which figured strongly in concentration of below-average employment changes) and the transposition of the Pacific and South Atlantic states, the rank order of

[1] See, for example, U.S., Department of Commerce, Area Redevelopment Administration, *Migration Into and Out of Depressed Areas; The Geographic Mobility of Labor: A Summary Report* (Washington: U.S. Government Printing Office, Sept., 1964); Gallaway, "Labor Mobility, Resource Allocation, and Structural Unemployment"; and Robert L. Raimon, "Interstate Migration and Wage Theory," *The Review of Economics and Statistics*, XLIV, 4 (Nov., 1962), pp. 428–38.

TABLE 35: Relation between Growth in Employment and Interstate Migration, 1955–60

(thousands)

Geographic area	Increase in nonfarm payroll employment	1960 residents who lived in a different state or abroad in 1955
Pacific	891	3,089
South Atlantic	824	3,244
Middle Atlantic	391	1,955
West and South Central	370	1,417
Mountain	335	1,248
West North Central	266	1,195
East South Central	234	846
New England	158	840
East North Central	136	2,311

SOURCE: *Manpower Report of the President, 1963*, p. 58.

employment changes by region matches the rank order of regions by number of migrant residents. The degree of adaptation is still in question, however, partly because there are scale biases and partly because supply and demand factors are not known. Is the labor force too mobile, too little mobile, or sufficiently mobile with respect to labor allocation? In other words, does too little or too much geographic mobility lead to unnecessary levels of unemployment?[2]

If migration is valued as a means for allocating labor resources, it may not always be required at the same level to perform the same function. The level of area mobility required when jobs are plentiful and geographically well distributed may be quite low when qualified workers are also well distributed. Quite likely, however, high voluntary mobility will accompany plentiful jobs. In this latter case a rise in area mobility could raise the frictional unemployment rate. If, however, job opportunities are geographically concentrated but plentiful, a migration rise could hold down the over-all unemployment rate. When demand drops, greater area

[2] The Knowles-Kalacheck Report asks the question, "Have unemployed workers become more immobile over time?" (p. 19). Stated this way, the study would equate the unemployment results of greater immobility with structural unemployment. However, there is the problem of what "more" means. For example, does it mean more perverse refusal to move to areas where jobs would be provided? This would raise the frictional, not the structural, level of unemployment. On the other hand, if less mobility is a symptom that the unemployed feel or know that they cannot fill existing openings, and do not move in vain, it is an appropriate response, since it would make no sense to move if the skills of the movers did not match the needs in other labor markets. Finally, mobility at a time of widespread and general job availability could actually raise frictional unemployment rates if moving per se caused short-term unemployment, and it would not be an adaptive mechanism.

mobility may or may not hold the unemployment rate down, depending on the distribution and quality of existing demand. But in any state of demand, if the available jobs are not matched by qualified workers, increased migration is an inappropriate adjustment that could not improve unemployment rates.[3]

In order to diagnose the reason for a change in migration rates it is necessary to know something about how the rates react to changing economic conditions. It is important to look at unemployment rates and the quality, quantity, and distribution of available jobs.[4] The question of geographic mobility is too complex to handle with a single statistic.

Mobility of Males in the Labor Force

The data presented here deal primarily with civilian males in the labor force from 1948 to 1964. Data for civilians not of labor force age are irrelevant to the discussion, and sufficient data on women are not available. The high labor force participation rates for males and their role as heads of families make them an appropriate subject of inquiry.

Information regarding migration is collected by the Census Bureau in its Household Survey in either March or April of each year. A migrant is defined as someone whose place of residence twelve months prior to the interview was in a different county from the present residence; migrants are classed as in-state or between-state, among other categories. The act of migration may have taken place at any time within the previous twelve months and could have involved more than one move.

The labor force status is determined in a different manner. The status of the individual in the week prior to the interview decides his labor force category, in line with the Household Survey definitions. Thus there is no

---

[3] In their test, Knowles and Kalacheck compare the average of unemployed male migration rates from 1957 to 1959 with the 1950–59 average. (The 1959 data were the latest then available, and the authors believed that 1950 was the earliest date for which data were available. In fact, data exist from 1948.) The authors find that "unemployed workers have been at least as geographically mobile since 1957 as earlier in the postwar period" (p. 77). They note, "Migration rates have been decidedly higher since 1952 than earlier" (p. 39). With earlier and later data available, however, we find that 1948 was as high as later years. The Knowles-Kalacheck results give the 1957–59, period a slightly higher average than 1950–59. But, if 1948–64 is compared with 1957–64, the results are reversed for unemployed males, averaging 10.6 percent from 1948 to 1964 and 10.4 percent from 1957 to 1964.

[4] Knowles and Kalacheck may be overly concerned with the migration rates of unemployed workers. After all, the allocative effect of area mobility should take the migrant from the unemployed category to the employed roster. Thus, a good allocation would raise the employed migration rate while it lowers the migration rate of the unemployed.

clear indication whether the act of migration caused, was caused by, or even involved the employment status. Unemployment reported currently could have been of any duration, and there may or may not have been a change of status since migration. An unemployed migrant, therefore, could have been unemployed when he migrated, employed when he migrated and unemployed because of the shift, employed when he migrated and unemployed after one or more periods of employment, or not in the labor force when he migrated and now looking for work. An employed migrant could have been employed when he migrated and retained or regained the same status at the interview date; or he could have been unemployed or out of the labor force twelve months earlier and now working.

When a worker moves and changes his labor force status between interview dates, both the employed and unemployed migration rates, as well as the male unemployment rate, are affected. For example, an unemployed worker who moves and finds work lowers the unemployed migration rate, raises the employed migration rate, and lowers the unemployment rate. But when a worker moves with no change in his labor force status he merely affects one migration rate. For example, if a worker remains unemployed the unemployed migration rate rises, but the employed migration rate and the unemployment rate are unchanged.

Motives for geographic movement are extremely varied, making it hard to separate cause from effect. These motives include preference for other regions, health, available housing and education, marriage, a way of life, family ties, employment opportunities, and keeping up with the Joneses. Many of the noneconomic factors that enter into migration decisions are eliminated by restricting attention to labor force males. Recent collection of data on motivation discloses that, of the migrants in 1963 who were eighteen to sixty-four years of age, 53 percent of employed and 69 percent of unemployed persons moved for reasons related to jobs.[5] If solely males were interviewed the percentages would probably be higher.

This investigation asks first what the trends have been from 1948 to 1964. Both employed and unemployed male migration rates and that of the population of labor force age are examined. Second, to what extent do economic factors account for migration? Third, is there any indication that area mobility operates as a labor allocator? Finally, do recent years show geographic mobility patterns indicative of structural or demand problems, or both?

[5] These include migration to take a job, to look for work, and because of a job transfer. See Samuel Saben (BLS), "Geographic Mobility and Employment Status, March 1962–March 1963," *Special Labor Force Report*, No. 44, Aug., 1964, p. A-9.

TABLE 36: Migration Rates of the Civilian Population Fourteen Years and Over by Age Groups, March or April, 1948–64

(percentages)

Year	Mo.	Civilians[a] 14 years and over			Migration rates[b] by age groups			
		Total migration rate	In-state migration rate	Out-of-state migration rate	14–24	25–44	45–64	65 & over
1948	A	6.2	3.2	3.1	9.4	7.3	3.3	3.1
1949	A	5.6	2.7	3.0	8.2	6.7	3.1	2.9
1950	M	5.5	2.9	2.7	8.4	6.6	3.0	2.2
1951	A	6.7	3.4	3.4	10.1	8.3	3.8	2.4
1952	A	6.3	3.0	3.3	10.1	7.8	3.1	1.9
1953	A	6.3	2.8	3.5	11.0	7.4	3.2	2.2
1954	A	6.3	3.1	3.2	10.4	7.3	3.3	3.3
1955	A	6.4	3.4	3.1	10.6	7.5	3.6	3.0
1956	M	6.7	3.6	3.1	11.7	7.6	3.5	2.8
1957	A	6.0	3.1	3.0	10.1	7.2	3.1	2.8
1958	M	6.5	3.2	3.2	10.4	7.9	3.5	2.6
1959	A	5.9	3.1	2.9	9.3	7.2	3.3	2.9
1960	M	6.2	3.1	3.1	10.2	7.5	3.1	2.8
1961	M	6.2	3.1	3.2	10.1	7.3	3.5	2.7
1962	A	6.0	3.0	3.0	9.4	7.1	3.4	2.9
1963	M	6.5	3.1	3.4	10.4	7.9	3.3	2.9
1964	M	6.2	3.2	2.9	11.8	7.7	3.2	2.7

[a] Civilians include military personnel living with their families or off post. These range from 1,149,000 in 1960 to 393,000 in 1949.
[b] Migrants are those who were living in a residence in a different county twelve months prior to the interview date.

SOURCE: Derived from U.S., Bureau of the Census, Current Population Reports, Series P-50 (for 1948 and 1949); and "Mobility of the Population of the United States," Series P-20 (for 1950 and thereafter).

Migration Trends

There is a hierarchy of migration rates at any point in time. For example, young men are more likely to migrate on entering the labor force, while young women move most often in connection with marriage. Migration rates are inversely related to age, and within the group twenty-five to forty-four years of age between-state mobility increases with the level of education. High levels of education are generally associated with higher mobility.

Table 36 presents migration rates by age groups for civilians of labor force age.[6] The inverse relationship of migration rates with age is apparent. Migration between states has been more important than within the states

[6] The data include members of the Armed Forces who lived with their families or off post. These ranged between 393,000 and 1,149,000.

TABLE 37: Male Unemployment and Migration Rates, March or April, 1948–64

(percentages)

Year	Unemployment rates		Migration rates[b]		
	Labor force	Migrants[b]	Labor force	Employed	Unemployed
1948	3.6	7.2	6.1	5.8	12.1
1949	5.0	8.0	5.6	5.4	8.8
1950	6.8	10.0	5.2	5.0	7.6
1951	2.4	3.5	6.7	6.6	9.8
1952[a]	2.4	3.2	6.6	6.5	8.8
1953[a]	2.5	4.6	6.7	6.6	12.5
1954	5.3	10.9	6.1	5.7	12.5
1955	4.7	7.9	6.1	5.9	10.2
1956	4.2	8.4	6.9	6.6	13.8
1957	4.1	7.0	6.1	5.9	10.4
1958	8.2	14.6	6.6	6.2	11.7
1959	5.2	9.1	6.0	5.8	10.6
1960	6.3	10.2	6.2	5.9	9.9
1961	7.9	12.8	6.4	6.1	10.3
1962	5.5	8.4	5.7	5.5	8.7
1963	6.4	10.5	6.5	6.2	10.7
1964	5.6	9.9	6.4	6.1	11.2

a The years 1952 and 1953 include 988,000 and 982,000 military personnel living with their families or off post.
b Migrants lived in a different county twelve months prior to interview date. Labor force category based on status at time of interview; follows Household Survey definitions.
SOURCE: Derived from Current Population Reports, Series P-50 and P-20.

in six out of the seventeen years covered. Averaged from 1948 to 1956, the migration rates are the same as those averaged from 1957 to 1964 for most of the population, while persons over sixty-five years show a slight increase in the later period, probably related to the development of retirement communities.

Table 37 presents the primary data—those for civilian males in the labor force. Data used to calculate unemployment rates were those collected with the migration data to keep the reference base consistent. These refer to a single month, rather than the annual averages used previously. The table shows that unemployed men are much more geographically mobile than employed men.[7] The direction of causality is ambiguous. The high participation of males in the labor force ties their migration rate to that of civilians fourteen years of age and over. Similarly,

[7] The size of the Armed Forces might also affect migration, even though civilian data are used. A civilian who was in the Armed Forces twelve months prior to the interview date is likely to appear as a migrant even if he returns to his parents' home. No military personnel are included except for 988,000 in 1952 and 982,000 in 1953, who were living with their families or off post.

high unemployment among youth affects the migration rates of unemployed males because of high mobility among youth. The coefficient of correlation between point changes in the migration rate of persons fourteen to twenty-four years old with point changes in the migration rate of unemployed males is 0.79 (significant at the 0.01 level; $N = 15$). Both series show a rise from 1948 to 1956 and a fluctuating but somewhat declining trend thereafter. There is a rise in 1963–64 in both rates, but the predicted value for youth migration is under-estimated by two standard errors. Aside from the slight downward trend from 1956 to 1964 in migration rates for unemployed males, there are no marked trends in migration.

Economic Factors and Migration

The economic responsiveness of male labor force migration can be evaluated through comparison of changes in male migration rates with changes in male employment and unemployment. The first relationship to be studied is the response of the male migration rate to percentage changes in male employment, using the same sample data.[8] When these two series are plotted together over time they show a surprising change. From 1948–49 to 1955–56 the two series move in the same direction except for 1951–52. The male migration rate rose and fell as employment rose and fell. Migration seemed to be a response to the pull of opportunity or was made possible by the permissive environment of employment expansion, but from 1956–57 to 1963–64 the reverse is true. The male migration rate falls as employment increases for males (except in 1960–61).

It is as if migration in the earlier period had risen largely as a response to the pull of economic growth but in later years rose as a response to the push of employment contractions. This could be the result of changes in the nature of skill availabilities or of changes in job availabilities or both. More widely distributed job openings are indicated by a declining trend in the concentration of above-average employment changes by area. More concentrated below-average employment declines by area in recessions suggest a reason for greater migration at those times. The reasons for the sharp behavioral shift are not absolutely clear, but a structural shift in behavior seems to have occurred.

[8] The full male labor force migration rate and the employed male migration rate are essentially the same, since unemployed migrants represent a small fraction of male migrants. Employed migrants are actually "successful" migrants. However, point changes in the employed male migration rate, regressed against point changes in the unemployed male migration rate (1948–49 to 1962–63), yield an r of 0.66 (significant at the 0.01 level). In other words, "unsuccessful" migrant behavior is not highly related to "successful" migrant behavior.

Statistical evidence of the shift comes from the regression of percentage changes in male employment with point changes in the male labor force migration rate. For fifteen observations (1948–49 to 1962–63), r is 0.05 and not significant; however, separating the periods, r is 0.77 for the eight observations from 1948–49 to 1955–56 and -0.73 for the remaining seven observations.[9] One can therefore say that there is an economic adaptation but that its character has reversed itself since 1956, perhaps owing to changes in the quality of available labor skills relative to labor demands.

The deviant years of almost two or more standard errors come in 1950–51 and 1962–63, when migration was above expected levels. In 1950–51 the employment of males and of male migrants both increased; mobilization and labor requirements of the Korean War help explain the deviation.[10] In 1962–63 the above-expected rise in migration is associated with a decline in male employment but a rise in migrant male employment. In other words, the adjustment was economic even in the deviant years.

Male professionals have the highest employed migration rate; for the period 1955 to 1960 it is 30.4 percent. The next highest migration rate is much lower, 19.1 percent for sales workers. Managers follow with 18.1 percent. The lowest rates are for farmers, 6.3 percent, and laborers, 13.7 percent.[11]

Employed labor force males who migrate usually move more within states than between states. (This suggests an affinity between employment, migration, and market knowledge.) The Korean period reversed this, first because of relatively high above-average employment change concentration, but second because of the influence of mobilization and demobilization on out-of-state migration. Employed males responded to the high geographic concentration of above-average employment gains in 1952–53 by increasing their out-of-state migration. Between 1956 and 1963 employed migrants and the population fourteen years of age and over show a trend increasingly in favor of out-of-state migration. This

[9] Note the change of sign. The r for 1948–49 to 1955–56 is significant at the 0.05 level and is 0.72 adjusted. For 1956–57 to 1962–63 r is nearly significant at the 0.05 level and is 0.66 adjusted. The 1963–64 change in male migration is predicted within 0.1 point. Regressing point changes for only the employed male migration rate against changes in male employment for the earlier period yields an r of 0.83, significant at the 0.01 level (0.79 adjusted). For the later period r is -0.63 (0.53 adjusted) and is not significant. In other words, the earlier period was dominated by successful employment responses, while the later period is less responsive to employment changes. Changes in the migration rate of unemployed males are not significantly related to male employment changes.

[10] In 1950–51 the Armed Forces increased by 88 percent, thus creating a high, unfilled demand for male labor skills.

[11] *Manpower Report of the President, 1965*, p. 271.

reflects either the selective and far-flung demand for special skills or the pushes and pulls of institutional factors. By 1964 employed in-state migrants were again more prominent.

Because out-of-state migrants are more likely to be well educated, this may be an indication of selective migration among the employed. It is interesting to note that the movement toward greater out-of-state employed migration started with the date that the relationship between migration and employment changes became inverse. Among unemployed migrants, out-of-state movers have continually out-numbered within-state movers. It is possible that where migration is over a long distance it often is not related to specific job opportunities. There is no trend in the rate spread, however, and the data may very well reflect changes in the size of the Armed Forces and teen-age male unemployment.

It is possible that employed male migrants are increasingly the more educated and in professional occupations. This tendency would be compatible with decreasing area mobility in employment growth years due to structural skill inadequacies. The highly educated are, after all, a small part of the male work force. A decline in unemployed male migration rates could be interpreted as an adaptive response to the quality of job availabilities if openings were concentrated in the higher skill occupations.

Further support for the argument that male migration rates are economically responsive but have undergone a shift comes through regressing point changes in the male unemployment rate, rather than changes in male employment, with point changes in the male labor force migration rate. This results in an r of -0.16 for the entire period, but -0.92 and 0.75 when the periods are split.[12] Thus the results show a similar response and an even stronger relationship.

The regression lines show that 1955–56 and 1962–63 were both above expected migration levels by two standard errors while 1956–57 was below by almost two standard errors. The unemployment rate regression eliminates the unusual employment effects in the Korean period. The sharp and deviant reversal of behavior in 1955–56 and 1956–57 suggests that migrants were learning a lesson. In 1955–56 excess migration seemed to be punished by unemployment. Employment increased for males and for male migrants, but the increased migration for employed and unemployed males was met both by a fall in the male unemployment rate and a rise in the migrant male unemployment rate.

[12] The r for 1948–49 to 1962–63 is not significant. For 1948–49 to 1955–56 r is -0.92, significant at the 0.01 level, -0.91 adjusted. For 1956–57 to 1962–63 r is 0.75, significant at the 0.05 level, and is 0.69 adjusted. Note that the change of sign again occurs. The change for 1963–64 is predicted within 0.2 point.

An explanation of the shift in migration patterns comes from an investigation of the jobs which were available to workers but were left unfilled. The Bureau of Employment Security, through the co-operation of its state affiliates, has listed at quarterly intervals since 1950 an inventory of job openings placed in clearance. These are jobs which could not be filled locally and which employers have agreed to make available to other workers. The jobs approximate local standards and have housing available in the area; thus, these are "real openings." [13]

The relative composition and level of the openings rather than their absolute level is of interest. These jobs indicate the degree to which migrants would be attracted or migration would be appropriate. The reader will appreciate that not only the level but the skill content of employment opportunities is important for migration, especially since migration is highest among young people who are new labor force entrants. Table 38 presents the vacancy data by broad occupational divisions. The jobs-in-clearance data show the chief reason for the unexpected rise in migration in 1950–51. The year 1951 stands at the highest level of unfilled jobs in clearance of any year represented; more than this, the change from 1950 to 1951 is over 200 percent.

The blue-collar jobs in clearance outnumber the white-collar jobs only through 1953. Thereafter, they are fewer in number, with a ratio which has declined from 0.8 in 1954 to 0.7 in 1957 and was at 0.4 from 1960 to 1963, rising again to 0.6 in 1964. If blue-collar jobs are strongly male jobs, there would be little pull on migration even in employment boom years after 1955, while recession years would encourage migration only among those qualified to move. The inverse nature of the movement after 1956, as has been shown, is more the result of changes brought about by the employed male migrant than by the unemployed migrant.

Point changes in the male labor force migration rate regressed against percentage changes in the total jobs in clearance series (1950–51 to 1962–63) yield an r of 0.71, significant at the 0.01 level. However, splitting the periods between 1950–51 to 1956–57 and 1957–58 to 1962–63 produces r's of 0.92 and −0.88, higher than those obtained with the employment or unemployment series. [14] Of even greater interest is the fact that the regression using only blue-collar jobs in clearance produces an r of 0.94

---

[13] The BES asserts that vacancies are not actively promoted unless there is a waiting applicant. The vacancies in clearance are therefore not as likely to be affected by administrative policies with respect to placement activities in state employment services as are the total of all job openings. That is, the jobs in clearance are likely to be "real" and the fluctuations from year to year are probably not administrative.

[14] The r's are significant at the 0.01 and 0.05 levels, respectively. The adjusted r's are 0.68, $N = 13$; 0.90, $N = 7$; and −0.85, $N = 6$. The regression equation overpredicts the migration rate change by 0.4 point in 1963–64.

TABLE 38: Nonagricultural Jobs Listed in Clearance with State Employment Services; Quarterly Averages,[a] 1950–64

Year,	Total	White collar	Blue collar	Service
1950	14,744	4,912	8,946	886
1951	45,652	16,209	27,521	1,922
1952	44,480	15,309	27,990	1,181
1953	39,964	13,171	25,492	1,301
1954	15,542	8,088	6,713	741
1955	20,520	12,229	7,476	815
1956	33,319	18,028	13,499	1,792
1957	27,354	14,881	10,920	1,553
1958	15,324	10,130	3,871	1,323
1959	20,021	12,734	5,768	1,519
1960	18,144	12,157	4,881	1,106
1961	17,764	12,286	4,503	975
1962	25,634	17,602	6,787	1,245
1963	22,476	15,024	5,919	1,533
1964	19,772	11,516	6,980	1,276

[a] Averages of state inventories listed in March, June, September, and December of each year.

SOURCE: U.S., Congress, Joint Committee, Subcommittee on Economic Statistics, *Higher Unemployment Rates, 1957–60: Structural Transformation or Inadequate Demand*, 87th Cong., 1st Sess. (Washington: U.S. Government Printing Office, 1961), p. 74. U.S., Bureau of Employment Security, *The Labor Market and Employment Security*, various issues, and *Employment Service Review*, various issues.

for the period 1950–51 to 1956–57, significant at the 0.01 level (0.93 adjusted). For the years 1957–58 to 1962–63, r is -0.85, significant at the 0.05 level (-0.81 adjusted), and the 1963–64 change is correctly predicted. The relevant equation is $X_m = 0.065 - 0.012 \, X_b$, where X_m is the point change in the migration rate and X_b is the percentage change in blue-collar vacancies.

With the divided total- and blue-collar job vacancy series the years that appear as major deviants are similar to those obtained using the unemployment rate: 1956–57 below and 1962–63 above expected levels of migration. Thus the attraction of unfilled blue-collar jobs is the best explanatory variable. The level of unfilled blue-collar jobs has been markedly lower than white-collar jobs since 1957. Even when they increase as in 1963–64 they are not a sufficient numerical attraction. On the other hand, in periods of rising unemployment, given already high unemployment levels, males in the labor force have been spurred to seek out more distant jobs.

In periods of declining employment and rising unemployment migration is now responsive to pushes. At this time job vacancies decline due to cyclical causes but may also decline because of the high mobility of those who are able to obtain employment in conjunction with a shift in location.

Another reason for rising migration at times of unemployment increases is that new arrivals bear the brunt of lay-offs and swell the ranks of those classified both as unemployed and as migrants.

Another way of saying this is that prior to 1957 a newly employed man in a year of rising employment and vacancies was more likely to have moved in the past year than in a recession year. Since 1957 both the employed and the unemployed are less likely to have moved in a good year, but rather in a year of employment and blue-collar vacancy declines. The newly employed migrant seems to be coming from a greater distance than formerly and seems more likely to be well educated.

It appears correct to say that male migration rates are responsive to economic variables, particularly those which reflect geographic changes in job opportunities; however, increased migration rates are now associated with inadequacies in demand. It is questionable whether a major employment boom would reverse the newer relationship; this did not occur in 1963–64. There is a marked possibility that the behavioral shift indicates structural problems.

Male Mobility and Adaptation

A series of tests can be set up to judge the allocative role of male migration rates. One is to regress the changes in employed male migration rates against unemployed male migration rate changes. Deviations from the usual pattern would indicate adaptive or maladaptive behavior. That is, a large deviant rise in employed migration relative to unemployed migration would suggest that migration had worked toward lowering the male unemployment rate. A large deviant decline in employed migration relative to unemployed migration would show an excess of unemployment associated with migration.[15]

The regression of point changes in the two series yields an r of 0.66 from 1948–49 to 1962–63 (significant at 0.05 level). The year 1952–53 shows a deviation of at least two standard errors in favor of unemployed migration while 1954–55 deviates in favor of employed migration; thus, one year appears to display better than "normal" adaptation, 1955, and one year displays excessive migration, 1953. In 1953 excessive migration may have raised the frictional level of unemployment. The 1963–64 figure deviates less than one standard error from its predicted value.

A visual comparison of unemployment rates for all labor force males by migration status is presented in Figure 4. Between-state migrants have

[15] The test assumes that if a regular relationship exists it can be regarded as a norm, or "neutral" basis for comparison. Ratios might serve the same purpose, with deviations from trend calculated.

a higher unemployment rate than within-state migrants, while migrants have a higher unemployment rate than all labor force males. The unemployment rates are in close harmony except for 1948–49, when the between-state unemployment rate fell; 1951–52, when migrant unemployment rates were reduced; and in 1955–56, when the unemployment rate for males declined but the migrant unemployment rate increased. In 1952–53 the migrant unemployment rates seem to have displayed a sharper increase than the over-all rate, possibly related to the start of demobilization. The maladaptive years appear to be 1952–53 and 1955–56.

Another test is to regress the unemployment rate for migrants against the male unemployment rate. The two rates are highly correlated. For sixteen observations, 1948 to 1963, r is 0.96. A deviation of over two standard

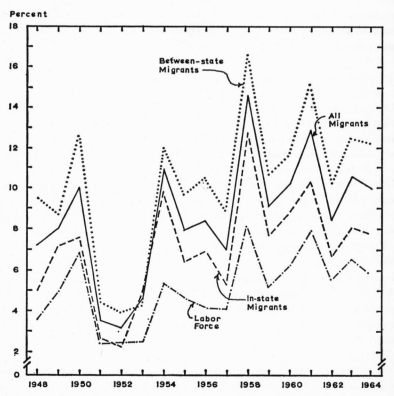

FIGURE 4: Unemployment Rates for Labor Force Males by Migration Status, March or April, 1948–64. (Source: Derived from U.S., Bureau of the Census, *Current Population Reports*, Series P-50 and P-20.)

errors above the regression equation, suggesting nonadaptive behavior, occurs in 1954. The 1964 prediction is accurate within one standard error. Thus, excessive migration may have contributed to higher unemployment in 1954. In 1953–54 concentration of above-average employment change by area was very low. The employed male migration rate declined while the unemployed male migration rate remained the same. In this recession year the result was an increase in unemployment rates for all males and male migrants, but the latter suffered proportionately more. Migration was penalized.

Regressing unemployed male migrants as a percentage of the male labor force against the male unemployment rate results in an r of 0.91 for the period 1948–63. The 1964 prediction is again within one standard error. In 1950 unemployed male migrants were below their expected labor force share by more than two standard errors, suggesting either extremely adaptive behavior or inadequate migration. The year 1956 shows the unemployed migrants' share of the labor force to be above expectations by almost two standard errors.

In 1956 migrants had clearly miscalculated. Either a rise in frictional unemployment occurred or structural changes were setting in. Both the employed and the unemployed migration rates rose from 1955 to 1956. This resulted in a decline in the male unemployment rate but a rise in the migrants' unemployment rate. Employment gains were not concentrated that year, so more migration did not seem to be called for. More important, demand for other than blue-collar workers carried the burden of the increase in job openings in clearance.

In 1955–56 the size of the Armed Forces was reduced. That year also followed the 1954–55 employment boom in the East North Central states. But the 1955–56 employment increase in that area fell disastrously below their usually well-above-average position in good years. In 1954–55 employment had risen 4 percent on a base which was 23 percent of all nonfarm payroll employment. In 1955–56 the rise was only 2 percent, yet the aggregate increases were 3.3 percent in 1954–55 and 3.4 percent in 1955–56. The above-average standard variation for the area fell from 222 percent to 45 percent. When it is recalled that this is a highly industrialized, blue-collar center, the structural story becomes stronger.

Conclusions

Migration seems to be largely adaptive from 1948 to 1963, except for three years, 1953, 1954, and 1956. In view of the inverse shift of the migration rate behavior from around 1956, it would appear that structural obstacles have induced migration rate declines in years of employment increases, not through perversity on the part of the labor force but for reasons related to the nature of skill availabilities and requirements.

The evidence suggests that structural changes in labor demand and supply have shifted the adaptive role of male migration since 1956 from providing wide distribution of male skill resources in high-demand years to a defensive movement out of contracted areas in low-demand years. There is more regional stability in years of employment increases, possibly because of a backlog of unemployed workers. The decline of employed male migration rates in recent years of employment increases suggests a mismatching of available unemployed labor with job openings elsewhere. These conclusions help to support the structuralist argument without denying the inadequacy of over-all demand. Migration rate behavior is not explainable without recourse to both structural factors and less-than-boom levels of demand.

It must be pointed out that this section has dealt with only male employment and male migration rates. With the increase in female employment there is less reason to expect that male labor force migration rates can alone be relied upon to play a strongly adaptive role in allocating labor. If married females move only when their husbands do, unfilled jobs for women could possibly be filled by currently unemployed women, immobile because of their husbands' opportunities. If this were the case, one would have to say that, in addition to any structural unemployment, the frictional level of full-employment unemployment had risen. Labor market adjustments would then have to be sought.

We frankly believe that the job vacancy data say otherwise. The bulk of the unfilled jobs are in the professions and specialized categories and not among traditionally female jobs.

EDUCATIONAL ADAPTATION

A fourth mechanism used by the labor force to adapt to changes in skill requirements is changes in its skills through education and training. It is an oversimplification to equate educational levels with particular skills, but broad generalizations can be made by linking educational levels with complexity of occupational requirements. This section discusses changes in the educational experience of the labor force in connection with changes in educational employment requirements. The questions raised are these: (1) Have there been marked changes in educational requirements for employment generally, and within occupational categories specifically? (2) Do differences in the educational levels of labor force groups indicate structural obstacles to employment?

Changes in Educational Requirements

In a purely demand and supply sense, the looser the particular labor market the higher the marginal educational requirements, while in a tight labor market marginal educational standards can be pushed down to minimum levels. Thus an a priori explanation offered by some demand theorists is that rises in educational requirements are due to inadequate aggregate demand and slack labor markets. There are limitations to the argument, however.

It cannot be assumed that rises in marginal or average educational requirements are solely due to supply-elastic employer preferences. Given the concept of port-of-entry jobs, that is, jobs for which hiring is done from outside the firm, and also given families of labor skills with limited transferabilities, technological change can produce an upward shift in minimum educational requirements.[16] This would come about when technological changes affect the content of skill families and the range of skills within each. That is, technological change will affect entry locations in the internal skill structure of the firm, the content of the port-of-entry job, and the educational distance between the entry job and the job at the upper limit within the skill family.

Since workers are expected to move upward within the firm along a continuum, a rise in the educational requirements at the top of a family of skills or an upward shift in the minimum educational requirements for the port-of-entry job itself will raise educational requirements at the entry job level. If this is so, inadequate demand will serve to raise requirements on an already raised minimum base. The implication for structural unemployment is that when minimal entry requirements rise or the lower level entry jobs shrink in their proportions to over-all employment the least educated are frozen out of employment, i.e., they are structurally unemployed. Their only alternatives are to raise their educational levels (or specific training), to leave the labor force, or to compete for the remaining low-level openings. A second argument against a solely aggregate demand explanation for rises in educational requirements is that the labor skill markets are not alike in relative tightness, and what is required is disaggregative analysis.

This section now turns to an examination of the educational attainments of the employed in order to investigate changes in requirements.

---

[16] See Dunlop, Paper presented at Research Conference. Dr. Dunlop, in his view of the internal occupational structure of the firm, suggests that ports of entry appear at various levels within the skill hierarchy. Between these points promotion occurs within the firm. At the ports, hiring occurs from outside the firm. Our conclusion is that ports of entry represent the lowest level of each skill family, the breaks occurring where the job requires educational or technical preparation beyond avenues available or offered within the firm.

Since it is difficult to ascertain educational requirements set by employers for new hirings, the actual achievements of the currently employed are used; however, marginal educational standards may be masked. Table 39 presents background information on the nature of the training of persons twenty-two to sixty-four years of age who had three or less years of college. The data reflect the current or last job held as of April, 1963.

As this table indicates, the occupation which has grown most—professionals—requires the greatest degree of formal training. Second in formal requirements are craftsmen, followed by clerical workers. The jobs requiring the least formal training are laborers, private household workers, and farm labor. Of these, only private household work is growing, and this is primarily female work. Most of the expanding jobs require a

TABLE 39: Ways in Which Civilians in the Labor Force with Three Years or Less of College Learned Their Current or Last Job, by Occupation of Civilians Twenty-two to Sixty-four Years in April, 1963

(percentages)

| Current or last occupation | Ways in which occupation was learned | | | |
	Formal[a]	On the job[b]	Casual[c]	No training needed
	Distribution within occupation			
Professional, technical	64.6	66.7	33.2	2.1
Managers, officials, propr.	36.2	57.1	55.7	4.0
Clerical	53.6	71.4	29.5	2.0
Sales	23.4	60.2	47.4	7.5
Craftsmen, foremen	40.6	64.8	47.5	1.8
Operatives	12.9	61.8	42.6	8.6
Laborers	6.9	40.0	50.5	18.1
Pr. household workers	10.3	9.3	56.4	27.9
Other service workers	24.6	45.5	42.7	13.5
Farmers, farm managers	20.6	17.6	79.7	8.4
Farm laborers, foremen	11.1	19.2	64.8	17.7
Total	30.2	56.2	45.4	7.5

NOTE: A small percentage in each category was listed as "not specified." Some persons listed more than one way of learning; therefore the percentages do not sum horizontally to 100.

a Formal includes school, apprenticeship, and Armed Forces.

b On the job includes those learning from persons on the job, those who had been enrolled in company training courses, and those who were promoted to the current position. This category overlaps with apprenticeship and casual learning.

c Casual includes mainly those who learned from a relative or friend or who "picked up" the occupation.

SOURCE: *Manpower Report of the President, 1964*, pp. 257–58.

high degree of on-the-job training, as well. Clearly, then, the labor force must have had to supply an upgrading in educational levels, by virtue of the occupational shifts alone.

A general upgrading in educational levels in the population has come about through two obvious mechanisms. These are (1) longer schooling for the younger population, and (2) the retirement and death of the older, less educated population. The gain in educational attainment was more rapid for men; women in the labor force had already attained high educational levels. For women, especially married women, there is a positive relationship by age group between education and labor force participation.[17] Between 1940 and 1954 the gap between white and non-white median years of school had closed by two and one half years. But since the mid-1950's both groups increased by one year, and the gap has remained fairly constant.[18]

The increase in the educational attainment of the employed may be a response to selective requirements imposed by employers, or may have been an employer response to the autonomous increase in school enrollment rates; both forces have probably been operative. In any case, the greater school enrollment rate over time for school age youth and normal demographic changes have upgraded the educational levels of the population. This is demonstrated in Table 40, which presents school enrollment rates for the noninstitutional civilian population of school age.

Table 40 indicates that the average percentage point gains in school enrollment rates for youth fourteen to twenty-four years old were about equal in the period 1948 to 1955 and from 1956 to 1963. On the other hand, the earlier period shows a higher net gain, 8.2 points, over the later period's 6.8 points. Over the period 1949 to 1964, high-school age youth increased their school enrollment rate by 11.5 points, while college and university age youth increased their much lower school enrollment rate by 10.8 points. In other words, the upper educational levels have not grown as rapidly as the middle levels. This suggests both an upgrading among the general population and some relative scarcity in persons taking upper-level educations.

The result of changes in school enrollment rates has been a redistribution of educational experience among age groups. Between 1957 and 1962 the proportion of high-school graduates in the labor force increased

[17] Denis F. Johnston (BLS), "Educational Attainment of Workers, March 1962," *Special Labor Force Report*, No. 30, May, 1963, pp. 504–5.

[18] The size of the gap (about one year for men twenty-five to twenty-nine years), however, does not account for all the differences between Negro and white living experiences. For example, adjusting for the education gap still does not explain income differences.

TABLE 40: Civilian School Enrollment Rate,ᵃ Youth Fourteen to Twenty-four Years, October, 1948, to October, 1964

October of year	Civilians 14–24	Point change over prior year	October of year	Civilians 14–17	Point change over prior year
1948	37.8%	—	1949	81.6%	—
1949	37.4	(0.4)	1957	89.5	—
1950	39.4	2.0	1958	89.2	(0.3)
1951	40.9	1.5	1959	90.2	1.0
1952	43.3	2.4	1960	90.3	0.1
1953	45.3	2.0	1961	91.4	1.1
1954	46.2	0.9	1962	92.0	0.6
1955	46.0	(0.2)	1963	92.9	0.9
1956	48.2	2.2	1964	93.1	0.2
1957	49.8	1.6		Civilians 18–24	
1958	50.2	0.4			
1959	50.2	0.0	1949	13.5%	—
1960	50.8	0.6	1957	20.2	—
1961	52.0	1.2	1958	20.6	0.4
1962	54.0	2.0	1959	20.0	(0.6)
1963	55.0	1.0	1960	21.0	1.0
1964	54.9	(0.1)	1961	21.6	0.6
			1962	24.0	2.4
			1963	24.4	0.4
			1964	24.3	(0.1)

ᵃ Persons of both sexes enrolled in school as a percentage of noninstitutional civilian population in age group.
Parentheses indicate negative numbers.
SOURCE: Derived from *Manpower Report of the President, 1965*, p. 220; and BLS, *Special Labor Force Reports*, Nos. 6, 16, 22, 34, 42, 55.

for every age group (Table 41). The share increased more for younger than older groups, although the reverse is true for increases in median school years completed. The proportion of those with college training has also grown, and the percentage point share increases have actually been larger than for high-school graduates. Thus, within the labor force and the employed, the shares going to those with advanced education have recently been rising more rapidly than those with secondary education.

Table 42 presents educational attainments for the employed eighteen years of age or over within occupations. The total increase of high-school graduates with no college, as a percentage of the employed, 1957 to 1962, was 2.8 points. This shift was accomplished, not by gains within those groups with already high educational levels, but by marked increases in the proportion of high-school graduates among service workers, farmers, laborers, craftsmen, domestic workers, operatives, and farm laborers. None of the white-collar jobs shows a percentage shift above the aggregate rise of 2.8 points. Indeed, the share going to high-school graduates declined

TABLE 41: Years of School Completed by Selected Labor Force Groups, March, 1957, and March, 1962

Labor force group	Year	Less than 4 yrs. HS	4 yrs. HS (12 yrs.)	Over 4 yrs. HS (over 12)	Median years
		(distribution within group)			
18 & 19	1962	35.9%	54.3%	9.7%	12.3
20–24	1962	30.5	44.5	25.1	12.4
25–34	1957	42.1	34.6	22.5	12.2
	1962	35.1	37.3	27.6	12.4
35–44	1957	49.2	32.7	17.1	12.0
	1962	42.7	34.5	22.9	12.2
45–54	1962	52.8	27.8	19.5	11.6
55–64	1962	64.5	18.4	17.1	9.4
65 & over	1957	72.8	12.1	12.3	8.5
	1962	69.6	13.7	16.7	8.8
Employed	1957	51.3%	29.5%	17.9%	11.7
	1962	45.4	32.3	22.4	12.1
Unemployed	1957	69.9	21.2	7.6	9.4
	1962	63.0	27.7	9.3	10.6
Not in LF	1957	60.2	26.5	11.7	10.2
	1962	57.6	28.1	14.3	10.7

NOTE: Data for 1957 do not total to 100 because of omission of persons not reporting educational attainment.

SOURCE: Derived from BLS, *Special Labor Force Report*, No. 30, and *Current Population Reports*, Series P-50, No. 78.

among professionals, managers, and sales persons. In the case of professionals the group with less than four years of high school increased its share, while the proportion of college-trained people also increased. It appears that scarcities on one hand and higher requirements on the other increased the proportions at either end of the educational spectrum.

There were increases in the shares going to persons with college training in all occupations; the aggregate increase was a gain of 4.5 percentage points. Those registering a rise above the aggregate shift include only managers-proprietors and sales workers. Both these groups have been upgraded in upper educational levels because of the changing nature of the jobs covered by these occupational titles. Entry requirements for both groups can be expected to have altered. The groups with the next highest rises in the share going to college-trained people are clericals and non-household service occupations. It is possible that these rises reflect increases in the labor force participation of married women with prior college training, as well as altered job content.

TABLE 42: Percentage Distribution of Employed Persons Eighteen Years and Over within Occupation Groups by Years of School Completed, March, 1957, and March, 1962

Occupation	Year	Less than 4 yrs. HS (below 12)	4 yrs. HS (12)	Over 4 yrs. HS (over 12)	Median years
Prof., tech.	1957	5.7%	18.9%	74.6%	16.+
	1962	6.9	16.9	76.1	16.2
Mgr., prop.	1957	37.4	34.0	27.2	12.4
	1962	33.2	33.9	32.8	12.5
Clerical	1957	23.5	56.7	18.8	12.5
	1962	21.2	56.8	22.0	12.5
Sales	1957	34.9	40.6	22.9	12.4
	1962	31.7	39.8	28.6	12.5
Craftsmen	1957	61.9	29.5	7.2	10.5
	1962	56.9	34.5	8.7	11.2
Operatives	1957	71.5	23.5	3.6	9.5
	1962	67.7	27.2	5.1	10.1
Laborers	1957	78.3	15.9	3.9	8.5
	1962	74.6	21.1	4.3	8.9
Service	1957	67.1	23.2	6.9	9.6
	1962	59.9	30.6	9.4	10.8
Pr. house.	1957	81.7	12.8	3.1	8.3
	1962	78.5	17.3	4.3	8.7
Farmers	1957	75.9	17.8	5.9	8.6
	1962	68.9	23.1	8.0	8.8
Farm labor	1957	80.5	14.9	3.8	8.2
	1962	77.3	18.4	4.2	8.5
Total	1957	51.3	29.5	17.9	11.7
	1962	45.4	32.3	22.4	12.1

NOTE: Percentages total within occupations. Data for 1957 do not total to 100 because of omission of persons not reporting educational attainment.

SOURCE: *Current Population Reports*, Series P-50, No. 78, and BLS, *Special Labor Force Report*, No. 30.

The pattern suggested by share shifts is partially reflected in the changes in median years of schooling.[19] Table 43 presents median school years by occupational groups. Occupations with the lowest educational requirements made the greatest gains in median school years. In the ten-year period 1952–62, the greatest rise came in service occupations other than household: from 9.2 years to 10.8 years of schooling. The next fastest rise

[19] The median can be ambiguous because there is no way of telling to what extent the median is also a modal figure. For example, among clericals the group with four years of high school is over 50 percent of the total; the distribution of those with college training did in fact shift upwards, but the median stayed the same at 12.5 because the mode contained the median in both years.

TABLE 43: Median Years of School Completed by Employed Persons Eighteen Years and Over by Major Occupation Group, October, 1952, and March, 1962

Occupation	October, 1952	March, 1962	Change: 1952–62
	Median years		Years
Total	10.9	12.1	1.2
Professional, technical	16+	16.2	0.2(max.)
Managers, officials, propr.	12.2	12.5	0.3
Clerical	12.5	12.5	0.0
Sales	12.3	12.5	0.2
Craftsmen, foremen	10.0	11.2	1.1
Operatives	9.1	10.1	1.0
Laborers	8.3	8.9	0.6
Pr. household workers	8.1	8.7	0.6
Other service workers	9.2	10.8	1.6
Farmers, farm managers	8.5	8.8	0.3
Farm laborers, foremen	7.5	8.5	1.0

SOURCE: *Manpower Report of the President, 1964*, p. 220.

came among craftsmen, followed by operatives. The smallest gains came in clerical (none at all), professional, and sales. The median year shifts reflect the movement toward greater proportions of high-school graduates. The spread from highest to lowest median years narrowed by 0.4 years.

Service occupations probably have absorbed younger and/or more educated displaced workers and also reflect the entrance of women who normally attain higher educational levels than men through the high-school range. The median year gain in the blue-collar occupations probably reflects the retirement of older workers and the competitive advantage of younger, more educated workers, as well as a change in job content; the shrinkage of blue-collar jobs presupposes the disadvantage of the less educated. The rise in the proportion of those with college training, however, reflects new requirements, especially in tight markets such as professionals. Median year figures do not reflect the latter changes.[20]

[20] A preliminary study of job vacancies was conducted by the National Industrial Conference Board in the Rochester, New York, area in September and October of 1964. It was done in a fairly tight labor market with the unemployment rate at about 1.4 percent in November, 1964. Minimum educational requirements for existing vacancies by occupation were sought as part of the study. Three to four years of high school were required for 75 percent of clerical and sales openings, 54 percent of skilled, and 52 percent of semi-skilled openings. For professional-managerial openings, 95 percent required more than high-school graduation. Among unskilled job openings 66 percent required nine or ten years of school, while only service occupations showed the bulk of its education requirements in the category of less than nine years of school: 81 percent required eight or less years. See John G. Myers, "Conceptual and Measurement Problems in Job Vacancies," paper delivered at the Research Conference on the Measurement and Interpretation of Job Vacancies, National Bureau of Economic Research, Feb. 11–13, 1965.

The general conclusions to be drawn about requirements are, first, that there have been upward shifts in the educational composition of the employed and of the population in general. Thus, regardless of the level of demand, increases in educational attainment are clearly a function of time and will be reflected in requirements for employment. On the other hand, the relative shifts within the employed by occupations suggest some loosening of requirements in tight skills with, at the same time, a wider range and a higher upper level in educational requirements by occupation. For the employed as a whole, educational upgrading has come about both as a result of educational trends and because of changes in the occupational content of total employment.

Labor Force Differences in Education

Whether educational differences create structural problems can perhaps be assessed through examination of educational levels among the employed, the unemployed, and those not in the labor force. Have the unemployed been falling behind the employed in educational levels?

The data in Table 41 suggest that the unemployed have a larger share of those with less than high-school education than do the employed. However, from 1957 to 1962 the share decline of those with less than four years of high school was greater for the unemployed (6.9 points) than the employed (5.9 points). For those classed as not in the labor force the drop in the lowest group's proportion was only 2.6 points. This may indicate that the potentially unemployed due to substandard education have left the labor force and/or that the labor force has witnessed the entry of the most educated portions of the labor force reserve, i.e., married women.

When the situation is explored further it can be seen that the share increases of those with college experience has been more important among the employed and those not in the labor force (which includes those still attending college and women not working) than for the unemployed. The unemployed show a relative educational disadvantage in the upper levels. The increase in the proportion of the unemployed who are high-school graduates without college was higher, however, than for those employed or not in the labor force.[21]

Changes in the gap between median school years completed by the employed and the unemployed, and the gap between the employed and those not in the labor force are interesting, although there is not sufficient data to adequately account for cyclical factors. Table 44 presents median

---

[21] It may be unnecessary to state the obvious, but unemployment rates within age groups are inversely related to years of school completed. See Johnston, "Educational Attainment of Workers, March 1962."

TABLE 44: Median Number of Years of School Completed by the Population Eighteen Years and Over by Labor Force Category, Selected Dates

	Population	Labor force Total	Employed	Unemployed	Not in labor force
Both Sexes					
Oct., 1952	10.6	10.9	10.9	10.1	10.0
March, 1957	11.0	11.6	11.7	9.4	10.2
March, 1959	11.4	12.0	12.0	9.9	10.5
March, 1962	11.9	12.1	12.1	10.6	10.7
March, 1964	12.0	12.2	12.2	10.9	10.9
Males					
Oct., 1952	10.1	10.4	10.4	8.8	8.5
March, 1957	10.7	11.1	11.2	8.9	8.5
March, 1959	11.1	11.5	11.7	9.5	8.5
March, 1962	11.6	12.0	12.1	10.0	8.7
March, 1964	12.0	12.1	12.1	10.3	8.7
Females					
Oct., 1952	11.0	12.0	12.0	11.5	10.4
March, 1957	11.4	12.1	12.1	10.4	10.7
March, 1959	11.7	12.2	12.2	10.7	10.9
March, 1962	12.0	12.2	12.3	11.5	11.2
March, 1964	12.1	12.3	12.3	11.9	11.5

SOURCE: Denis F. Johnston (BLS), "Educational Attainment of Workers, March 1962," *Special Labor Force Reports*, No. 30, May, 1963, p. 506, and No. 53, May, 1965, p. 519.

years for both sexes and for each sex separately, covering October, 1952 (a Korean War date), March, 1957 (one month before the cyclical low in the unemployment rate), March, 1959 (mid-recovery), March, 1962 (presumably well past mid-recovery), and March, 1964.

The size of the median year gap between the employed and the unemployed was greatest at the near cyclical peak month in 1957. For men the Korean period shows the lowest gap, 1.6 years. Note that at least four years of high school (twelve years of school) is the median achievement for the total employed and each employed group by sex by 1962, and for females for all five dates. On the other hand, each median for the unemployed and those not in the labor force is below the twelve-year mark.

Males not in the labor force display a median year gap with respect to employed males that is greater than the employed-unemployed gap; it increased between 1952 and 1962. The implication seems to be that, among males, structural unemployment related to inadequate levels of education have been minimized by declines in labor force participation.

This point is further clarified in Table 45, which presents median years of school for civilians eighteen years and over by age groups and by labor force status. Median years tend to equal or be higher for those not in the labor force when one of the alternatives to labor force participation is full-time school enrollment. This is apparent for males from eighteen to twenty-four years of age. In 1952 and 1959 this was true for males

TABLE 45: Median School Years for Selected Groups in the Civilian Noninstitutional Population, October, 1952, March, 1959, and March, 1962

| Group | Median school years | | | |
	October, 1952	March, 1959	March, 1962	Change 1952–62
Civilians 18 years and over				
18 and 19 in labor force	—	12.1	12.3	—
not in labor force	—	11.8	12.2	—
20–24 in labor force	—	12.4	12.4	—
not in labor force	—	12.4	12.4	—
25–34 in labor force	12.1	12.3	12.4	0.3
not in labor force	12.2	12.3	12.3	0.1
35–44 in labor force	11.4	12.1	12.2	0.8
not in labor force	11.4	12.1	12.2	0.8
45–54 in labor force	—	10.8	11.6	—
not in labor force	—	9.8	10.5	—
55–64 in labor force	—	8.9	9.4	—
not in labor force	—	8.7	8.7	—
65 and over in labor force	8.3	8.6	8.8	0.5
not in labor force	8.1	8.2	8.3	0.2
Males 18 years and over				
18 and 19 in labor force	—	11.7	12.1	—
not in labor force	—	12.0	12.3	—
20–24 in labor force	—	12.2	12.4	—
not in labor force	—	14.1	14.1	—
25–34 in labor force	12.1	12.3	12.4	0.3
not in labor force	12.7	12.7	12.0	(0.7)
35–44 in labor force	11.2	12.1	12.2	1.0
not in labor force	9.6	10.0	9.1	(0.5)
45–54 in labor force	—	10.4	11.1	—
not in labor force	—	8.3	8.5	—
55–64 in labor force	—	8.8	9.0	—
not in labor force	—	8.2	8.4	—
65 and over in labor force	8.2	8.5	8.7	0.5
not in labor force	7.5	8.0	8.1	0.6

Parentheses indicate negative figures.

SOURCE: *Current Population Reports*, Series P-50, No. 78; BLS, *Special Labor Force Reports*, Nos. 1, 30.

twenty-five to thirty-four, perhaps reflecting the veterans' use of the "G.I. bill of rights" and their continuation through to graduate school. The male groups thirty-five to forty-four and forty-five to fifty-four show the widest gap in median years, with those not in the labor force way below in educational levels. This is echoed in the total of male and female age groupings but is partly washed out by the lesser contrast and higher educational levels among women. Most significant is the fact that the gap increased over the years shown. Among males twenty-five through forty-four years of age the median years attained by those not in the labor force have actually declined.

One is forced to conclude, therefore, that men with substandard education, probably from farms and among nonwhites and laborers, have faced structural unemployment and that many have eventually chosen to withdraw from the labor force. The patterns indicate a selective process with respect to education in recent years. This emphasizes the role of participation rates as an adaptive force in conjunction with educational achievement.

Whether this educational adaptation is fully adequate is another question. Recent work on this topic has centered on the plight of the high-school dropout. The dropout rate declined from 1960 to 1963 but was as high as 22 percent even in 1963.[22] While the school attendance rate for fourteen- to seventeen-year-olds is increasing, the experience of those who drop out is growing worse. Unemployed dropouts sixteen to twenty-four years old were one half of the unemployed in this age group who were not in school in October, 1962. The unemployment rate of dropouts sixteen to twenty-one years of age in February, 1963, was twice as high as for high-school graduates, at 27 percent.

Income levels throughout life are directly related to the recency of the dropout and inversely related to the number of years of school completed. A relationship exists between steadiness of work and educational level, which reflects the characteristics of jobs open to less educated workers. For that reason, unemployment rates and education are related. Duration of unemployment, however, is less closely related to education since once the job loss is incurred, the reasons for the loss influence the re-employability of the individual. In addition, specialized skills at higher levels can make re-employment difficult. But, except for females over eighteen, the highest incidence of long-term unemployment does occur among individuals with less than eight years of schooling.

[22] *Manpower Report of the President, 1965*, p. 224. The school dropout rate is defined here as the number of school dropouts as a percentage of the noninstitutional population of June high-school graduates not enrolled in college plus dropouts, as of October of the year of graduation or dropout. The rates in 1960, 1961, 1962, and 1963 were 27.2, 27.9, 23.3, and 22.2 percent, respectively.

The Bureau of Labor Statistics found that the high-school dropout is ill-equipped to find employment for a number of reasons. First, he does not meet minimum educational levels, as four years of high school increasingly becomes a requirement for employment. In addition, only 30 percent of dropouts in February, 1963, had taken vocational or commercial programs while in school; among high-school graduates 38 percent had taken such programs. The dropouts were less likely to have entered training programs after leaving school, and they were more likely to be below the usual grade for their age and showed profiles of dissatisfaction and difficulties with school. The characteristics of the dropouts suggest inadequacies in the school system as much as deficiencies in the youth involved.[23]

Conclusions

The changing occupational content of employment and the direction of technological change have shifted skill requirements from those learned casually and on the job to those requiring formal training. This has raised educational standards. In the presence of skill scarcities, some employers have taken on themselves the support of special training and education as a kind of fringe employment benefit. This is a way to upgrade the internal labor force; however, these benefits accrue to those already possessing an initial educational advantage: high-school graduation at least. Changes in educational requirements have been met by an upgrading of general educational levels in the labor force but those with lower levels of attainment face structural unemployment or must leave the labor force.

CONCLUSIONS

The labor force's four mechanisms of adjustment—participation rates, job mobility, geographic mobility, and educational attainment—have been found to be adaptive but not adequate to eliminate what appear to be bottlenecks of labor skill scarcities at the top and superabundance of unskilled labor at the bottom of the skill hierarchy. Evidence of such dislocations has existed since 1955. These problems, developing as they did within a framework of inadequate levels of over-all demand, were accentuated thereby, but they would have been present even in a period of more rapid rates of output growth.

[23] An interesting and disturbing sidelight is that the unemployment rate for non-white youths who graduated from high school was almost as high as the rate for non-white dropouts, the rates being 25.6 and 26.1 percent, respectively, in February, 1963. For fuller details on the experience of dropouts see BLS, *Special Labor Force Reports*, Nos. 6, 32, 34, 46, 47, 54.

CHAPTER 8

EVIDENCE OF SKILL SHORTAGES

Chapter 1 suggested that the structurally unemployed comprise (1) those with obsolete skills and skills needed in declining proportions with respect to output, and (2) those with skills which are complements of skills in short supply. Chapter 5 concentrated primarily on finding preconditions for the existence of the first group; Chapters 6 and 7 gave indirect indications that both groups currently exist. This chapter deals with direct evidence of skill shortages. It assumes that some complementarity of skills exists, with only limited substitution possible; thus, evidence of skill scarcities in conjunction with high unemployment is the test for the existence of the second group of the structurally unemployed.

The areas explored here are job vacancy data, the skill composition of the labor force reserve compared with employment and vacancies, hours of work by occupation, and annual income changes by occupation. These are the areas in which structural skill scarcities should be manifest as distinct from general labor shortages at full employment levels.

JOB VACANCY DATA

Complete information on available, unfilled openings would provide the clearest indication of selective unsatisfied labor demand. If such a measure were available by occupation, industry, and location, it would be possible to differentiate frictional from structural unemployment.[1]

Unfilled job listings have certain specific limitations. For example, given general awareness of shortages, openings for certain skills might not show up in listings since operations are often built around existing staff.

---

[1] Of course, vacancies because of substandard wages and working conditions or because of employer discrimination would have to be taken out of the frictional category.

Structural skill shortages are hidden when demand unemployment exists along with them because output is adjusted to a lower level and the shortages would be operative only with an increase in demand. Openings for nonkey posts would not appear until key posts were filled. The major problem, however, is not the inadequacy of job vacancy data but the absence of a comprehensive series.

At the moment there are only two sources that provide time series on unfilled openings. One is the National Industrial Conference Board's (NICB) Index of Help Wanted Ads. This is not broken down by occupation.[2] The second is inventories of nonfarm job openings placed in clearance, referred to in Chapter 7, collected by the Department of Labor's Bureau of Employment Security (BES) with the co-operation of state agencies. The jobs listed are those which cannot be filled locally, and they are classified by six occupational groupings.[3] Both series are assumed to represent nonfarm job openings since agricultural jobs do not generally appear in help-wanted ads.

Two approaches are possible for analysis: aggregate and by occupation. When total vacancies are used, the examination must take into account over-all unemployment rates. Examination of vacancies by occupation is necessary if structural shortages can exist side by side with inadequate demand, for total unfilled vacancies may decline while certain kinds of skills may show a rise in vacancies. An increase in an index of job vacancies would prove the increase of frictional unemployment if the component job skills within the vacancy group stayed in rough proportion to each other. If, on the other hand, the composition of the vacancies shifted significantly, this would indicate structural changes.[4]

[2] The NICB monthly index is based on help-wanted ads in newspapers from 1951 to 1964 in thirty-three areas in the United States, and from fifty-three areas thereafter. The data appear in the NICB publication, *The Conference Board Record*, and in a monthly bulletin.

[3] The BES series is available from 1950 for the months of March, June, September, and December. The jobs are those that have been posted but are unfilled in state employment offices. Therefore, they represent employers willing to use the agencies, jobs which could not be filled locally, and jobs whose particulars meet BES standards. The data appeared in *The Labor Market and Employment Security*, and now appear in the *Employment Service Review*. The series representing job orders placed by employers with state agencies, are more apt to fluctuate with administrative policy and staffing.

[4] The Knowles-Kalacheck Report states that if employers are not able "to fully satisfy their demand for professional and highly skilled labor . . . [there will] be a rise in the number of unfilled job vacancies, the volume of which will be greater than in the comparable phase of earlier cycles" (p. 13). Knowles-Kalacheck and Simler ("The Structural Hypothesis and Public Policy") insist that for structural unemployment to exist vacancies rise as unemployment rises. This is an implicit use of a model which plots vacancies on one axis against unemployment on the other. The 45-degree line rising from the origin is then often said to be a locus of points of "full" employment. However, this would be true only if the unemployed are equipped to take the

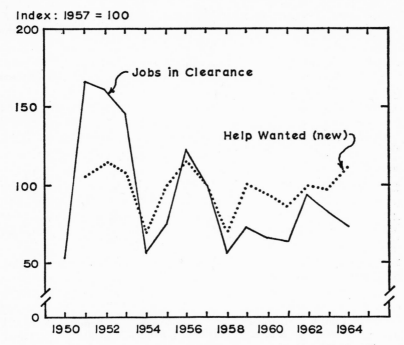

Index: 1957 = 100

FIGURE 5: Indexes of Job Vacancies, 1950–64. (Source: Table 46.)

Aggregate Indexes

The help-wanted and jobs-in-clearance indexes are presented in Part A of Table 46 and Figure 5. The two indexes generally move together, though not with the same amplitude.[5] This could easily be explained by the differences in the kinds of jobs each represents. Employers are notoriously loath to use the state agencies for better job postings, especially white-collar jobs. Thus the Korean period shows a spread between the two series, which is clearly a reflection of the need for blue-collar help. This situation is completely reversed after 1957 and the help-wanted index is

vacant jobs. Thus, the model and the authors do not differentiate structural from frictional unemployment. Departures from the 45-degree line cannot differentiate inadequate demand unemployment from structural unemployment because skill complementarities are not taken into account. A shortage in a key skill can result in openings for the skill plus its complements, but listed vacancies will reflect only the skill in short supply and not the complements—if these are available among the unemployed. The number of unemployed can thus be greater than the number of vacancies, but the unemployment can still be due to structural rather than demand causes.

[5] There is no basic difference in movement between the old and the new help-wanted series.

TABLE 46: Indexes of Job Vacancies, 1950–64

A. Aggregate indexes: 1957 = 100

Year	BES nonfarm job openings in clearance[a]	NICB help-wanted ads[b]		Civilian unemployment rate
		Old series	New series	
1950	53.9	—	—	5.3%
1951	166.9	111.1	105.6	3.3
1952	162.6	119.5	114.2	3.1
1953	146.1	111.3	108.2	2.9
1954	56.8	71.6	70.4	5.6
1955	75.0	100.7	99.7	4.4
1956	121.8	117.3	115.4	4.2
1957	100.0	100.0	100.0	4.3
1958	56.0	72.1	70.3	6.8
1959	73.2	101.2	99.0	5.5
1960	66.3	94.2	93.4	5.6
1961	64.9	85.9	86.2	6.7
1962	93.7	100.1	98.8	5.6
1963	82.2	—	97.5	5.7
1964	72.3	—	110.6	5.2

B. BES jobs in clearance by occupation[a]

Year	Prof. & mgr.	Clerical & sales	Services	Skilled	Semi-skilled	Unskilled
1950	27.1	53.5	57.0	79.1	80.2	114.9
1951	87.9	182.3	123.8	245.3	184.6	520.0
1952	94.9	130.8	76.0	248.3	191.9	527.6
1953	83.7	105.2	83.8	184.1	234.8	730.7
1954	53.8	56.4	47.7	64.0	50.0	71.5
1955	81.4	84.9	52.5	69.5	66.8	62.8
1956	121.7	119.4	115.4	124.4	115.9	138.9
1957	100.0	100.0	100.0	100.0	100.0	100.0
1958	74.9	44.4	85.2	37.0	28.1	41.8
1959	94.6	54.1	97.8	56.6	51.0	20.8
1960	88.6	57.5	71.2	50.7	38.0	5.1
1961	90.8	53.8	62.8	46.0	36.3	8.8
1962	126.4	90.0	80.2	65.2	69.9	9.0
1963	109.2	72.3	98.7	57.1	60.3	7.6
1964	84.4	52.9	82.2	66.9	60.5	44.5

[a] Bureau of Employment Security, U.S. Department of Labor, jobs listed for clearance with state agencies. They must meet requirements: (1) a local shortage in the skill requested; (2) employers willing to recruit out-of-area applicants; (3) wages and conditions of work not far below local standards; (4) housing available in the area. Data are yearly averages for March, June, September, and December.

[b] National Industrial Conference Board's Index of Help Wanted Ads; Old series based on newspaper ads in thirty-three areas in the U.S.; new series has new weights and twenty additional areas.

SOURCE: Derived from *Higher Unemployment Rates, 1957–60*, p. 74; U.S. Bureau of Employment Security, *The Labor Market and Employment Security*, and *Employment Service Review*, various issues; and National Industrial Conference Board.

the higher one, probably reflecting the emphasis on white-collar jobs, special skills, and the professions. In 1963–64 the two indexes diverge, perhaps reflecting greater placement efforts on the part of state agencies but also reflecting the differences in the kinds of jobs represented.

When the jobs-in-clearance index for 1950–63 was regressed against the unemployment rate, r was -0.88, significant at the 0.01 level.[6] The index was over-predicted for 1964, but within one standard error. The behavior of the index in recession years is of interest. In 1954 the index was about one standard error below expectations, in 1958 it was close to one standard error above, and in 1961 it was a little over one standard error above the predicted value. In other words, there has been an autonomous rise in the index at cyclical troughs, but not of a size which can eliminate chance as an explanation. In the three years when the unemployment rate was 5.6 percent, 1954, 1960, and 1962, the index stood at 56.8, 66.3, and 93.7; thus evidence of an autonomous rise again appears.[7]

Regression of the NICB help-wanted index (new series from 1951 to 1963) against the unemployment rate yields a coefficient of correlation of -0.78, significant at the 0.01 level. It is understandable that this series, probably more selective in coverage, should yield a lower r than the BES series.[8] Each year from 1959 to 1963 shows a deviation of the actual index above the expected value, although none is above one standard error. In 1964, however, the index is almost two standard errors above the expected value.

The years 1954, 1960, and 1962 with an unemployment rate of 5.6 percent show indexes of 70.4, 93.4, and 98.8, reflecting an upward shift in vacancy levels since 1957. The recession year deviations also reflect this phenomenon. For 1954 the index is below expectations by over 2 standard errors. In 1958 it is below by somewhat over 1 standard error, and in 1961 it is above by 0.5 standard error. The divergence of the two indexes in 1964, with the vacancy index over-predicted and the help-wanted index

---

[6] The regression equation is as follows: $I_j = 231.2 - 27.8\ U$, where I_j is the index of jobs in clearance and U is the unemployment rate.

[7] The Knowles-Kalacheck Report notes that at the same levels of unemployment, jobs in clearance were greater in number in 1959 and 1960 than in 1950 or 1954 when similar unemployment rates obtained, and that this is also true of the help-wanted index. One would imagine that this would help to prove the case for the structural side. Instead, the authors state they have disproved the structural argument because "the number of nonfarm job openings was lower in 1959–60 than in 1955–57 in every major occupational category" (p. 78). The unemployment rate of 1959–60 averaged 5.5 percent, while the average for 1955–57 was 4.3 percent. Since the authors demand a higher vacancy index at higher unemployment rates, they feel justified in their conclusion.

[8] The adjusted r values are -0.87 for the BES series and -0.76 for the NICB series. The latter regression equation is: $I_h = 138.4 - 8.5\ U$.

under-predicted by their respective regression equations, suggests continued shortages in selected skills. Despite higher unemployment rates, the economy seems to be facing increasing levels of unfilled jobs even at recession levels of unemployment.

If the vacancy data are valid at all, then either (1) workers are refusing these jobs because they are unattractive, or (2) workers are not able to fill them. If not able, they either (*a*) do not have the skills required or (*b*) are too far away from them. Reason (1) may be discounted, judging from the work on mobility and other sources. Job demands of the unemployed do not appear to be out of line with existing conditions and wage rates.[9] Moreover, only jobs which are near par in these respects with others in their areas can enter the jobs-in-clearance roster. The second reason in fact describes structural unemployment.

Job Vacancies by Occupation

If structural skill shortages can exist along with inadequate demand, the over-all level of vacancies may be less revealing than the composition of the vacancies. The question is, does the skill composition of vacancies reflect structural skill shortages independent of the level of vacancies?

This examination utilizes the distribution of BES indexes of jobs in clearance by occupation from 1950 to 1964. The years compared are 1954 with 1958, and 1955 with 1959 and 1964 when the aggregate indexes were nearly the same and the cycle phase was similar. From Table 46, Part B, a clear rise is evident in the professional index from 1954 to 1958, and from 1955 to 1959 or 1955 to 1964, but not from 1959 to 1964. The same is true for service occupations. On the other hand, clerical and sales jobs show a reverse response, with the index falling from 1954 to 1958 and from 1955 to 1959 and 1964. Particularly dramatic are the declines in the indexes from 1954 to 1958 and from 1955 to 1959 for the three blue-collar groups. The indexes rose somewhat from 1959 to 1964; therefore holding the over-all vacancy index constant provides clear evidence of a structural shift in the composition of vacancies at least from 1954 to 1959.

The professional index is at its highest level in 1962, followed by 1956 and 1963. None of the other occupations reflects comparable levels in any year after 1957. The clerical and sales index is highest in 1951, followed by 1952 and 1956. Service workers were most in demand in 1951, 1956, and 1957. The years with greatest blue-collar demand are clearly the years of Korean mobilization and demobilization.

[9] See Stein, "Work History, Attitudes, and Income of the Unemployed."

TABLE 47: Percentage Distribution of BES Jobs in Clearance by Occupation, 1950–64

Year	Prof. & mgr.	Clerical & sales	Services	Skilled	Semi- skilled	Unskilled
1950	21	12	6	42	13	6
1951	22	13	4	43	9	9
1952	25	10	3	43	10	9
1953	24	9	3	36	14	14
1954	40	12	5	32	7	4
1955	46	14	4	26	8	2
1956	43	12	5	29	8	3
1957	42	12	6	28	9	3
1958	56	10	9	19	4	2
1959	54	9	8	22	6	1
1960	60	10	5	20	5	0*
1961	60	10	5	20	5	0
1962	57	12	5	20	6	0
1963	56	11	7	20	6	0
1964	50	9	6	26	7	2

* Zero indicates less than 0.5 percent.
SOURCE: Same as Table 38.

Table 47 shows that the distribution of job vacancies has clearly undergone a dramatic change, regardless of the level of over-all unemployment and of total vacancies. Jobs for professionals and managers were about 23 percent of vacancies from 1950 to 1953, about 43 percent of vacancies from 1954 to 1957, and about 56 percent of all vacancies from 1958 to 1964. This group displays three clear-cut phases. The clerical-sales share has not changed much over time, nor has that of the service occupations. A marked change has come among the skilled occupations—they have essentially reversed roles with professionals in hard-to-fill jobs. The phases appear to be from 1950 to 1953, when the share averaged 41 percent; 1954 to 1957, with an average of 29 percent; and 1958 to 1963, with an average of 20 percent. In 1964 the share was as high as in 1955. Semi-skilled and unskilled occupations show similar but less dramatic declines since they were an already small share of job vacancies in clearance. The nature of their skills would make recruiting over distances unlikely except in periods of over-all tight labor supply.

Comparison of 1954 with 1958 and 1955 with 1959 and 1964 shows a strong share increase for professionals, a major decline for craftsmen in the recession years, and a less dramatic rise for professionals and no loss for craftsmen in the recovery years. Structural shortages are clearly evident with respect to professionals.[10] It appears, then, that unemployment of their skill complements probably added to structural unemployment from 1955 to 1964.[11]

Recent Labor Department Research on Job Vacancies

The Department of Labor undertook an experimental program of job vacancy data collection in 1964–65 and conducted a special survey of job openings at local employment service offices as of the end of July, 1964. The latter survey was designed to investigate the occupational characteristics of unfilled jobs. Preliminary results pertinent to this section have been reported.[12]

The survey of unfilled openings listed with local employment service offices covered fifty-two large metropolitan areas and twenty-six smaller areas. About two-thirds of the areas had unemployment rates between 3.0 to 5.9 percent; one sixth included those with less than 3.0 percent and one sixth those with 6.0 percent or more. The results showed that 70 percent of jobs unfilled for fifteen days or more were in occupations for which special training, education, or skills were required. Thirty percent were for professionals, 24 percent for clerical and sales, and 16 percent for skilled blue-collar occupations. About 56 percent of all openings were unfilled because of lack of qualified applicants and about 22 percent because of sub-standard conditions. By way of contrast, the survey found 8 percent of the experienced unemployed in the professional-managerial group. These occupations were 30 percent of vacancies open at least

---

[10] Knowles and Kalacheck comment that the ". . . rise over time in the series in nonfarm job openings, and presumably also in the help-wanted index, is accounted for by changes in the demand for professional and managerial workers. The number of job openings available for all other workers was actually somewhat smaller in 1959 and 1960 than in 1950 or 1954. Demand for professional workers has shown some independence of the general labor market trends" (p. 74).

The authors go on to point to the role of missile, space, and electronic data-processing industries in causing the strength of demand for professional workers, but they seem to feel that unless the aggregate series rises markedly, occupational shifts are irrelevant. This is because they insist on the "adequacy" of over-all demand as a prerequisite for structural unemployment.

[11] These results have been criticized by those who say that the BES has placed great emphasis in recent years on the collection of professional vacancies. Two answers are in order. First, the BES develops job openings only when there are applicants. Thus, unfilled vacancies in clearance should not be affected. Second, if the emphasis does affect the index it would show up from the 1961 period. The upward shift in the professionals' share of vacancies occurred in two steps, both prior to 1961. If anything, greater placement attempts would bias the unfilled jobs in a downward direction.

[12] See Vladimir D. Chavrid and Harold Kuptzin, "Employment Service Operating Data as a Measure of Job Vacancies," paper presented at Research Conference on the Measurement and Interpretation of Job Vacancies, National Bureau of Economic Research, Feb. 11–13, 1965.

fourteen days. The semi-skilled were about 31 percent of the experienced unemployed but 12 percent of the vacancies; unskilled were 13 percent of the unemployed and 3 percent of openings. Thus, structural imbalances were evident even on a broad, six-occupation breakdown.

The Department of Labor's experimental job vacancy program also uncovered structural imbalances. The program provided for two surveys in fiscal 1965 in sixteen areas. Tentative conclusions were that most vacancies reported were of relatively long duration and considered hard to fill.[13] Specific occupations listed most often included engineers, registered nurses, draftsmen, laboratory technicians, physical therapists, stenographers, typists, machinists, tool and die makers, and several types of mechanics and repairmen. A survey was made in October of 1964 in Birmingham, Milwaukee, Portland, and Providence. The small and select regional character of this sample makes generalization difficult with respect to the global occupational content of vacancies; however, the survey did point up another aspect of the structural problem. There was marked evidence of regional imbalances with respect to labor demand and supply for specific occupations. In one area demand exceeded supply for particular occupations while the reverse situation obtained in another area. Thus there was an indication that the imbalances on a broad occupational basis probably understate the degree of structural imbalance in the economy—even at less-than-adequate rates of output growth.

THE LABOR FORCE RESERVE

The distribution of employment by occupation tells something about the skills both needed and available in the labor force. Additional data on the total supply of labor skills can shed light on the origin of skill scarcities. Something analogous to an unused labor supply schedule exists for 1951, although it is not a schedule in the sense that quantities are set against prices. The Census Bureau collected data in 1951 that presented the past work experience of individuals not in the labor force who were twenty years or over.[14] Among other breakdowns, occupation groups were represented according to the respondents' last job or, in the case of those who had not worked since World War II, the highest paid past job. For the purposes of this section all those over sixty-five years of age were eliminated; the remainder constituted a skill reserve for the labor force.

---

[13] *Ibid.*

[14] U.S., Bureau of the Census, "Work Experience of the Labor Reserve: March 1951," *Current Population Reports*, Series P-50, No. 38, 1952.

These data, used along with employment and vacancy data, provide insights about the nature of skill scarcities. To avoid problems of non-comparable magnitudes and coverage, only percentage distributions were considered. Farm occupations were eliminated from the reserve and employment data, also for purposes of comparability. The more detailed groupings were combined so as to correspond to the jobs in clearance categories. The results are presented in Table 48 and Figure 6.

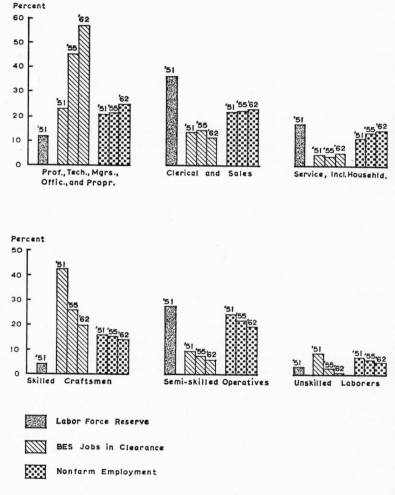

FIGURE 6: Distribution of the Nonfarm Labor Force Reserve, Employment, and Jobs in Clearance by Occupation, 1951, 1955, and 1962. (Source: Table 48.)

TABLE 48: Distribution of the Nonfarm Labor Force Reserve, Employment, and Jobs in Clearance by Occupation, 1951, 1955, and 1962

(percentages)

Category and occupation	Distribution		
	1951	1955	1962
Civilians 20–64 years in March, 1951, not in labor force, by last job worked[a]			
Prof., tech.; Mgr., offic., propr.	11.7		
Clerical; Sales	36.2		
Service (incl. pr. house.)	17.9		
Skilled (craftsmen)	3.7		
Semi-skilled (operatives)	27.7		
Unskilled (laborers)	2.5		
Total	100.0		
BES nonfarm job openings in clearance			
Prof., tech.; Mgr., offic., propr.	22.3	45.9	57.0
Clerical; Sales	13.2	13.7	11.6
Service (incl. pr. house.)	4.2	4.0	4.9
Skilled (craftsmen)	41.9	26.4	19.8
Semi-skilled (operatives)	9.5	7.6	6.4
Unskilled (laborers)	8.9	2.4	0.3
Total	100.0	100.0	100.0
Household Survey nonfarm employment			
Prof., tech.; Mgr., offic., propr.	20.4	21.7	24.5
Clerical; Sales	21.2	22.1	22.9
Service (incl. pr. house.)	12.2	13.0	14.0
Skilled (craftsmen)	15.7	14.9	13.8
Semi-skilled (operatives)	23.3	21.9	19.1
Unskilled (laborers)	7.3	6.3	5.6
Total	100.0	100.0	100.0

[a] Or by highest paid job if last job was held during World War II.

SOURCE: Derived from sources for Tables 16 and 38; and U.S., Bureau of the Census, "Work Experience of the Labor Reserve: March 1951," *Current Population Reports*, Series P-50, No. 38, 1952.

In 1951 the United States was at the start of the Korean War, and the demand for skilled craftsmen was the highest of all the occupations in short supply. The labor force reserve offered little additional supply since craftsmen, primarily men, were already largely absorbed into the labor force.[15] Thus the proportion of craftsmen in employment was far below the proportion in jobs in clearance. On the other hand, there were

[15] Most of the reserve craftsmen were in the group sixty-five years and over and were eliminated since they were not real prospects for re-entry.

abundant sources to draw on for operatives and most white-collar occupations. The labor force reserve was heavily concentrated among women who had worked during World War II. They had been clerical workers and semi-skilled operatives, primarily. Thus, in these two areas and in service occupations, the share in the labor force reserve was higher than the share in jobs in clearance and in employment, and the employment shares were higher than the vacancy shares.

Laborers were in short supply in 1951, as many probably went into the Armed Forces or chose more lucrative blue-collar jobs. Selective Service drew away the new entrants who normally would have taken laborers' jobs. Very few women hold laborers' jobs. At the other end of the training scale, the reserve supply of professionals and technicians, though not insignificant, did not match the need for them. Their share in employment was about equal to their share of jobs in clearance in 1951 but both shares were above that in the labor reserve.

The year 1955 may have been pivotal from the point of view of technological change. The largest absolute employment increase of 1954–55 went to operatives, but it marked the start of the trend to professional and white-collar employment at the expense of the manual occupations. Looking back at the labor force reserve data it is easy to see what occurred. There is evidence of a shift, not only in the composition of skill requirements, but a shift in labor skill bottlenecks from craftsmen to professionals and technicians.

As the demand for clerical, sales, and service workers grew, women in the labor reserve with earlier experience were drawn into employment. Since these occupations represented a major part of the labor force reserve, their jobs-in-clearance share remained smaller than their employment share; the employment shares, in turn, were below the reserve shares. This development was made possible by the rising trend in female participation rates, especially among older women. By way of contrast, the shift in labor requirements away from blue-collar work is shown by more dramatic drops in the shares of jobs in clearance than in employment. The drop from 1951 to 1955 is particularly marked for craftsmen and laborers. But, at least for craftsmen, there was a continuing need which kept its share of jobs in clearance in 1962 (19.8 percent) higher than its share of nonfarm employment (13.8 percent). It is likely that the content of craftsmen jobs changed and this may be why the proportion of jobs in clearance remained high (for example, repairmen and mechanics are classed as craftsmen). With operatives, since there was an abundance of the needed skills in the labor reserve, the decline in demand is parallel to the decline in employment, but the unfilled jobs share has never indicated anything like a shortage of operatives. It was and remains minimal.

The situation among professionals, technicians, managers, officials, and proprietors provides the major contrast. Here the rise in the share of jobs in clearance between 1951 and 1955 is of major proportions. This is the new bottleneck. It seems clear that the labor force reserve could not supply the growing need, nor were new labor force entrants able to provide a boost in the employment share comparable to the rise in the unfilled demand share. There could easily have been a greater increase in this employment category had the population been able to supply the skills. If the supply of craftsmen and laborers was structurally blocked in 1951, should the later shortage in the professional-managerial group be considered a qualitatively different kind of block? We think so. First, the 1951 blocks were partly related to the mobilization of men; but, second, the basic difference lies with the preparation needed in the unfilled occupations (see the training attainments listed in Table 39).

Both 1951 and 1962 had in common a shortage of skills that require a great deal of training, which is why the skills were in short supply. But craftsmen are primarily developed on the job and in casual procedures. On the other hand, the need for laborers in 1951 drew on one of the lowest pretraining occupations. Professionals and technicians, however, require not only long training but formal training. This group seems least able to draw naturally from the declining occupations. In addition, managers and officials require years of special experience, while the self-employed are declining and do not enter the category of skill shortages. We might rely on the labor market to shift workers into operative and craft training from laborers' jobs and from the farms, but we cannot assume that it will get them into schools to become professionals or technicians. Besides, the length of training time involved is also longer. Thus, the jobs-in-clearance data show a continued bottleneck in this area.

HOURS OF WORK

If certain skills are in scarce supply this shortage will appear not only in unfilled vacancies, but, as Knowles and Kalacheck suggest, the work week of the group in short supply will be lengthened.[16] However, the test suggested by the authors looks for overtime hours in the nonmanufacturing industries.[17] This is a less-than-satisfactory approach for a number of reasons.

In the first place, the shortage is probably by skill, rather than by industry. The shortage of skilled professionals might be reflected in the

[16] *Higher Unemployment Rates*, pp. 12–13.
[17] *Ibid.*, p. 22.

manufacturing work week rather than in nonmanufacturing. To the extent that females, new entrants, and displaced workers have entered the service-producing industries, there is no reason to expect strongly increased work weeks in the nonmanufacturing sector as a whole. Second, given the rise in voluntary part-time work in most service-producing industries, an increase in the work week would be a better argument for the demand position since a lay-off of part-time help could lengthen the work week. [18] Third, changes in the work week can also be a function of technological changes related to shift needs or can be related to collective bargaining and premium pay conditions. Fourth, shorter hours per week and per year have been a trend for the entire century, and, given the postwar increase in voluntary part-time work, one would not expect to find evidence of increased hours of work strong enough to reverse the secular trends. [19]

It is necessary to go behind the long-run trends. Table 49 presents a breakdown of hours worked per week for May, 1948, and May, 1963, by industry, divided into four sub-categories. The data show a shift to part-time work in the service-producing industries and a general decline in the length of the work week. But there has been a selective increase in the proportion of nonfarm wage and salary workers who put in more than forty-eight hours a week. Their share has shown an increase over the postwar period. This phenomenon is described by Ewan Clague, Commissioner of the Bureau of Labor Statistics:

> There is no basis for believing that this uptrend, which appears to have been more pronounced since the mid 1950's is the result of more dual job-holding or better survey techniques. . . . A major factor responsible for this trend appeared to be both an increasing proportion of professional and technical workers in nonfarm employment, and a lengthening of hours among those highly skilled workers. [20]

[18] See David J. Farber, *Annual Paid Man-Hours of Employment and Annual Wages, 1946–54*, U.S., Department of Health, Education, and Welfare, Social Security Administration, Bureau of Old-Age and Survivors' Insurance, 1962.

[19] The Knowles-Kalacheck Report states, "The average length of the workweek for employed persons in both manufacturing and nonmanufacturing industries has . . . declined between successive cyclical peaks in 1953, 1957 and 1960" (p. 75). The trend to part-time work explains much of this, and in manufacturing the work week, though fairly stable, responds to the level of output. In addition, there has been pressure from labor to negotiate cuts in the standard work week or to increase paid vacations and holidays. The authors go on to comment, "Changes in the rate of growth of nonmanufacturing output do not seem to have had a significant impact on year-to-year changes in the length of the workweek" (p. 75).

[20] "Hours of Work in the United States and Abroad," *Monthly Labor Review*, 86, No. 8 (Aug., 1963), p. 929 [summary of prepared report].

TABLE 49: Hours of Work per Week: Wage and Salary Workers in Nonagricultural Industries, May, 1948, and May, 1963 (percentage distribution)

Industry	Percentage distribution within industry groups							
	1–35 hours		36–40 hours		41–48 hours		49 hrs., over	
	1948	1963	1948	1963	1948	1963	1948	1963
Mining; forest; fisheries	11.3	7.9	37.4	53.3	42.6	14.9	8.8	23.8
Construction	16.2	16.9	49.7	52.9	24.9	15.0	9.3	13.3
Manufacturing	9.1	9.4	64.5	62.1	19.6	16.8	6.8	11.8
Utilities	6.3	9.7	41.7	62.9	37.9	11.8	14.0	15.6
Trade	14.7	24.1	32.4	37.2	36.1	18.7	16.7	20.0
Finance	7.8	12.5	54.8	62.7	27.1	10.0	10.4	14.9
Service industries	23.7	30.7	37.4	42.0	24.7	12.5	14.3	14.7
Government	5.3	8.7	65.5	70.0	19.7	9.8	9.5	11.5

SOURCE: U.S., Bureau of Labor Statistics, "Hours of Work in the United States and Abroad," *Monthly Labor Review*, 86, No. 8 (Aug. ,1963), p. 929.

As Table 49 indicates, the increase in working over forty-eight hours is in contrast to the decrease in the group working forty-one to forty-eight hours. And the rise in the over-forty-eight hour group is marked in those industries which have experienced major production employment losses, such as mining and manufacturing, as well as in service-producing industries.

Table 50 presents data on workers who put in forty-nine hours or more of work per week, by occupation, for the month of April in 1952 and 1963. The occupations that both increased employment and require specialized training show the greatest increase in persons working over forty-eight hours, namely professional and technical workers. The greatest share increases went to professionals, followed by nonhousehold service workers.

A survey that collected data for May, 1963, on payment of overtime premium pay found that about 26 percent of all wage and salary workers put in over forty hours a week that month, but only 29 percent of overtime workers received premium pay.[21] Of those working overtime, 56 percent normally work overtime without premium pay, while 17 percent normally work overtime with premium pay. Of the occupations with heavy distribution of those working over forty-eight hours—professionals, managers, craftsmen, operatives, and farmers—only the blue-collar workers received a considerable portion of premium pay. In other words, the overtime for over forty-eight hours has increased in the areas of short supply without a great penalty to employers.

[21] James E. Blackwood and Carol B. Kalish, "Long Hours and Premium Pay," *Monthly Report on the Labor Force*, July, 1963, pp. 17–24.

TABLE 50: Persons at Work Forty-nine Hours or More per Week by Occupation, April, 1952, and April, 1963

Occupation	Percentage distribution		Thousands of persons		Percentage change
	1952	1963	1952	1963	1952–63
Prof., tech.	6.9	12.7	744	1,507	103
Mgrs., offic., propr.	22.7	24.0	2,438	2,844	17
Clerical	3.6	3.8	388	447	15
Sales	6.2	7.0	666	832	25
Craftsmen	9.2	10.2	990	1,208	22
Operatives	11.6	12.5	1,242	1,477	19
Laborers	2.5	2.3	264	272	3
Pr. household	1.6	1.9	270	221	30
Other service	6.8	8.6	726	1,014	40
Farmers	22.1	12.0	2,368	1,421	(40)
Farm laborers	6.8	5.0	730	587	(20)
Total	100.0	100.0	10,726	11,829	10

Parentheses indicate negative figures.
SOURCE: U.S., Bureau of Labor Statistics, "Hours of Work in the United States and Abroad," *Monthly Labor Review*, 86, No. 8 (Aug., 1963), p. 929.

CHANGES IN ANNUAL EMPLOYMENT INCOME

If certain skills are in short supply it would be reasonable to expect that wages for these skills would be bid up, especially while demand was able to sustain the job openings. On the other hand, there is no reason to expect that all occupations showing employment gains would show unusual wage increases. This is because wages in a free market would represent a balance of supply and demand. Therefore, the labor force reserve, job vacancies, and the transferabilities and substitutabilities of skills would all enter into the determination of differential wage movements.

Certainly the movement of aggregate wages is not a sufficient test of skill shortages.[22] If different labor skills are required in fairly fixed proportions, and if demand were slack besides, skill shortages would not necessarily bid up aggregate wages since the aggregate wage change is affected by relative weights as well as specific wages. There is no denying the evidence of slack demand from 1952 to 1963; one would not look to stable average wages as proof that skill bottlenecks were absent.

[22] In his testimony before the Subcommittee on Economic Statistics, John Kendrick supported his denial of structural unemployment by pointing to the less rapid rise of wages and prices in 1960 than in 1956–57. He concluded that "the labor force structure was not frustrating an expansion that would otherwise have taken place" (*Employment and Unemployment: Hearings*, p. 343).

This section explores the movements of average annual wages by occupation and sex from 1950 to 1960 in an attempt to find whether there is evidence of wage movements which signal the existence of skill shortages. It does not set out a theory of wages. It suggests, however, that the elasticities of labor skill coefficients and skill transferabilities influence supply and demand for particular kinds of labor, and, therefore, that differential movements in employment income can be indicative of skill availabilities.

There is downward pressure on wages for a skill needed in smaller proportions through the action of the displaced, but this effect is minimized if the skill holders can move to other labor skill markets. Where the displaced skill is organized by unions, the downward pressure is minimized in the originating market but is more heavily brought to bear in alternative markets. For example, one expects the unionized, operative workers' wages to resist downward pressure, but wages of alternative, nonunionized occupations to be affected by displaced operatives.

The greater specificity of both professional and managerial skills should easily have given rise to wage increases, all other things being equal. First, they became wanted in greater proportions; second, they are least affected by the downward wage pressure of market entrants coming from declining occupations; third, the labor reserve is also short of these skills. An inadequate supply should raise the rates in response to a shifted demand for these skills. It is easy to see how skill shortages could put upward pressure on specific wages, but aggregate demand repercussions could quickly develop to dampen aggregate labor demand and to keep the wages of even the bottleneck skills from spiraling. This would certainly be true for average wages in the economy as a whole.

The data utilized here are average year-to-year percentage changes in average annual income by occupation and sex for the periods 1950–55 and 1955–60. These are compared with the corresponding average percentage changes in employment by occupation and sex. The two cross-section series were examined for regularities and irregularities.[23]

---

[23] The reader will note that no use is made of hourly wage rates or data by industry. These alternatives were not used because all industries have been experiencing changes in their skill composition which could strongly affect industry averages. The industries also may not have equally suffered from skill shortages or uniformly benefited from labor productivity changes. Average hourly figures are not used since regularity of employment, permanence, and regularity of overtime work all are ignored by the measure.

Gallaway uses wage rates to test for structural blockages and finds a competitive market adjustment in wages by area, but not by occupation or industry (Gallaway, "Labor Mobility, Resource Allocation, and Structural Unemployment"). He does not consider the problem of skill shortages; instead, he suggests that the evil may be in union market power.

Table 51 presents the average annual rates for the two time segments. The first question asked is whether the relationship of employment growth to annual wage and salary income growth is different in the two periods. Average employment growth in 1950–55 by occupation is roughly related to employment growth in 1955–60. The coefficient of rank correlation is 0.67 for sixteen observations and is significant at the 0.01 level. On the other hand, the rank correlation for the two income periods is −0.41, almost significant at the 0.05 level. Income increases by occupation in the first period were only minimumly and inversely related to their position in the second period. Thus, there is some indication that a different set of forces dominated the later period.

The rank correlation of employment and income changes for 1950–55 is 0.16 and is not significant; thus in the earlier period employment growth

TABLE 51: Average Annual Percentage Change in Wage and Salary Income by Occupation and Sex, 1950–55 and 1955–60[a]

Occupation and sex		1950–55		1955–60	
		Employment	Income	Employment	Income
Prof., tech.	M	6.0	4.6	5.7	5.6
	F	4.0	5.5	4.4	5.3
Mgr., prop.	M	0.1	3.9	1.8	7.1
Clerical	M	(1.4)	5.7	2.5	3.8
	F	4.0	4.7	3.5	3.4
Sales	M	0.6	6.4	2.0	2.8
	F	1.2	0.9	2.2	4.6
Craftsmen	M	1.7	6.2	0.6	4.2
Operatives	M	1.0	5.6	(1.2)	4.2
	F	1.4	5.3	(1.0)	3.4
Laborers	M	1.0	5.8	0.1	3.4
Non-house. service	M	0.5	4.6	1.9	2.8
	F	4.1	4.6	5.1	5.4
Pr. household	F	1.9	4.3	2.7	1.9
Farmers	M	(2.8)	1.1	(5.7)	6.0
Farm laborers	M	(3.2)	3.1	0.3	4.2

[a] Average annual wage and salary income in current dollars by current or last occupation. Parentheses indicate negative figures.

SOURCE: Derived from *Manpower Report of the President, 1964*, p. 199, and U.S., Bureau of the Census, *Trends in the Income of Families and Persons in the United States 1947 to 1960*, Technical Paper No. 8, prepared by Herman P. Miller (Washington: U.S. Government Printing Office, 1963).

seemed to have little relationship to income growth. If this is true it rules out any marked skill shortages. The product moment coefficient of correlation yields an *r* of 0.34, also not significant. The scatter of points does not suggest any regularity even if extreme cases were eliminated. For 1955–60 the rank order correlation is still lower, 0.06; the product moment coefficient is 0.02. The scatter of points suggests, however, that elimination of four observations might change the results. These points represent male and female professionals, male managers, and female service workers. With the remaining twelve points the product moment coefficient of correlation is −0.89, significant at the 0.01 level.[24] Thus, there is some indication that the more the increase in employment, the less the increase in average annual income. This phenomenon suggests excess labor supply. The four eliminated occupations all show income growth well above the regression line computed for the twelve observations. They are from four to five standard errors above expectations in income growth. The male and female professional and male managerial occupations can thus be said to display indications of shortage; female service occupations perhaps show signs of shortage due to sub-standard working conditions, which are now being redressed in the market.

These admittedly very rough results offer refutation of the argument that the less skilled occupations are being priced out of the market because of social wage floors. Harold Demsetz suggests that "minimum-wage laws and union wage rates make it impossible or difficult for a growing component of our labor force to offer its services at wage rates sufficiently low to be employed."[25] In fact, the lower skill occupations are behind in income gains. The relationship of income and employment growth is inverse in the 1955–60 period, and within this female household workers show extremely low income growth. Minimum wage protection does not cover private household workers, yet their employment increase from 1950 to 1960 was less than spectacular, at 18 percent compared with 28 percent for white-collar workers. In addition male sales workers, male and female operatives, male laborers, and male service workers all show negative income deviations from the regression line.

The unfilled jobs are primarily in the highly skilled and highly productive occupations, not in those jobs that are filled by low-quality labor. The greatest rises in average income came among male and female managers, male and female professionals, craftsmen, and female non-household service workers. These were the skills of short supply and increasing demand, as well as limited transferability. Male operatives

[24] If the same four occupations are eliminated from the 1950–55 correlation the *r* obtained is 0.39 and not significant.
[25] Demsetz, "Structural Unemployment," p. 90.

were in the middle range of increases, while farm laborers were at the bottom. The former combined high productivity gains with unionism, while the farm workers were in a declining industry with no unionism.

CONCLUSIONS

Available job vacancy data indicate structural skill shortages by area and by occupation. Indications of shortages in professional and managerial labor first appeared in 1954, with a further rise in 1958. These skill shortages persisted in the presence of admittedly slack over-all labor demand. A continuing need for craftsmen and a rising need for professionals suggest that our training of labor force entrants is not adequate to keep unemployment to a minimum at any level of demand. We have not been able to make up for the lack of these skills in the labor force reserve that existed in 1951.

The data suggest that overtime hours beyond forty-eight per week have increased for skills in short supply. The increases have been strongest for professionals, but appear in some degree among most nonfarm occupations. This development, running counter to other work-week trends and in the face of obvious weaknesses in over-all demand, supports the hypothesis of specific lacks in selected skills or in specific locations.

The explanation of wage changes is an extremely complicated task, but the contrasting evidence of the periods 1950 to 1955 and 1955 to 1960 supports the proposition that income changes have signaled the existence of skill shortages among the more highly trained occupations, while other skills have been available in adequate or excess supply.

The tests of skill shortages offered here need not all have been positive to establish evidence of structural skill shortages; however, each did produce some positive results. Although each result was not in itself conclusive, the additive effects support the proposition that the period after 1956 shows evidence of structural skill shortages.

CHAPTER 9

DIRECT EVIDENCE
OF STRUCTURAL UNEMPLOYMENT

This study would be unnecessary if a comprehensive and direct measure of structural unemployment were available. But measures such as unemployment rates by occupation refer to the last job held by the unemployed; regional data are statistically inadequate; and data on duration of unemployment are based on length of current rather than terminated spells of unemployment. There is no ongoing series on job vacancies comparable to the unemployment series with which to differentiate frictional from structural unemployment. There is no information on skill complementarity that would make it possible to estimate unemployment due to key skill scarcities. Finally, even a meaningful analysis of variance using unemployment by age, sex, color, occupation, and education is impossible since the existing data do not permit entries in each cell in any one year or over time.

Thus, in the absence of comprehensive, direct measures, the preceding chapters have built up indirect evidence of structural unemployment. The purpose of this chapter is to piece together the little direct evidence that exists. Much of it is fragmentary or suggestive. The areas covered are duration of unemployment, unemployment by occupation, age, and sex, the inexperienced unemployed, and unemployment by color.

LONG-TERM UNEMPLOYMENT

Duration of unemployment is indicative both of the state of over-all job opportunities and the rehirability of the unemployed. For example, in a recession great numbers of people lose jobs and are laid off, thus swelling

175

the ranks of the unemployed. If demand does not regain full employment levels, and if the unemployed remain in the labor force, duration of unemployment will increase as inadequate demand persists. On the other hand, if workers are structurally unemployed, the shortage of their skill complements and their maladaptation to new job openings will also result in prolonged spells of unemployment—independent of the level of potential demand. Thus the symptoms with respect to duration will be the same, after the fact.

Because of the way the unemployment data are collected, either a larger percentage of the labor force unemployed for a given duration or else a longer duration of unemployment for a given percentage of the labor force will raise the over-all unemployment rate. The monthly unemployment rate measures the unemployed as a percentage of the labor force at a point in time. The yearly rate is a twelve-month average. When there are increases in the number of persons unemployed during the year the rate will rise; when the same number of unemployed is carried over more months the rate will also rise. The indication is that higher unemployment rates since 1955 are a result both of larger numbers of persons unemployed in the year and of longer duration of unemployment for those who are unemployed.

Changes in the duration of spells of unemployment cannot be measured directly since the available data represent currently accumulated unemployment of spells not necessarily yet completed. Once a year there are data which add together the unemployment experienced by individuals during the calendar year, but the length of individual spells does not emerge, and the calendar year cuts off spells at either end; thus, alternative measures of duration must be used.

"Average duration of unemployment" is a twelve-month average of the total number of weeks of unemployment already experienced by the currently unemployed, divided by the number of persons currently unemployed. The yearly measure is sensitive to the timing of increases in new unemployment, such as at the start of a recession, as well as the duration of individual spells of unemployment. From 1947 to 1963 the average duration of unemployment series lags the over-all unemployment rate at five out of eight turning points. There is coincidence in 1948, 1953, and 1961 (see Table 52). Despite these differences, the two series correlate from 1947 to 1963 with an r of 0.82, significant at the 0.01 level. Where the regression equation of average duration on the over-all rate under-estimates average duration, duration would appear to have increased relative to the numbers usually unemployed at the given unemployment rate. This occurs in 1955 with a deviation of almost two standard errors. Duration is over-estimated in 1949, when the deviation is

TABLE 52: Measures of Long-Term Unemployment, 1947–64

Year	Average duration (weeks)	Long-term unemploy-ment rate[a]	Very long-term unem-ployment rate[b]	Long-term unemployed as % of total unemployed	Unemploy-ment rate
1947	9.8	0.66	0.27	16.9	3.9
1948	8.6	0.50	0.19	13.3	3.8
1949	10.0	1.10	0.41	18.5	5.9
1950	12.1	1.24	0.57	23.3	5.3
1951	9.7	0.48	0.22	14.4	3.3
1952	8.3	0.37	0.13	12.0	3.1
1953	8.1	0.33	0.12	11.3	2.9
1954	11.7	1.26	0.49	22.7	5.6
1955	13.2	1.07	0.51	24.2	4.4
1956	11.3	0.79	0.34	18.9	4.2
1957	10.4	0.82	0.35	19.1	4.3
1958	13.8	2.12	0.97	31.0	6.8
1959	14.5	1.50	0.82	27.3	5.5
1960	12.8	1.35	0.64	24.3	5.6
1961	15.5	2.14	1.12	31.9	6.7
1962	14.7	1.56	0.81	27.9	5.6
1963	14.0	1.49	0.76	26.1	5.7
1964	13.3	1.31	0.65	25.1	5.2

NOTE: Definitions of unemployment are adjusted to those adopted in 1957.
[a] Unemployed fifteen weeks or more as percentage of labor force.
[b] Unemployed twenty-seven weeks or more as percentage of labor force.
SOURCE: *Economic Report of the President, 1964*, p. 235; *Manpower Report of the President, 1965*, pp. 193, 209; and BLS, *Special Labor Force Report*, No. 52, April, 1965, p. A-39.

almost three standard errors. In that year the rate was more strongly affected by the numbers of unemployed.

In the years 1947 to 1954, seven out of eight estimates over-predict average duration; in' the nine-year period 1955 to 1963, six estimates under-predict average duration. The average duration for 1964 is also under-predicted. Thus an autonomous shift toward greater duration is suggested. For years of the same unemployment rate (5.6 percent), average duration rose from 11.7 weeks in 1954 to 12.8 weeks in 1960, and to 14.7 weeks in 1962. The highest average duration came in 1961, although the highest unemployment rate was in 1958.[1]

Data from the Household Survey, giving the number currently un-employed who have been without work for fifteen or more weeks, are used to calculate the rate of long-term unemployment. Among those unemployed fifteen weeks or more, those unemployed twenty-seven weeks or more are called the "very long-term unemployed." The rates do not

[1] It is impossible to make a similar comparison by occupation group, since the necessary data exist only from 1958. Such a comparison would be revealing.

measure structural unemployment per se because (1) they can also reflect prolonged inadequacies in demand, and (2) they do not account for either those becoming newly unemployed who will go on to long-duration unemployment or those whose unemployment is interrupted by temporary work.

Table 52 presents long-term and very long-term unemployment rates. The long-term series lags turning points in the over-all rate twice, in 1950 and 1960. Years with the same unemployment rate show the long-term rate rising from 1.26 in 1954 to 1.35 in 1960, and again to 1.56 in 1962. The very long-term rate lags at three turning points, 1950, 1955, and 1960. The years of the same over-all rate show a rise from 0.49 in 1954, to 0.64 in 1960, and to 0.81 in 1962.

Simler regressed the long-term and the very long-term rates from 1947 to 1957 against the over-all rate and obtained simple R^2's of 0.87 and 0.70, respectively.[2] The effect of the previous year's rate was then taken into account by a variable representing the prior year's over-all rate. The effect was to raise the R^2's (now multiple correlation coefficients) to 0.89 and 0.84, respectively. In all four cases, however, when the 1947–57 regression equation was used to predict the 1958–63 values of both long-term rates, each actual rate was higher than predicted.[3] These results suggested that "time has been a statistically significant factor underlying the rise in the long-term unemployment rate."[4] Thus another variable, time, was added to the equation predicting the long-term rate, raising R^2 to 0.926. Predictions through 1963 no longer showed systematic deviations.

Simler's results indicate that duration has risen, independent of the rise in the numbers of unemployed reflected in the over-all rate, and this has taken place gradually over time. The "duration of long-term unemployment has become longer," he concluded.[5] These results suggest the operation of a factor that is related to time. Since the effects are observed before high levels of unemployment appear (i.e., before 1957), persistent inadequacy of demand is ruled out or is accounted for by the lagged variable.[6] A structuralist position would argue that changes of the kind outlined earlier have been responsible for the shift over time. Simler suggests something else, however. He uses the increasing proportion of

[2] Simler, "The Structural Hypothesis and Public Policy."

[3] The actual rates were higher, as well, from 1954 to 1957 (long-term) and 1955 to 1957 (very long-term) for the simple regressions, and from 1952 to 1957 (long-term) and 1953 to 1957 (very long-term) for the multiple regressions.

[4] Simler, "The Structural Hypothesis and Public Policy," p. 990.

[5] *Ibid.*, p. 996.

[6] The effect of structural unemployment on the over-all rate itself is not accounted for in the equation to the extent that the over-all rate is higher as a result of longer duration unemployment.

workers forty-five years of age and over in the labor force as his "time variable."[7] The value of the older group's proportion correlates with time from 1947 to 1957 with an R^2 of 0.98. Used as the third independent variable in the multiple regressions, the R^2 obtained for the long-term unemployment series is 0.933 as compared with 0.926, using time. Thus the Simler approach, by a simple transformation of the time variable, eliminates consideration of the qualities of the long-term unemployed and substitutes consideration of the composition of the labor force.

The reasoning is open to question if only because it ignores the effect of total labor force composition in favor of a change in one segment. In addition, using the labor force proportion forty-five years of age and over as a variable in both equations, Simler's unexplained residuals show under-prediction of both long-term rates in five out of six observations from 1958 to 1963. Use of time as a variable to predict the long-term rate resulted in three out of six under-predictions. In other words, systematic effects were not eliminated by substitution of the older worker proportion for time in the equations.

The following test of Simler's hypothesis was performed. Very long-term unemployment rates by age and sex from 1958 to 1964 were applied to the labor force as it was in 1953 by age and sex. The resulting over-all, very long-term unemployment rate was then compared with the actual rate in each year. If proportions of age groups in the labor force are the responsible variable, then the calculated rates for the years 1957 to 1964 should be considerably lower than the actual rates and the difference should have increased over time. The results were as follows. In 1960 and 1962 the actual rate was higher than the calculated rate by 0.02 percent of the labor force. In 1959, 1961, 1963, and 1964 the difference was 0.03 point. In 1958 the difference was 0.04 point. Thus there is no evidence that a constant labor force composition similar to that in 1953 would have brought about a reduction in long-term unemployment of major proportions. Actually, the deviations unaccounted for by Simler's regression equation using the older worker share are positive and larger than the calculated differences in our test in three out of six years: 1958, 1961, and 1962.

It is much more reasonable to assume that shifts in long-term rates themselves have accounted for the rise in long-term unemployment. When very long-term rates by age and sex from 1957 to 1964 are regressed against the over-all very long-term rate,[8] the results suggest that men

[7] Simler, "The Structural Hypothesis and Public Policy," pp. 990–93.

[8] Data exist only from 1957 to 1964; therefore any observed trend would be based on a period subsequent to the initial structural impact. There is no basis of comparison with earlier years.

forty-five to sixty-four have displayed an autonomous rise in very long-term unemployment relative to the total. Men twenty to forty-four show an autonomous decline. Youth also show a rise, but later than that for older men.[9]

In order to separate the effect on the unemployment rate of duration rather than numbers, the percentage among the unemployed who were unemployed fifteen weeks or more (see Table 52) was regressed against the long-term unemployment rate. This avoided reference to the over-all unemployment rate. If the percentage share is over-estimated from the resulting regression equation, unemployment has been inflated by numbers of long-term unemployed in the labor force rather than by duration relative to the number of unemployed. This would be expected in recession years. An under-estimation of the share of the long-term unemployed among the unemployed would suggest a rise in structural unemployment independent of demand conditions as reflected in the over-all rate itself.

The regression from 1947 to 1964 yields an r of 0.97. The deviations suggest a rise in structural unemployment.[10] The deviations discriminate

[9] Very Long-Term Unemployment by Age and Sex Regressed against the Over-all Very Long-Term Unemployment Rate, 1957–64

Group		r	Behavior of deviations of actual less estimated rates
Males	14–19	0.91	positive or zero 1962–64
	20–24	0.96	negative 1961–64
	25–44	0.95	negative 1961–64
	45–64	0.99	positive 1960–64
	65 & over	0.92	no trend
Females	14–19	0.71	positive or zero 1961–64
	20–24	0.88	no trend
	24–44	0.98	no trend
	45–64	0.95	no trend
	65 & over	0.41	no trend

SOURCE: Derived from *Manpower Report of the President, 1965*, pp. 195, 210.

[10] Deviations of the Actual Less the Computed Value for the Long-Term Unemployed as a Percentage of the Labor Force, Based on Regression against Long-Term Unemployment Rate

1947	0.5	1953	(1.4)	1959	1.4
1948	(1.3)	1954	(0.5)	1960	0.1
1949	(2.9)*	1955	3.2*	1961	(1.3)
1950	0.3	1956	1.0	1962	1.3
1951	0.0	1957	0.9	1963	0.3
1952	(1.1)	1958	(1.9)	1964	1.3

* Over two standard errors.
Parentheses indicate negative deviations.

recession years from nonrecession years only after 1954 and suggest a major rise in the structural rate in 1955. From 1955 to 1964 the only negative deviations come in 1958 and 1961. From 1947 to 1954 there are only two positive deviations, and these are very small.

The conclusion is that higher unemployment rates after 1954 are partly accounted for by an autonomous rise in duration of unemployment related to structural unemployment and independent of the rise in the duration of unemployment resulting from persistent inadequacies in demand.

UNEMPLOYMENT BY OCCUPATION

The strongest argument offered by the Knowles-Kalacheck report against the structural case is that the unemployment rates themselves deny the structural hypothesis. Using unemployment rates by occupation and industry, the authors show the following: (1) Unemployment has not displayed a tendency to be more concentrated over time by occupation or industry—independent of the over-all unemployment rate for experienced workers. (2) The regression of unemployment rates by industry and occupation against the over-all experienced worker rate from 1948 to 1957 predicts the rates from 1958 to 1960 satisfactorily. (3) Time is not a significant partial correlate with the rates. This section offers rebuttals to the Knowles-Kalacheck arguments. It deals with the nature of the data, the tests offered, interpretation of the results, and presents additional evidence.

The reader is reminded that when the unemployed are listed by industry and occupation they are classified by the last job held.[11] This means that even one day's work in a different category will shift the incidence of unemployment. Workers who have abandoned the search for work because of discouragement are listed as out of the labor force unless they *volunteer* the information that they would look for work if they thought it was available. A worker is classed as employed even if he works without pay as long as this amounts to fifteen hours in the survey week. Finally, new entrants to the labor force who are unemployed are not classified by occupation but as "inexperienced."

These conditions of enumeration are a precondition for the phenomenon of rises in the unemployment rates in occupations which offer temporary employment, lower skill requirements, and unpaid work—after there is an elapse of time from initial displacement. Such occupations probably

---

[11] Further discussion will deal only with occupations, since movement across skill categories is more relevant to the discussion; however, results are similar by industry.

include service occupations, self-employment (which appears with the managerial group), farm employment, and possibly clerical work.

Both Knowles-Kalacheck and Gallaway offer evidence that unemployment rates by occupation did not shift in their relative distribution from 1948 to 1960.[12] Let us examine the meaning of the data. If certain skills and certain educational levels are being structurally displaced, two effects would be no new hires of workers with the skills and educational levels involved and lay-off of those currently employed with these endowments. This would raise unemployment rates among inadequately trained new entrants and those currently in the affected jobs. Over the course of time the displaced workers would (1) seek and find other employment, (2) remain unemployed, or (3) leave the labor force. Unemployed new entrants have similar alternatives. If (1) occurs but the work found is only temporary, structural unemployment would exist but the unemployed would be classified by a different occupation. If (2) occurs the duration of unemployment in the original category would grow. If (3) occurs the skill level of those not in the labor force would fall relative to those in the labor force but structural unemployment would not be reflected in the rate of unemployment after withdrawal occurred. In the light of these alternatives, structural unemployment would be reflected in more concentration of unemployment only in case (2). But even here, if structural changes spread from the factory to the office, more and more occupational categories would be affected and unemployment would be less, not more, concentrated.

Knowles and Kalacheck used as an index of dispersion of unemployment rates the average deviation of unemployment rates by occupation. Occupational unemployment rates were subtracted from the experienced worker rate, weighted by the occupation's labor force share each year and the average deviation was then computed. The years covered were 1948 to 1960. The index of the average deviations was regressed against the experienced worker unemployment rate.[13] The authors claim that the over-all level of unemployment adequately explains the observed concentration of unemployment; but does it?

Unemployment rate concentration is related to the over-all rate largely because the categories most responsive to changes in demand are the largest categories, namely the blue-collar occupations. Weighting by labor force share each year takes no account of changes in employment shares over time and would, in the test used, work to lower concentration. In a recession condition, as opposed to one of structural blocks, workers in

---

[12] *Higher Unemployment Rates*, pp. 49–58, and Gallaway, "Labor Mobility, Resource Allocation, and Structural Unemployment," p. 712.

[13] *Higher Unemployment Rates*, p. 50. The calculated coefficient of correlation was 0.98.

an occupational category would tend to "hold-on" until recall from a lay-off. But with prolonged unemployment due to inadequate demand or structural unemployment, workers would be likely to seek other work, even temporary work, or leave the labor force. This would be especially true after benefits ran out. Temporary work would change workers' occupational categories and lower the concentration of unemployment rates by occupation.

Within the originating, contracting occupations structural unemployment would more likely be differentiated from recession unemployment by an increase in the share represented by the long-term unemployed relative to the rate of long-term unemployment. Those who would have entered the declining occupation but who had not yet found work would swell the ranks of the inexperienced unemployed and would not be listed by occupation. When there are skill shortages and skill complementarities, all but the skill in short supply would show a rise in unemployment. Differing patterns of complementarity would have differing effects. Thus the pattern of concentration more realistically to be expected would be an autonomous rise in unemployment in the contracting occupations at the initial impact of structural change, followed after a period of time by a lower level of unemployment concentration. In other words, an autonomous and sustained rise in unemployment rate concentration is an unrealistic test of structural unemployment.

Using Knowles and Kalacheck's own figures, we estimated their dispersion index from the regression equation based on the experienced worker rate. The resulting deviations show the pattern predicted here. From 1955 to 1958, the actual index is under-predicted. In the next two years it is over-predicted. The earlier years show no grouping of deviations of the same sign, although five out of seven from 1948 to 1954 are over-predicted.[14]

In another test Knowles and Kalacheck regressed each unemployment rate by occupation against the experienced worker rate.[15] The results

[14] Dispersion Index Predicted from Experienced Worker Unemployment Rate, 1948–60, Actual Less Predicted Index

Year	Deviation	Year	Deviation	Year	Deviation
1948	(6)	1953	(1)	1957	10
1949	2	1954	(3)	1958	12
1950	(17)	1955	11	1959	(5)
1951	(7)	1956	6	1960	(6)
1952	3				

Parentheses indicate negative figures.
SOURCE: Derived from *Higher Unemployment Rates*, p. 50.

[15] *Ibid.*, p. 65.

indicated generally high coefficients of correlation, but the lower r's for some occupations might have been considered to be indicative of structural differences. They were not regarded as such.

Craftsmen had the highest r, 0.99, followed by operatives, 0.98, and laborers, 0.97. Employment in these occupations is highly responsive to demand conditions and represents high proportions of total unemployment at any time. In 1953 these occupations accounted for 14.5 percent, 26.5 percent, and 14.8 percent of unemployment, respectively. Farmers and professionals showed the lowest correlation with the experienced worker rate, 0.52 for farmers, and 0.67 percent for professionals. These accounted for 0.6 percent and 3.0 percent of unemployment in 1953, respectively.

We computed the coefficient of rank correlation between the eleven r's and the respective shares of unemployment in 1953. The result was 0.88. Thus 77 percent of the correspondence between an occupation's unemployment rate and the over-all rate is explained by that occupation's share of unemployment.

Knowles and Kalacheck used their regression equations to predict unemployment rates in 1958, 1959, and 1960. They found an over-estimation each year among professionals, craftsmen, and domestic workers.[16] No conclusion was drawn from this, however.

In a situation where various series normally move in sympathy—in response to cyclical fluctuations in demand and because of complementarity—such errors as indicated and the identity of the less correlated series might give one pause to reflect. In addition, since structural changes occurred as early as 1955, the regression equations themselves were influenced by newly emerging behavior patterns in 1955, 1956, and 1957, or three out of ten observations between 1948 and 1957.

Knowles and Kalacheck overcame part of the problem by regressing the occupational rates in a multiple correlation against time and the experienced worker rate for 1948 to 1957. A negative and statistically significant partial correlation coefficient with time would have indicated a structurally favored occupation; a positive, significant coefficient would have indicated a structurally disadvantaged one. Four partial coefficients proved to be significant with time.

Three white-collar occupations showed negative and significant partial coefficients: managers, -0.70; sales workers, -0.57; and professionals, -0.77. Farm laborers showed a significant positive coefficient, 0.70. Operatives had a coefficient of 0.44 and craftsmen -0.48, but both were not significant at the 0.05 level (because N was so low). The introduction of a time variable appreciably raised the coefficient of correlation,

16 *Ibid.*, p. 57.

in the case of professionals from a simple r of 0.67 to a multiple r of 0.88. It was raised from 0.87 to 0.94 for managers, and from 0.73 to 0.83 for sales workers.[17] Thus Knowles and Kalacheck actually did obtain evidence of a structural shift in favor of specific white-collar occupations and a suggestion of an unfavorable shift for operatives and farm laborers. The negative time coefficient for craftsmen is in line with evidence of skill scarcities in that occupation.

There is evidence that suggests the incidence of unemployment has shifted to occupations offering temporary work. A study was made of job tenure in January, 1963, in which males and females were grouped by occupation and by median years on their current job as follows:[18]

Males		Females	
Farmers	18.0 years	Farm labor	9.9 years
Managers	8.4	Managers	5.8
Craftsmen	6.9	Craftsmen	4.8
Professionals	5.4	Operatives	4.1
Clerical	5.3	Professionals	3.7
Operatives	5.1	Clericals	3.0
Service	3.6	Sales	2.9
Sales	3.5	Service	1.9
Laborers	2.5	Household workers	1.7
Farm labor	1.5	(No laborers recorded)	

When workers below twenty-five years of age and those forty-five years and over are eliminated, the starting dates of jobs held in January, 1963, reveal the jobs offering temporary or recent entry to prime age workers. A starting date within the past six months suggests the result of voluntary shifts, the temporary nature of prior work, and the jobs available to the displaced. For males twenty-five to forty-four years of age the distribution within each occupation shows that a date of hire within the past six months was the mode for four occupations. These were farm laborers with 42 percent in this category, nonagricultural laborers with 24 percent, sales workers with 17 percent, and service workers with 16 percent. Among females twenty-five to forty-four years old the six-month tenure period was the mode for service workers (35 percent), sales workers (32 percent), operatives (20 percent), and professionals (20 percent).[19]

[17] *Ibid.*, p. 65.
[18] Harvey R. Hamel (BLS), "Job Tenure of American Workers, January, 1963," *Special Labor Force Report*, No. 36, Oct., 1963, p. 1149.
[19] *Ibid.*, p. A-12.

We suggest that structural unemployment was felt in the blue-collar occupations from 1955 to the early sixties but shifted to the expanding low-skill occupations thereafter because of the way unemployment is enumerated.

THE INEXPERIENCED UNEMPLOYED

The influx of new labor not yet committed to specific jobs should ease structural changes in the labor market. This requires, however, that entering youth be able to move to those areas of employment which are opening and that they can be utilized there. The new entrants must come equipped to fill the new jobs. Youth are expected to have high rates of unemployment as they shift about to get experience but it is assumed that the duration of their unemployment will be brief. In the past, entering labor force members were able to find employment with given training and education. If the entrants' skill mix remains the same but the requirements are changed, however, structural unemployment would result, although no "displacement" would be apparent.

New entrants find that many of the jobs in the expanding fields are already taken by workers displaced from declining occupations. Thus unemployment rates in the old areas could decline relatively, but at the expense of the rate for the inexperienced labor force. Unfortunately there is no published unemployment rate for new labor force entrants. This is because there are no data on the numbers of new entrants who do find jobs which can be added to the number of unemployed to make up a labor force figure. Instead, we must use an indirect measure of the inexperienced rate: the difference between the over-all unemployment rate and the experienced worker rate. The latter is the number of those unemployed who have had at least two weeks of work experience, as a percentage of those employed plus unemployed with at least two weeks of work experience. The difference between the experienced rate and the total rate is accounted for by the inexperienced unemployed as a percentage of the labor force. Table 53 presents the two rates.

In the normal cyclical sequence the difference between the over-all unemployment rate and the experienced worker rate will be greater at troughs. New entrants have a harder time finding work under low demand conditions. On the other hand, the absolute share of the unemployed accounted for by the inexperienced unemployed is generally lower at cyclical troughs simply because the ranks of the unemployed are swollen by regular labor force participants.

If new entrants are not adequately equipped to fill new openings and are being pushed out of entry jobs by displaced workers the spread in the

TABLE 53: Civilian Unemployment Rate Regressed against Experienced Worker Rate and with Time, 1947–64

Year	Unemployment rates				Deviations: Actual Less Calculated X_1's	
	Experienced workers (X_2)	Total (X_1)	Difference ($X_1 - X_2$)	Time^a (X_3)	A^b	B^c
1947	3.6	3.6	0.0	−8.5	(0.3)	(0.2)
1948	3.0	3.4	0.4	−7.5	0.2	0.2
1949	5.1	5.5	0.4	−6.5	(0.2)	(0.1)
1950	4.9	5.0	0.1	−5.5	(0.4)*	(0.3)*
1951	2.9	3.0	0.1	−4.5	(0.1)	(0.1)
1952	2.5	2.7	0.2	−3.5	0.0	0.0
1953	2.4	2.5	0.1	−2.5	0.0	(0.1)
1954	4.6	5.0	0.4	−1.5	(0.1)	(0.1)
1955	3.8	4.0	0.2	−0.5	(0.2)	(0.2)
1956	3.4	3.8	0.4	0.5	0.1	0.1
1957	3.8	4.3	1.5	1.5	0.1	0.1
1958	6.2	6.8	0.6	2.5	(0.1)	(0.1)
1959	4.9	5.5	0.6	3.5	0.1	0.0
1960	5.0	5.6	0.6	4.5	0.1	0.0
1961	5.9	6.7	0.8	5.5	0.1	0.1
1962	4.9	5.6	0.7	6.5	0.2	0.1
1963	4.9	5.7	0.8	7.5	0.3	0.2
1964	4.4	5.2	0.8	8.5	0.3	0.2
r	—	—	—	—	0.988	0.991
beta coef.	1.02	—	—	0.02		

NOTE: Unemployment 1947–56 not adjusted to new definitions adopted in 1957.
* Two standard errors or more.
ᵃ Time centered at mid-1955.
ᵇ $X_1 = -0.230 + 1.155\,X_2$.
ᶜ $X_1 = -0.099 + 1.124\,X_2 + 0.013\,t$; time centered at mid-1955.
Parentheses indicate negative figures.
SOURCE: Derived from *Manpower Report of the President, 1965*, pp. 202–5, 207.

two rates would increase independently, regardless of the stage of the cycle. The inexperienced workers' share of unemployment would also grow relative to the over-all rate. The data suggest that this is occurring. The inexperienced workers' share of unemployment rose from 4.4 percent in 1953 to 16.0 percent in 1964. The aggregate unemployment rate regressed against the experienced worker rate yields a simple coefficient of correlation of 0.988; however, the deviations of the actual less the calculated over-all rate show a systematic positive deviation after 1955 (except for 1958, a recession year). Introducing time as a variable raises the correlation to 0.991 but the new deviations show the same pattern (see Table 53). Thus an autonomous rise in unemployment appeared among new labor force entrants about 1955–56.

Computing the correlation coefficient from 1947 through 1955 yields an r of 0.991 (the same as the multiple correlation with time from 1947–64). Next, the years 1956 to 1964 were projected using the regression coefficients obtained for the earlier nine-year period. The results show a systematic under-estimation from 1956 to 1960 and an additional rise in the period 1961–64.[20]

The first autonomous rise occurs about the time of the structural changes discussed earlier; the second rise comes at about the time the blue-collar, long-term rates show a relative fall. This suggests that new workers have indeed been squeezed out of entry jobs by displaced workers. Even if there were no structural unemployment at all among experienced workers from 1956 to 1964, as much as 0.2 to 0.5 percent of the labor force were structurally unemployed inexperienced workers. That is, had conditions similar to 1947–55 prevailed, they would have been employed. Thus, assuming a minimum frictional rate of 2.9 percent, an average of 15 percent of the remaining unemployment from 1959 to 1964 was accounted for by structurally unemployed new entrants. This does not count structural unemployment among experienced workers.

Regressing the over-all very long-term rate against the very long-term experienced worker rate from 1957 to 1964 yields an r of 0.996. The deviations of the actual less the calculated rate again show a trend: -0.02, -0.03, -0.01, 0.00, from 1957 to 1960, and 0.01, 0.01, 0.03, and 0.02 from 1961 to 1964.

Regressing the very long-term share of unemployment among the *inexperienced* unemployed against the comparable share of the very long-term unemployed among the *experienced* unemployed shows a positive bias. The coefficient of correlation is 0.76; the deviations from 1957 to 1964 are as follows: -0.01, -0.02, 0.00, 0.01, 0.00, 0.01, 0.01, and 0.00. There are no negative deviations after 1958. In other words, longer duration unemployment among the inexperienced unemployed has risen relative to that among the experienced unemployed since 1958.

[20] Actual Less Computed Values of Over-all Rate Based on Regression against Experienced Work Rate, 1947–55

Year	Deviation	Percentage of total unemployment rate after 2.9 percent is subtracted
1956	0.2	22.2
1957	0.3	21.4
1958	0.3	7.7
1959	0.3	11.5
1960	0.3	11.1
1961	0.5	13.2
1962	0.4	14.8
1963	0.5	17.9
1964	0.5	21.7

Automation studies indicate that employers who automate often are proud of the fact that they have not always had to get rid of workers. They try to leave this to "normal attrition." But a nationwide practice of attrition means that the burden of unemployment will have to be carried more and more on the shoulders of the new entrants. This is more of a problem when demand is slack but is also a problem as long as the new requirements cannot be filled by the young. The problem appears to be growing.

Unemployment among Youth

The relationship of teen-age unemployment to the experienced worker rate was studied because many new labor force entrants gain their first work experience between the ages of fourteen and nineteen. This is the group that will probably not go on to college or will work while continuing school. It also includes the dropouts at the time they terminate schooling. Table 54 presents unemployment rates by sex for fourteen- to

TABLE 54: Unemployment Rates for Fourteen- to Nineteen-Year-Old Youth by Sex Regressed against Experienced Worker Rates, 1947–64

| Year | Unemployment rates | | | Actual less calculated | |
	Experienced workers	Males 14–19	Females 14–19	Males 14–19	Females 14–19
1947	3.6	9.1	7.1	(0.7)	(2.1)
1948	3.0	8.3	7.3	(0.1)	(0.5)
1949	5.1	11.9	11.2	(1.6)	(1.5)
1950	4.9	11.0	10.4	(2.0)	(1.8)
1951	2.9	7.0	7.4	(1.1)	(0.2)
1952	2.5	7.6	7.0	0.5	0.3
1953	2.4	6.8	6.0	(0.1)	(0.5)
1954	4.6	11.2	10.0	(1.1)	(1.5)
1955	3.8	9.9	9.0	(0.4)	(0.7)
1956	3.4	9.6	9.9	0.2	1.0
1957	3.8	11.3	10.1	1.0	0.5
1958	6.2	15.2	13.1	(1.0)	(2.1)
1959	4.9	13.8	12.3	0.8	0.1
1960	5.0	14.0	12.9	0.7	0.5
1961	5.9	15.4	14.8	(0.1)	0.3
1962	4.9	13.3	13.2	0.3	1.0
1963	4.9	15.5	15.7	2.5*	3.5*
1964	4.4	14.5	15.0	2.7*	3.9*
r	—	—	—	0.90	0.83

NOTE: Rates 1947–56 not adjusted to definitions adopted in 1957.
* Two standard errors or more.
Parentheses indicate negative figures.
SOURCE: Derived from *Manpower Report of the President, 1965*, pp. 202–5.

nineteen-year-old youth and deviations of the rates based on regression against the experienced worker rate.

Deviations for males and females display the same sign except in 1961. The deviations are all positive after 1955 except for recession years, but the negative recession deviations for males decline in absolute size from trough to trough. The two most recent years, 1963 and 1964, show positive deviations beyond two standard errors for both sexes. The evidence, therefore, is that the youth unemployment rate strongly reflects unemployment among the inexperienced unemployed.[21]

Higher youth unemployment is thus not merely a reflection of youth mobility; it appears to display growing structural problems. The youth market may have grown to unsupportable proportions; that is, labor force composition may have affected the unemployment rates themselves. This would come about if a significant section of the youth is becoming increasingly unacceptable for new entry jobs. The same level of preparatory education may be less and less satisfactory over time, resulting in a larger pool of nontransferable labor competing for a declining number of jobs. A growing pool of inappropriately trained youth would raise youth unemployment rates and the share of the labor force accounted for by the inexperienced unemployed.

Education

Evidence to support the hypothesis that structural inadequacy is reflected in the plight of the inexperienced unemployed comes from scanty but suggestive evidence. Table 55 presents the labor force experience of graduates and dropouts sixteen to twenty-four years of age, excluding those enrolled in college. Presumably, all other things being equal, the graduate would do better than the dropout at any time and especially in a slack labor market. However, even in the four years 1960–63, an autonomous rise is evident in the ratio of the dropout rate of unemployment relative to graduates' rates. While the over-all rate for youth sixteen to twenty-four years old fell from 1961 to 1962, the unemployment rate continued to rise steadily each year for dropouts, and only the over-all rise in unemployment in 1963 over 1962 halted the climb in the ratio of dropout to graduate unemployment rates. The evidence thus suggests that youth handicapped by inadequate training are structurally unemployed—beyond the effects of slack demand conditions.

[21] When the regression equations are applied to the years 1956–64 and the calculated unemployment rates are applied to the respective fourteen- to nineteen-year-old labor force in those years, the effect on the total labor force rate would be a reduction of unemployment by 0.1 percentage point in 1956, 1957, and 1958; 0.2 point in 1959–62, and 0.4 point in 1963 and 1964. Thus the effect on the over-all rate is greater using the inexperienced unemployed than using teen-age unemployment taken alone.

TABLE 55: Unemployment Rates of High-School Graduates Not Enrolled in College and School Dropouts (Sixteen to Twenty-four Years of Age) as of October of Year of Graduation or Dropout, 1960–63

Year	Total rate	Graduates	Dropouts	Ratio dropouts to graduates
1960	11.2	15.2	18.2	1.20
1961	13.0	17.9	26.8	1.50
1962	11.3	14.1	28.6	2.03
1963	12.2	18.0	31.7	1.76

SOURCE: *Manpower Report of the President, 1965*, pp. 198, 224.

AGE AND SEX

Age and sex are related to unemployment because of labor market characteristics associated with these factors. Age and educational levels are inversely related, but age and experience are directly related. Thus unemployment rates in general decline with age as stability is achieved in a person's labor market role, but they also decline with educational levels. Very long-term unemployment rates are highest among the very young and the very old. Recent structural changes may have made the less educated unable to move out of contracting employment areas or unable to enter the labor market successfully, thus affecting the re-employability of older workers as well as the employability of new entrants.

The problems of the older worker, aside from ill health, are very much related to the work performance expected from them. The older worker often possesses obsolete skills and outmoded past training. His educational level is lower than that of younger workers. He is more reluctant to move geographically and less interested in taking retraining. Having had a history of long employment, he is less able to "sell" himself to an employer. His health is worse and his strength is not what it once was. The fact that seniority protects the older worker can mean that, if his plant shuts down, the younger workers will have already left and found the available positions. The older worker thus emerges to find that jobs are more difficult to obtain.[22]

Employer attitudes have intensified the age problem in that the better, growing occupations seem to have more severe age restrictions for hiring. Although muscles and brawn are less required in finance, real estate, insurance, trade, and public utilities, Jane N. and Arthur M. Ross found

[22] International Labour Office, *Unemployment and Structural Change, Studies and Reports*, New Series, No. 65 (Geneva: International Labour Office, 1962), p. 61.

that age barriers were most common in these areas and that hiring limits were more restrictive in larger establishments and more felt by women than men.[23] Although ability declines more slowly in clerical, sales, professional, and managerial occupations, these, along with unskilled laboring work, most frequently specify upper age limits.

The so-called immobility of older workers is based on some valid reasoning. Aside from moving costs per se, older workers as home owners face loss, through resale, on their major tangible asset after a lifetime of work. In areas of high unemployment, real estate values make the sale of a home prohibitive. Older workers are reluctant to move because of deep family and community ties and hopes of recall; they are not anxious to take retraining because they are fairly convinced that their age would be a barrier to re-employment in any case.[24]

Unemployment rates for five age groups over nineteen years by sex were regressed against the over-all unemployment rate in an inspection for possible shifts in incidence. The deviations of the actual less the calculated rates are presented in Table 56. There are major differences in the relationship of the group rates to the over-all rate, primarily by sex, but the patterns are also differentiated by age.

In the 1949 recession women's rates are over-estimated and males' under-estimated by the regression lines, with young men clearly suffering the effects of low seniority. In 1954 the male experience is similar except that older men fifty-five to sixty-four are badly hurt, as in the following year. Women were also adversely affected. By 1958 labor force withdrawal of the two older male age groups probably held down their relative rates and men twenty-five to forty-four (who are primarily operatives) were most seriously hurt. Women's rates were generally lower than anticipated. In 1961 the situation is different; male rates are over-estimated while female rates are under-estimated by the regression lines.

The data suggest that male labor force withdrawal is a mechanism which has held down unemployment rates. Men fifty-five to sixty-four years of age show negative deviations from 1956 to 1964, except for 1961, and 1960–61 was one of only two instances in the period when the labor force rate for this group increased. For men forty-five to fifty-four the participation rate has been declining, as it has for men twenty to twenty-four. The two groups including men twenty-five to forty-four show little trend and little change in labor force participation rates. Women twenty

[23] U.S., Senate, Special Committee on Unemployment Problems, *Studies in Unemployment*, 86th Cong., 2nd Sess. (Washington: U.S. Government Printing Office, 1960), p. 104.

[24] Walter H. Franke, "Labor Market Experiences of Unemployed Older Workers," *Proceedings of the Fifteenth Annual Meeting*, Industrial Relations Research Association (Pittsburgh: Dec., 1962), p. 174.

TABLE 56: Unemployment Rates by Age and Sex Based on Regression against Civilian Rate, 1947–63; Actual Less Calculated Rates, 1947–64

	Males					Females				
Year	20–24	25–34	35–44	45–54	55–64	20–24	25–34	35–44	45–54	55–64
1947	1.8*	0.4	0.1	0.0	(0.5)	(0.9)	(1.1)*	(0.9)*	(0.7)*	(0.7)*
1948	0.6	(0.1)	(0.1)	0.1	(0.1)	(0.4)	(0.2)	(0.4)	(0.1)	(0.1)
1949	0.6	0.0	0.1	(0.3)	0.3	(1.0)	(0.7)	(0.7)	(0.6)*	0.0
1950	(0.8)	0.0	(0.1)	0.2	0.5	(0.7)	(0.2)	(0.4)	0.4	0.4
1951	(1.6)	(0.2)	(0.2)	0.3	(0.1)	(0.2)	0.6	0.8*	0.7*	0.9*
1952	(0.6)	(0.1)	0.1	0.3	(0.3)	0.4	(0.1)	0.3	(0.2)	(0.3)
1953	0.1	0.2	0.2	0.6	0.2	0.5	(0.1)	0.0	(0.2)	(0.3)
1954	1.3	0.2	0.3	0.2	0.7*	(0.4)	0.3	0.2	0.2	0.4
1955	0.2	(0.2)	0.2	0.3	0.7*	(0.1)	0.2	0.1	0.0	0.2
1956	(0.1)	(0.1)	(0.2)	0.2	(0.1)	0.4	0.0	0.1	0.3	0.2
1957	0.5	(0.2)	0.0	0.3	(0.2)	0.1	0.5	0.1	(0.1)	(0.2)
1958	1.2	0.5*	0.4*	(0.2)	(0.2)	(0.8)	(0.1)	0.1	(0.1)	0.1
1959	(0.6)	0.0	0.0	(0.1)	(0.1)	0.4	(0.1)	0.2	0.1	0.3
1960	(0.6)	0.0	0.0	(0.2)	(0.1)	0.4	0.2	(0.2)	0.0	(0.4)
1961	(0.7)	(0.2)	0.0	(0.5)	0.1	0.3	0.0	0.3	0.2	0.1
1962	(0.6)	(0.3)	(0.2)	(0.4)	(0.1)	1.2*	0.4	0.2	0.1	(0.3)
1963	(0.9)	(0.4)	(0.4)*	(0.8)*	(0.5)	0.9	0.7	0.0	0.0	(0.3)
Projected										
1964	(0.7)	(0.9)*	(0.6)*	(0.7)*	(0.5)	1.3*	0.6	0.4	0.0	(0.1)
r	0.93	0.98	0.98	0.98	0.95	0.95	0.92	0.95	0.94	0.86

NOTE: Rates from 1947–56 not adjusted to definitions adopted in 1957.
* Two or more standard errors.
Parentheses indicate negative figures.
SOURCE: Derived from *Manpower Report of the President, 1965*, p. 205.

to twenty-four seem to carry a recent, heavy burden of unemployment relative to past experience, which is somewhat puzzling.[25] The major rise in recent years, however, is among youth fourteen to nineteen years of age.

The changes in labor force composition by age, sex, and color have largely been offsetting with respect to over-all unemployment.[26] However, changes in the relative unemployment rates of the groups may not have been offsetting. Unfortunately the regression of each rate by age and sex

[25] The female rate regressed against the male unemployment rate shows an autonomous trend rise in female unemployment from 1961 to 1964.

[26] Unemployment rates by age, sex, and color for the years 1957 to 1964 were applied to the labor force of 1955. The results showed a rise of 0.1 point in the rate for 1959, 1960, and 1961—due to the changed proportions among white males in the labor force compared with the 1955 composition. In 1962 and 1963, 0.2 point was attributable to changed proportions among white males and females, and in 1964, 0.2 point was attributable to the different proportions of white males and females, and Negro males.

against the over-all rate cannot account for the effect of structural unemployment in the over-all rate itself.

Deviations of calculated very long-term rates from 1957 to 1964 indicate that males forty-five to sixty-four years of age and possibly males fourteen to nineteen, sixty-five and over, and females fourteen to nineteen are carrying the burden of very long-term unemployment shifts relative to the over-all very long-term rate. Table 57 indicates that teen-age youth of both sexes are carrying both a greater over-all rate and a higher "structural" rate relative to the population, while older men are carrying a part of the structural burden that is not reflected in the total unemployment rate of older men.

TABLE 57: Very Long-Term Unemployment Rates by Age and Sex Regressed against Over-all Very Long-Term Rates; Actual Less Calculated Rates, 1957–64

	Males					Females				
Year	14–19	20–24	25–44	45–64	65 & over	14–19	20–24	25–44	45–64	65 & over
1957	(0.15)	0.05	0.04	(0.01)	0.02	(0.12)	(0.17)	0.03	0.01	(0.12)
1958	(0.09)	0.20*	0.07	(0.06)*	(0.16)	(0.18)	(0.11)	0.02	(0.07)	(0.05)
1959	0.08	(0.01)	0.09	(0.04)	(0.24)*	(0.11)	0.03	(0.10)*	0.09*	(0.35)
1960	(0.02)	0.04	0.03	0.01	(0.05)	(0.08)	0.13	(0.03)	(0.06)	(0.07)
1961	(0.11)	(0.08)	(0.03)	0.04	0.18	0.00	(0.03)	0.04	0.03	0.01
1962	0.00	(0.04)	(0.01)	0.02	(0.01)	0.15	(0.02)	0.02	(0.04)	0.29
1963	0.20*	(0.04)	(0.07)	0.00	0.13	0.13	(0.02)	(0.01)	0.02	(0.13)
1964	0.09	(0.12)	(0.12)*	0.03	0.12	0.21	0.19	0.03	0.02	0.41*
r	0.91	0.96	0.95	0.99	0.92	0.71	0.88	0.98	0.95	0.41

* About two standard errors or more.
Parentheses indicate negative figures.
SOURCE: Derived from *Manpower Report of the President, 1965*, pp. 195, 210.

The data in Table 45 (in Chapter 7) suggest that unemployment rates have been kept lower than might be expected for men because males at either end of the age scale have sharply cut their participation rates and because the least qualified men have been the ones to withdraw from the labor force. Between 1959 and 1962, for example, men in the labor force in each group between twenty and sixty-four years of age have increased their median years of school more than men not in the labor force. In fact, among men twenty-five to forty-four, those out of the labor force have shown a decrease in median school years. There is a great likelihood that if these men were to be questioned they would indicate withdrawal due to discouragement. The way the unemployed are enumerated, therefore, may provide a built-in bias against the recording of structural unemployment, and the bias may be increasing over time.

UNEMPLOYMENT AMONG NEGROES

Unemployment rates for Negroes have been higher than for whites in every postwar year. This has been due to a variety of factors including disadvantages by virtue of education, occupational composition, and geographic location. But, in addition to all these, discrimination is a separate factor leading to higher unemployment rates. The purpose of this section is to evaluate changes in Negro unemployment relative to changes in white unemployment over the postwar years.

The white and nonwhite[27] unemployment rates presented in Table 58 indicate something of the bare bones of the situation which takes its toll of Negro life and material well-being. It is the link between civil rights and economics. Negroes were 11 percent of the civilian labor force in the early 1960's but were about 21 percent of the unemployed and 25 percent of those working part-time for economic reasons. Except for workers eighteen to twenty-four years old with under eight years of education,

TABLE 58: Unemployment Rates for Negroes and Whites, 1948–64

Year	White	Negro	Actual less computed Negro rate based on regression against white rate
1948	3.2	5.2	(1.0)
1949	5.2	8.2	(2.4)*
1950	4.6	8.5	(0.8)
1951	2.8	4.8	(0.6)
1952	2.4	4.6	0.1
1953	2.3	4.1	(0.2)
1954	4.5	8.9	(0.2)
1955	3.6	7.9	0.8
1956	3.3	7.5	1.0
1957	3.9	8.0	0.2
1958	6.1	12.6	0.0
1959	4.9	10.7	0.7
1960	5.0	10.2	0.0
1961	6.0	12.5	0.1
1962	4.9	11.0	1.0
1963	5.1	10.9	0.5
1964	4.6	9.8	0.5
r	—	—	0.95

NOTE: Unemployment 1948–56 not adjusted to definitions adopted in 1957.
* Two or more standard errors.
Parentheses indicate negative figures.

SOURCE: Derived from *Manpower Report of the President, 1965*, p. 204.

[27] "Nonwhite" is a euphemism used by official sources; however, Negroes account for about nine-tenths of the category. The terms are used here as equivalents.

unemployment rates by years of schooling in 1962 were higher for non-whites in each educational group and three times as high for high-school graduates twenty-five to fifty-four years of age.[28]

A regression of the Negro rate against the white rate from 1948 to 1964 yields an r of 0.95, as indicated in Table 58. The reader will observe that from 1955 to 1964 every deviation calculated from the regression equation is positive. In other words, there has been an upward shift in Negro unemployment relative to white unemployment beyond the level accounted for by over-all demand or increases in white structural unemployment.

The regression line was calculated for the years 1948–54 (r was again 0.95), and the Negro unemployment rates from 1955 to 1964 were estimated using this equation. Differences from the actual rate ranged from 1.1 percent of the Negro labor force in 1957 to 2.4 percent in 1962. Had the predicted rates been real, the over-all rate, adjusted for estimated Negro unemployment, would have been lower by about 0.2 point in most of the years.[29] The effect on the global rate is small since Negroes make up a much smaller percentage of the labor force than of unemployment. The autonomous rise in Negro unemployment, however, accounts for 5 percent of the difference between a 2.9-percent unemployment rate and the actual rate in 1958, and as much as 22 percent in 1956.

Negroes are concentrated in unskilled and semi-skilled occupations that are subject to layoffs and short hours. Those with limited education are feeling the impact of higher skill requirements. In addition, they have been leaving agriculture, with its lower unemployment rates, in great numbers. To illustrate, 21 percent of all Negro workers were in agriculture

[28] Johnston, "Educational Attainment of Workers, March 1962," p. 513.

[29] Actual Less Computed Value of Negro and Over-all Unemployment Rates Based on 1948–54 Regression of Negro Rate against White Rate

Year	Actual less calculated rates		Difference as percentage of over-all rate after 2.9 percent was subtracted
	Negro	Over-all	
1955	1.5	0.2	18.2
1956	1.6	0.2	22.2
1957	1.1	0.1	7.1
1958	2.0	0.2	5.1
1959	2.1	0.2	7.7
1960	1.4	0.2	7.4
1961	2.0	0.2	5.3
1962	2.4	0.3	11.1
1963	2.0	0.2	7.1
1964	1.7	0.2	8.7

NOTE: Rates for 1955 and 1956 not adjusted to definitions adopted in 1957.

in 1948 compared with 12 percent in 1962. Negroes are more concentrated in the less organized industries where seniority is not enforced in lay-offs, or in occupations in organized industries where employment is declining and their seniority is not well established.

While "nonwhite workers have been entering the professional, technical and clerical fields faster than other white-collar occupations," Negroes are still a small part of white-collar employment.[30] In 1960 they had only 3.7 percent of white-collar employment but 10 percent of all nonagricultural employment. "Nonwhite women have made larger proportionate gains than have nonwhite men, but they are still more underrepresented."[31] In managerial jobs for men and sales jobs for women, where the disparity has been greatest, "there has been no appreciable change during the past decade."[32]

Negro unemployment rates are not accounted for solely by differences from whites in occupational composition. Negro unemployment rates that were current in 1962 by occupation were applied to the Negro labor force, which was adjusted so that the employment proportions by occupation corresponded to those of whites. This "standardization" cut the Negro unemployment rate from 11.0 percent to 8.1 percent.[33] In 1962 the white rate was 4.9 percent; thus the difference was only cut in half. The remaining difference comes from the fact that unemployment rates are higher for Negroes in every occupational group.

Table 59 presents Negro and white unemployment rates by occupation for 1960 and 1962. In both these years the over-all unemployment rate was 5.6 percent. As the table indicates, not only was the Negro rate much higher in each occupation in both years, the difference ranging from 4.6 points for craftsmen to 0.2 point for farmers in 1960, but the gap increased from 1960 to 1962 with only one exception, clericals. Unemployment rates fell over the two years for white craftsmen, operatives, laborers, domestic workers, farmers, and farm laborers. But it rose for each Negro occupation except clericals and farm laborers. Some of the differences may be due to the breadth of occupational categories but much is clearly related to discrimination. The fact that employers in expanding occupations have been the least organized by unions, have had the least obligation to government with regard to employment practices (except government employment itself), and in many cases could be most selective in hiring has shown up in the unemployment rates.

[30] Matthew A. Kessler (BLS), "Economic Status of Nonwhite Workers, 1955–62," *Special Labor Force Report*, No. 33, pp. 1–2.

[31] Carol A. Barry (BLS), "White-Collar Employment: I. Trends and Structure; II. Characteristics," *Special Labor Force Report*, No. 12, 1961, p. 41.

[32] *Ibid.*

[33] Kessler, "Economic Status of Nonwhite Workers, 1955–62," p. 4.

TABLE 59: Unemployment Rates by Occupation and Color, 1960 and 1962

Occupation	1960			1962		
	White	Negro	Difference	White	Negro	Difference
Professional	1.7	2.9	1.2	1.7	3.1	1.4
Managerial	1.3	2.7	1.4	1.4	3.6	2.2
Clerical	3.6	7.3	3.7	3.8	7.1	3.3
Sales	3.6	5.9	2.3	4.0	10.2	6.2
Craftsmen	5.0	9.6	4.6	4.8	9.7	4.9
Operatives	7.5	11.2	3.7	6.9	12.0	5.1
Laborers	11.5	15.0	3.5	11.0	15.8	4.8
Pr. household	3.4	6.6	3.2	3.1	7.1	4.0
Other service	5.1	9.1	4.0	5.3	10.8	5.5
Farmers	0.3	0.5	0.2	0.2	1.0	0.8
Farm labor	4.1	8.2	4.1	3.9	5.8	1.9

SOURCE: U.S., Bureau of Labor Statistics, "Labor Force and Employment," *Special Labor Force Reports*, Nos. 14 and 31, 1961 and 1963.

TABLE 60: Median Years of School Completed among Employed Workers Eighteen Years and Over by Occupation and Color, March, 1959 and 1964

Occupation and color		1959	1964	Difference: W — N		Median change: 1959–64
				1959	1964	
Total	White	12.1	12.3	3.5	2.2	0.2
	Nonwhite	8.6	10.1			1.5
Prof., tech.	White	16.2	16.1	0.0	(0.1)	(0.1)
	Nonwhite	16.2	16.2			0.0
Managerial	White	12.4	12.5	4.0	1.8	0.1
	Nonwhite	8.4	10.7			2.3
Clerical and sales	White	12.5	12.5	0.0	0.0	0.0
	Nonwhite	12.5	12.5			0.0
Craftsmen	White	11.0	11.6	1.7	1.0	0.6
	Nonwhite	9.3	10.6			1.3
Operatives	White	10.1	10.6	1.4	0.5	0.5
	Nonwhite	8.7	10.1			1.4
Laborers	White	9.0	9.9	2.2	1.5	0.9
	Nonwhite	6.8	8.4			1.6
Service workers	White	10.1	11.0	1.3	1.7	0.9
	Nonwhite	8.8	9.3			0.5
Farm occupations	White	8.7	8.9	3.2	2.8	0.2
	Nonwhite	5.5	6.1			0.6

Parentheses indicate negative figures.
SOURCE: *Manpower Report of the President, 1965*, p. 227.

Data on median years of schooling completed by Negroes and whites by occupational grouping indicate that Negroes are being penalized for lower educational attainment—a major factor related to structural unemployment—but that faster gains among Negroes than among whites have not been rewarded. Table 60 presents the median years of school completed by each occupational group by color in 1959 and 1964. In 1959 all but two occupational categories of whites showed higher median school years than Negroes, ranging from 4 years among the managerial-proprietor group to 1.4 years for operatives. Among professionals and clericals there was no difference; yet the difference in unemployment rates in 1959 was 1.7 percentage points for professionals and 4.5 points for clericals. Between 1959 and 1964 the Negro gain in median years was more rapid than for whites in all but two occupation groups: (1) clerical-and-sales, where there was no change, and (2) service workers, where displaced white manual workers probably helped raise the white median. In 1964 Negro professionals actually showed higher median school years completed than whites.

Since the problem of school dropouts is of great significance to young workers, reasons for dropping out of school for persons sixteen to twenty-one years old are of interest. Among whites the most important reason in February, 1963, was being "not interested in school" (24 percent).[34] Among Negroes marriage or pregnancy was the most important reason (28 percent). The second most important reason for whites was marriage or pregnancy (23 percent); for Negroes it was economic need (20 percent). Negroes ranked higher in the category labeled "difficulties with school authorities" and "wanted to go to work," but not particularly different in "poor grades" or "due to own illness." Thus it seems clear that the vicious cycle of poverty, social deprivation, and inadequate education was still at work.

Negro very long-term unemployment rates by sex have also been higher than white rates. The data for the years 1957–64 are presented in Table 61,

[34] Main Reason for Dropping Out of Elementary or High School, Persons Sixteen to Twenty-one Years in the Noninstitutional Population not Enrolled in School, February, 1963

(percentage distribution)

	Not interested in school	Poor grades	Difficulties with school authorities	Wanted to go to work	Economic need	Marriage or pregnancy	Own illness	Other
White	24.1	8.2	3.5	7.5	17.8	22.9	5.4	10.6
Nonwhite	10.1	8.1	8.6	8.2	19.8	27.7	5.8	11.7

SOURCE: U.S., Bureau of Labor Statistics, "Out-of-School Youth, February 1963," *Special Labor Force Report*, No. 46, p. A-6.

Part A. For Negro men the rate was about three times that of white men; Negro women had from two to three times the white female rate. Part B of Table 61 presents the results of regression of the very long-term unemployed's share of total unemployment within each of the four groups

TABLE 61: Very Long-Term Unemployment among Whites and Nonwhites by Sex; and Cross Correlations by Sex, 1957–64

	Very long-term unemployed as:							
A.	Percentage of labor force in group				Percentage of unemployed in group			
	White		Nonwhite		White		Nonwhite	
Year	Male	Female	Male	Female	Male	Female	Male	Female
1957	0.31	0.28	0.90	0.63	8.49	6.37	10.70	8.53
1958	0.90	0.71	2.55	1.29	14.83	11.42	18.58	11.95
1959	0.71	0.61	2.54	1.14	15.42	11.43	22.01	12.10
1960	0.57	0.46	1.82	1.06	11.86	8.68	16.93	11.19
1961	1.01	0.87	2.89	1.64	17.63	13.37	22.46	13.79
1962	0.69	0.58	2.38	1.64	14.98	10.69	21.77	14.72
1963	0.65	0.53	2.12	1.63	13.86	9.26	20.04	14.36
1964	0.59	0.53	1.46	1.49	13.23	9.55	16.03	13.82

B. Very long-term unemployed as percentage of total unemployment in group predicted from very long-term rate of group; actual less estimated shares

C. Nonwhite very long-term rate by sex predicted from white very long-term rate by sex; actual less predicted rates

	Male		Female		Nonwhite	
Year	White	Nonwhite	White	Nonwhite	Male	Female
1957	(1.00)	(1.20)	(0.24)	(0.18)	(0.13)	(0.27)
1958	(1.61)	(2.62)	(0.33)	(0.47)	(0.18)	(0.22)
1959	1.22	0.87	0.87*	0.53	0.36	(0.23)
1960	(0.69)	(0.16)	(0.09)	0.07	0.04	(0.10)
1961	(0.10)	(0.66)	(0.30)	(0.59)	(0.15)	(0.10)
1962	1.02	1.53	0.49	0.34	0.25	0.31
1963	0.37	1.26	(0.34)	0.03	0.11	0.37
1964	0.80	0.97	(0.05)	0.28	0.29	0.23
r	0.93	0.93	0.98	0.98	0.94	0.68[a]

* Two or more standard errors.
[a] With an r of this value an additional observation would result in a significant correlation at 0.05 level.
Parentheses indicate negative figures.

SOURCE: Derived from *Manpower Report of the President, 1965*, pp. 195, 204, 210.

against its respective very long-term unemployment rate. The patterns displayed echo that of the over-all economy, namely a rise in numbers relative to duration in 1957 and 1958, reflecting demand conditions, and again in 1960 and 1961, with duration more important than numbers in the other years. White females, however, display a relative freedom from structural unemployment symptoms while nonwhite females show positive deviations in all but three years. Part C of Table 61 indicates the behavior of Negro very long-term unemployment rates by sex relative to white rates. Negro male rates are higher relative to white in all but recession years but are highly correlated. On the other hand, Negro female rates show a strong upward shift relative to white female rates from 1962 to 1964, with a resulting lower coefficient of correlation.

The behavior of Negro unemployment rates relative to white rates not only shows a recent autonomous rise, but the behavior of labor force participation rates by color, age, and sex also indicate that Negro unemployment rates would have been still higher had not Negro men withdrawn at a much more rapid rate than white men. As Table 62 demonstrates, nonwhite males show a labor force rate decline between 1948 and 1964 in all but two age groups and a higher rate of withdrawal in each of these than for white men. Only in the group twenty to twenty-four years of age is there a greater increase in the Negro labor force participation rate. The picture is similar among females, except that female participation rates increased over the period. The gain in participation rates was greater for white women on the whole, but greater for nonwhite women twenty to twenty-four years old.

TABLE 62: Percentage Point Changes in Civilian Labor Force Participation Rates by Age, Sex, and Color, 1948–64

Age group	Males		Females	
	White	Nonwhite	White	Nonwhite
14–19	(9.7)	(20.6)	(3.8)	(7.7)
20–24	1.3	3.8	3.7	6.5
25–34	1.5	0.4	3.7	2.2
35–44	(0.4)	(2.8)	8.2	5.1
45–54	0.2	(3.1)	16.9	11.2
55–64	(3.5)	(8.0)	16.1	10.8
65 & over	(18.6)	(20.7)	1.3	(4.8)
Total	(6.3)	(9.2)	5.8	1.6

Parentheses indicate negative figures.

SOURCE: Derived from *Manpower Report of the President, 1965*, p. 196.

Conclusions

The dramatic rise in Negro unemployment, one that would be considered catastrophic if it were general, points up the vulnerability of Negroes in a period of rapid labor force restructuring. The rise in unemployment among new labor force entrants is also of depression levels. When the effect of autonomous shifts in unemployment for Negroes and the inexperienced unemployed are added, the autonomous increase represented by these two groups accounts for 0.4 percent of the labor force in 1957, 0.5 percent in 1958, 1959, and 1960, and 0.7 percent in 1961, 1962, 1963, and 1964. In other words, the 5.2-percent rate of unemployment in 1964 could have been 4.5 percent if Negroes and new entrants had experienced conditions similar to those operating before 1955. This leaves out an adjustment for older workers, the poorly educated, those in distressed areas, those with obsolete skills, and those out of work because of skill bottlenecks. Of course, the categories overlap; however, there is reason to believe that structural unemployment might account for as much as half the increase in unemployment rates above the frictional minimum in nonrecession years.

CHAPTER 10

MINIMUM UNEMPLOYMENT

The foregoing chapters have offered evidence that the postwar period did not witness an autonomous rise in frictional unemployment, and that since 1956 there have been increases both in demand unemployment and in structural unemployment. If it is assumed that these conclusions are correct, implications must be drawn with respect to the possibility of achieving full employment at stable prices. The demand theorists have been identified with the position that unemployment can be reduced to about 4 percent through aggregate fiscal means without affecting over-all prices. At the other pole the structuralists have been associated with the claim that inflationary pressures would appear before 4 percent is reached. A third position is presented here, namely that simultaneous treatment of structural and demand problems could make possible an unemployment rate as low as 2.9 percent (achieved in 1953) without inflation.[1] This chapter discusses some of the questions involved.

MINIMUM UNEMPLOYMENT AND THE
INFLATIONARY MINIMUM

The complexity of industrial markets is such that there will be some unemployment at full employment. The seemingly Keynesian test of full employment—an increase in over-all prices when demand is increased— is therefore inadequate when labor markets are not perfectly competitive. More than this, when there are skill complementarities and limited substitutability of skills, specific labor shortages make a simple one-to-one

[1] This point of view is held by a growing number of economists.

relationship between over-all wages and over-all unemployment rates impossible.

If wage changes and unemployment rates are not uniquely related, a full-employment policy need not stand as an alternative to other policies which require price and/or wage stability. An unfortunate aspect of the structural-demand argument has been the underlying assumption by many of the discussants that unemployment levels and price levels are uniquely related. As a result, the demand position has been associated with a call for fiscal and monetary ease in the absence of any inflationary danger, while the structuralists have been associated with a call for early tightening of controls, stemming from a concern with inflation and balance of payments problems. Many demand theorists fear admitting the structuralists' diagnosis because to them it implies inflation at ever higher unemployment levels.

There is a growing body of literature that shows the extremely loose relationship between unemployment rates and changes in over-all wages as represented in "Phillips curves."[2] United States data, generally average hourly rates in manufacturing, have not shown clear relationships nor stability over time. Economists have required additional variables to explain wage or price movements. Tests of the Phillips relationship have largely discounted the earlier view of Samuelson and Solow that it would take about 8-percent unemployment to keep money wages from rising.[3] Eckstein and Wilson used unemployment and profits to explain wages but required the addition of a wage-round mechanism and the assumption of pattern bargaining.[4] Charles Schultze suggests that wage increases follow the pattern set by firms with high productivity gains.[5] Other authors have

[2] The Phillips curve is generally drawn as a negatively sloped curve which is roughly parallel to each axis, i.e., the upper branch of a rectangular hyperbola with asymptotes parallel to the axes. The implication usually drawn from Phillips curves is that below certain unemployment rates wages increase very rapidly for only small changes in unemployment, and that above certain unemployment rates large changes in unemployment can be effected through small changes in wages.

[3] Paul A. Samuelson and Robert M. Solow, "Analytical Aspects of Anti-Inflation Policy," *American Economic Review*, L, 2 (May, 1960), pp. 177–94.

[4] Otto Eckstein and Thomas A. Wilson, "The Determination of Money Wages in American Industry," *The Quarterly Journal of Economics*, LXXVI, 3 (Aug., 1962), pp. 379–414. The study might be more limited in its application than it first appears since the authors deal only with manufacturing production wage changes. Pattern bargaining probably relates to highly interchangeable occupations and cannot be generalized to the whole economy.

[5] Schultze, *Recent Inflation*, pp. 67–69. This author also deals primarily with manufacturing production workers. Schultze notes that higher, more uniform, wage increases appear in heavy industries rather than in lighter industries in spite of divergent employment tendencies. He suggests that in oligopolistic industries wage increases are substitutes for price competition and are used to discourage entry.

simply demonstrated that the Phillips predictions are neither uniquely determined nor accurate.[6]

Rather than being a means of determining unemployment, average wage changes for the economy as a whole may better be considered a force in income distribution, as suggested by Keynes.[7] Micromovements in wages, on the other hand, must be symptomatic to some extent of the net effects of relative supplies, demands, and transferabilities of skills.

The concept that wage increases and unemployment rates are somehow uniquely related in the economy as a whole should be tested by looking at relevant aggregate data. If the argument is significant at all, it is because any relationship between wage changes and unemployment rates will be translated into a relationship between unemployment rates and price changes for the economy as a whole. That is, the economist must "trade-off" the desire for full employment against the desire for price stability. For the trade-off to be necessary, there must be a unique relationship between the unemployment rate and wage changes, the unemployment rate and price changes, and thus between changes in wages and changes in prices. We tested these assumptions, using as proxies for the wage and price variables the GNP implicit price deflator[8] and average annual compensation per employee.[9] The relationship of price changes to the unemployment rate from 1929–30 to 1963–64 is presented in Figure 7.

Do the two series appear to be uniquely related? We think not. Is there justification for using a Phillips curve to describe the relationship? Probably not. A unique, long-term relationship between the variables is clearly ruled out since the data are separable into at least two clusters.

[6] See, for example, W. G. Bowen, *Wage Behavior in the Postwar Period*, Industrial Relations Section, Department of Economics (Princeton, N.J.: Princeton University Press, 1960); Keith B. Griffin, "A Note on Wages, Price and Unemployment," *Bulletin of the Oxford University Institute of Statistics*, Aug., 1962; Philip Ross, "Labor Market Behavior and the Relationship Between Unemployment and Wages," *Proceedings of the Fourteenth Annual Meeting*, Industrial Relations Research Association, New York, 1961.

[7] Keynes, *General Theory*, pp. 13–15.

[8] We used the revised National Income Division series, which divides current dollar GNP by constant, 1958-dollar GNP. This measure is probably more representative of aggregate prices than the consumer price index or the wholesale price index.

[9] The variable used is current dollar compensation of employees divided by the sum of Household Survey employment, plus the Armed Forces, minus the self-employed and minus unpaid household workers. This figure reflects average annual employment income of persons employed by others. Its weaknesses are that (1) hours worked are not reflected; part-time and part-year employment is weighted equally with full-time and full-year employment, and (2) there is no adjustment for the skill mix. However, the figure is a rough counterpart of the unemployment rate. Use of average hourly earnings of production workers in manufacturing was rejected because this measure is limited to one part of one sector of the economy and cannot record the intersectoral, interoccupational market adjustments which would be reflected in an aggregate indicator.

A Phillips-type curve might be picked out of the lower cluster, but it would involve using a discontinuous time period and overlooking many of the observations. Two straight lines, almost parallel, could just as easily be picked out.

Assuming that the thirties and the World War II period are of a qualitatively different nature, we focused on the seventeen observations from 1947–48 to 1963–64. As indicated in Table 63, changes in the GNP deflator show a low correlation with the unemployment rate, at −0.49

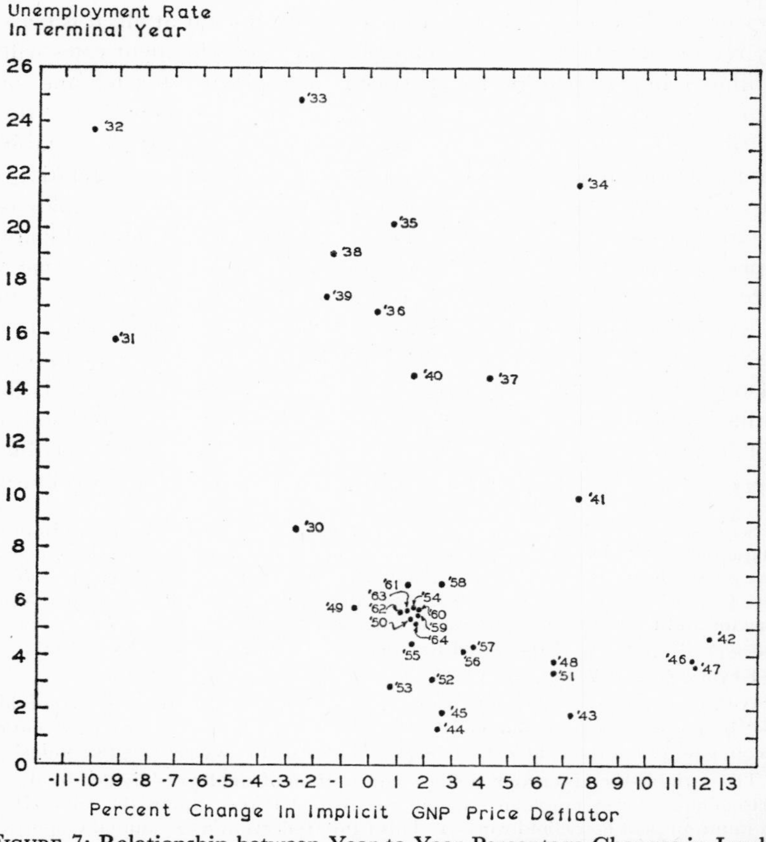

FIGURE 7: Relationship between Year-to-Year Percentage Changes in Implicit GNP Price Deflator and the Terminal Year Unemployment Rate, 1929–30 to 1963–64. (Note: Dates refer to terminal year. Unemployment rates from 1948 to 1963 adjusted to definitions adopted in 1957.) (Source: Derived from U.S., Office of the President, *Economic Report of the President*, 1965 [Washington: U.S. Government Printing Office, 1965], p. 214; and *Survey of Current Business*, Aug., 1965, pp. 52–53.)

(significant at the 0.05 level). Thus, even in the postwar years, unemployment and price changes were not uniquely related. The regression equation suggests that an unemployment rate of 5.6 would be needed to hold prices steady, but, in fact, prices rose in 1953–54, 1958–59, 1959–60, 1961–62, and 1962–63 when the rate was between 5.5 and 5.7 percent. In the two years when prices moved less than 1 percent, 1948–49 and 1952–53, the unemployment rate was 5.9 and 2.9 percent, respectively.

Deviations from the regression line show that the Korean and post-Korean years 1951–52 and 1952–53 had unemployment rates much lower

TABLE 63: Civilian Unemployment Rate Related to Percentage Changes in GNP Deflator[a] and Annual Average Compensation per Employee,[b] 1947–64

Yearly change	(1) GNP price deflator[a]	(2) Annual comp. per employee[b]	Year	(3) Civ. unemployment rate	Deviations of actual less calculated values based on regression equations		
					Unemp. rate based on		(6) Col. 1 based on Col. 2
					(4) Col. 1	(5) Col. 2	
1947–48	6.7	6.1	1948	3.8	0.2	(0.5)	3.6
1948–49	(0.6)	1.1	1949	5.9	0.1	(0.3)	(1.2)
1949–50	1.4	5.4	1950	5.3	0.1	0.7	(1.4)
1950–51	6.7	10.1	1951	3.3	(0.3)	0.6	1.6
1951–52	2.2	6.0	1952	3.1	(1.9)	(1.2)	(0.9)
1952–53	0.9	7.2	1953	2.9	(2.5)	(1.0)	(2.7)
1953–54	1.5	0.0	1954	5.6	0.4	(1.0)	1.4
1954–55	1.5	4.6	1955	4.4	(0.8)	(0.5)	(0.9)
1955–56	3.4	4.3	1956	4.2	(0.4)	(0.8)	1.2
1956–57	3.7	5.4	1957	4.3	(0.2)	(0.3)	0.9
1957–58	2.6	2.4	1958	6.8	2.0	1.1	1.3
1958–59	1.6	5.5	1959	5.5	0.4	1.0	(1.2)
1959–60	1.7	3.1	1960	5.6	0.5	0.1	0.1
1960–61	1.3	2.5	1961	6.7	1.5	1.0	0.0
1961–62	1.1	4.0	1962	5.6	0.3	0.5	(1.0)
1962–63	1.3	3.3	1963	5.7	0.5	0.3	(0.4)
1963–64	1.7	4.4	1964	5.2	0.1	0.2	(0.6)
Coefficient of correlation					−0.49	−0.77	0.61
Two standard errors					2.1	1.5	2.9

[a] Percentage change in the implicit GNP deflator is based on current dollar GNP divided by constant dollar GNP, 1958 = 100 (revised National Income Accounts data).
[b] Percentage change in current dollar compensation of employees, based on revised National Income Accounts, divided by total employment according to Household Survey, plus Armed Forces, minus self-employed and unpaid family workers.
Parentheses indicate negative figures.

SOURCE: Derived from U.S., Department of Commerce, *Survey of Current Business*, Aug., 1965, pp. 28–29, 52–53; and *Manpower Report of the President, 1965*, pp. 193, 200.

than would be expected. Stated another way, prices rose much less than would be anticipated from the low unemployment rates; on the other hand, prices in 1957–58 rose much more than would be expected from the unemployment rate. The years from 1957 to 1964 all show positive deviations or an upward drift in price changes relative to the unemployment rate, with the largest deviations coming in recession years. This suggests structural bottlenecks.

Looking behind the price change data, we find a closer correlation between changes in average employee compensation and the unemployment rate; r is -0.77 (see Table 63). However, explaining 59 percent of the variation does not truly suggest a unique relationship. [10] The regression equation suggests that average annual employment income will rise at unemployment rates below 6.6 percent. Wages rose, however, in 1957–58 and 1960–61 when the rate was 6.8 and 6.7 percent, respectively, but they held steady in 1953–54 with an unemployment rate of 5.6 percent. The major deviations from the regression line come in the 1951–54 period, when wages rose less than was expected, and in 1957–59 and 1960–61, when average wages rose more than was expected from the unemployment rate. The positive trend from 1957 to 1964 is again evident.

The moderately close relationship between wage changes and the unemployment rate is not carried over to an equally strong relationship between price changes and the unemployment rate because wage and price movements in the postwar period are correlated at only 0.61 (significant at the 0.01 level). This means that changes in one explain only 37 percent of the variation in the other. As Table 63 indicates, price changes of 6.7 percent were accompanied by wage changes of 6.1 and 10.1 percent, and variations between 1.5 and 1.7 percent in prices have corresponded to variations between 0.0 and 4.4 percent in wages.

These results indicate that there is little need to speculate about a "necessary" level of unemployment which must be lived with if prices are to be kept stable. The level of unemployment at which all unemployment would be frictional should not be confused with the level of unemployment needed to keep prices stable. The latter, the inflationary minimum, varies according to circumstances in the labor market; the former, the full employment minimum, is a more stable figure. The two are confused because frictional and structural unemployment are confused. The inflationary minimum is equal to the full-employment minimum when there is no structural unemployment. In the presence of structural, the two rates diverge by the amount represented by structural unemployment.

---

[10] Neither does the scatter of points define a Phillips curve. The straight line is better.

Confusion is reflected in the belief that prices must rise before full employment is reached. Wages can increase before full employment is reached for two different reasons. The first is if noncompetitive imperfections in the markets make possible autonomous wage increases. The imperfections can be (1) union control, (2) employers' use of their position to utilize wage increases in lieu of price competition, or to prevent entry, or (3) a rise in minimum wages. The other reason is skill bottlenecks.

It is supposed that unemployment is necessary to curb wage inflation, yet "cost-push" inflation is possible both at full-employment and at less than full-employment levels. Charles Schultze comments that "if rising wages or administered prices themselves continue to generate monetary demand sufficient to clear the market, despite the rising aggregate supply price of full employment output, cost-push inflation and full employment can coexist."[11] So full employment is possible with no inflation or with limitless inflation—depending on the circumstances.

Wages can increase before full employment is reached where there are skill bottlenecks. Since technical coefficients are different in different industries, bottlenecks will be reached earlier with one composition of output than another. But this latter point tells more about the importance of selective government spending with regard to ouput composition than it does about wage policy.

Unemployment levels can be reduced without wages or prices being affected if the distribution and composition of labor skills is changed through increasing mobility or retraining. In other words, bottlenecks in labor skill supplies can create partial wage inflations; if these partial shortages are overcome, over-all wages need not rise and unemployment can be reduced.[12] Wage and price changes need not always be related. Capital shortages and autonomous shifts in the profit rate can put pressure on prices rather than wages. Because of the effect of capacity rates on unit costs, rapid shifts in the composition of demand can be inflationary through the combined effects of bottlenecks and under-utilized capacity.[13]

If increased demand flows to markets where a full complement of labor skills is available, employment and output can expand without a wage rise. If new demand goes to markets with an over-all tight labor supply or

[11] Schultze, *Recent Inflation*, p. 21.

[12] "If it is the balance between the partial disequilibria in the submarkets, and not the unemployment in itself which is decisive for the development of money wages, there is no reason why we should not be able to obtain a 100 percent employment with stable money wages" (Bent Hansen, "Full Employment and Wage Stability," *The Theory of Wage Determination*, ed. John T. Dunlop [London: Macmillan & Co., Ltd., 1957], Chapter 5, pp. 73, 78).

[13] This is the import of Schultze's study, *Recent Inflation*.

shortages in skills with fixed coefficients, wage increases and price increases can occur. It becomes important where the increased demand is felt.[14]

Given skill bottlenecks and nontransferability of skills, lower wages could theoretically be used to offset the rate of technical displacement of workers. But, if the saving in total labor or in capital costs is of a magnitude such that it could not be matched by wage declines, a cut in wages would merely transfer income from wages to profits but not relieve the unemployment. A cut in product prices resulting from cost savings would transfer income from producers to consumers, but need not relieve the unemployment. While the old technology was still available, lower wages could encourage the use of old rather than new machines, thus only delaying the introduction of technological change.

If output is relatively inelastic with respect to wages in many industries, a wage increase would raise total employee compensation (and spending) more than would an equivalent percentage wage decline through the resulting increase in employment. Thus the best means of reducing unemployment might be wage increases, not decreases. The less important are labor costs in total costs the more likely this is to be true. The less competitive the product market the more likely this is to be true.

THE FULL-EMPLOYMENT MINIMUM

Chapter 3 presented evidence that the frictional rate of unemployment did not autonomously rise between 1948 and 1964; it demonstrated, however, that the short-term rate changes with the over-all rate. Thus it is not easy to pick out a single unemployment rate and call it the rate which is compatible with full employment, that is, a rate at which unemployment is purely frictional. The rate identified as the full-employment minimum has changed. It was formerly assumed that full employment was the lowest achievable rate of unemployment under normal conditions, and an historical judgment was introduced. Under these circumstances the rate of 2.9 percent achieved in 1953 was chosen. But "normal" is not a precise word, and 2.9 percent has rarely been mentioned in recent years.

---

[14] "What happens to prices and production depends on both supply and demand. Under given conditions of supply, prices and output will rise and fall together along with demand, and their relative movements will be correlated with the level of economy-wide resource utilization. Under given conditions of demand, autonomous cost increases will raise prices and reduce output, and vice versa for autonomous decreases. An initial change on either side is unlikely to leave the other unaffected, however, and this means that one must be alert to several forms of interaction between the two. . . . Assertions that single factors are responsible [for observed behavior should be] received with skepticism (Hickman, *Growth and Stability*, p. 370).

The persistence of higher unemployment rates themselves and fear of rising prices have combined to weaken the earlier goal of 2 to 3 percent. In 1958 Daniel Bell wrote that 2 or 3 percent of the labor force was a "normal" minimum rate of unemployment.[15] In 1960 the Senate Special Committee pointed out that there were many economists who believed that "an unemployment rate of three percent is both attainable and compatible with economic stability in a free society."[16] But even at that time the goal of 2- to 3-percent unemployment was fading.[17]

In 1962 the Subcommittee on Economic Statistics of the Joint Economic Committee never seriously raised the question of a rate below 4 percent.[18] The "many economists" of 1960 had all but vanished in a wave of concern about balance of payments and inflation. The literature which puts forward a purely demand diagnosis accepts, for the most part, a 4-percent frictional minimum. Most of those who raise the possibility of achieving a 3-percent rate point to the need for policy geared to alleviating structural unemployment.[19]

This section deals critically with two studies which reject 1953 as an example of full employment with stable prices. Albert Rees states that 1951–53 was a time of over-full employment due to the Korean mobilization.[20] (The unemployment rates were 3.3, 3.1, and 2.9 percent.) The term "over-full" is used to describe high employment levels when excess demand has pushed up prices. The World War II years are such years— when the labor force and capacity were both being strained to the limit.

Knowles and Kalacheck chose the 1957–60 period for their investigation partly because their "normal" periods are 1955–57 and 1948. The rates in 1951–53 are considered to be the result of "the exceptional influence of the Korean war."[21] The various developments of those years are said to

---

[15] Daniel Bell, "The Invisible Unemployed," *Fortune*, LVIII, July, 1958, p. 105.

[16] U.S., Senate, Special Committee on Unemployment Problems, *Report*, 86th Cong., 2nd Sess. (Washington: U.S. Government Printing Office, March 30, 1960), p. 37.

[17] William Miernyk stated in December, 1959: "In a recent survey conducted by the Joint Economic Committee, 60 per cent of a sample of economists indicated that they would be prepared to accept a level of unemployment amounting to *more than* 5 percent of the labor force, if necessary, as a condition for achieving a high degree of price stability. More than 13 percent of the respondents . . . were prepared to accept . . . seven percent or more in order to achieve stable prices!" ("The Incidence of Persistent Unemployment," *Proceedings of the Twelfth Annual Meeting*, Industrial Relations Research Association, Washington, 1959, pp. 22–23).

[18] *Employment and Unemployment: Report.*

[19] See, for example, National Planning Association, *The Rise of Chronic Unemployment*, p. 37; John T. Dunlop in *Studies in Unemployment*, U.S., Senate, Special Committee on Unemployment Problems, 86th Cong., 2nd Sess. (Washington: U.S. Government Printing Office, March 30, 1960), pp. 4, 14.

[20] Albert Rees in *Studies in Unemployment*, pp. 32–34. The Korean war ended in July of 1953 and thus directly influenced about half the year.

[21] *Higher Unemployment Rates*, p. 5.

have "led to widespread labor shortages and to the relaxation of hiring standards. . . ."[22] The authors then go on to accept "the neighborhood of 4 percent" as the full employment level—short of either wage increases or actions to improve labor market efficiency.[23]

Let us consider 1953. The very short-term unemployed were 1.4 percent of the labor force that year (Table 5). This indicates that a good deal of voluntary movement was taking place without intervening unemployment; the unemployed were finding jobs rapidly. Long-term unemployment accounted for 0.3 percent of the labor force, the lowest rate achieved in the postwar period. Average duration was also at its lowest point, eight weeks. It is reasonable to suppose that the remaining 1.2 percent of the labor force unemployed were seasonally unemployed, or unemployed for reasons such as market shifts or irregular disabilities lasting from five to fourteen weeks. In other words, the unemployed were primarily frictionally unemployed.

Capacity utilization in manufacturing was at its postwar high of 93 percent[24] but the GNP price deflator rose by only 0.9 percent. Surely the 0.9-percent price rise was not a sign of strain. The 1950–51 shift in the composition of output, brought about by the mobilization of 1950–51, was accompanied by a 6.7-percent rise in the GNP price deflator—at a higher level of unemployment (3.3 percent) than in 1953, and with a capacity rate in manufacturing of 91 percent. In 1951–52 the price deflator rose by 2.2 percent; the capacity rate in manufacturing stood at 90 percent. As indicated in Table 63, the changes in the GNP deflator and wages in 1951–52 and 1952–53 were unusually low with respect to the unemployment level.

The 1950–51 price rise was clearly tied to structural bottlenecks. Real consumer expenditures were only able to rise by 1.0 percent, making way for the shift from consumer to war goods. Real government expenditures rose by 43 percent and nonresidential construction by 11 percent. The evidence of excess demand is limited to the consumer sector. In 1950–51 the Consumer Price Index rose 8 percent; the commodity component rose 9 percent. In other words, the 6.7-percent rise in the GNP deflator in 1950–51 was not so much a symptom of over-full employment as of a structural shift in the composition of demand while demand increased. By 1953 real personal consumption expenditures were being permitted to regain their former place. They increased by 4.8 percent in 1952–53.

[22] *Ibid.*, pp. 5, 6.

[23] *Ibid.*, pp. 7, 8.

[24] Federal Reserve Board's measure. U.S., Congress, Joint Economic Committee, Subcommittee on Economic Statistics, *Measures of Productive Capacity: Report*, 87th Cong., 2nd Sess. (Washington: U.S. Government Printing Office, July 24, 1962), p. 16.

Government expenditures rose by 8.4 percent. In 1951–52 the Consumer Price Index rose 2.2 percent and the commodity group rose 1.3 percent; by 1952–53 the rise in the index was only 0.8 percent, and the index fell 0.3 percent for commodities.

The year 1952–53 marked a decline of 47,000 in the Armed Forces. The returning men were largely absorbed by the transformation of production back to a peace-time basis; the civilian labor force grew by 1.1 percent. It can be argued that unemployment was low because the Armed Forces were at their second highest postwar size in 1953— 3,547,000—but the size of the Armed Forces in 1954 was larger (3,350,000) than in 1951 (3,099,000), and no one has suggested that 1954 was a year of "over-full" employment. Thus there is no strong reason to put 1953 into the hopper with 1951 and 1952. An easing back to a normal composition of production was evident while the economy was buoyed by continuing government outlays. Industrial resources did not appear to be severely strained nor in severe disuse. In the monetary sphere, in contrast with the excess liquidity of the period just after World War II, 1953 was also a "normal" year. In the opinion of the National Industrial Conference Board, by 1953 "the prewar relationship of liquid assets to income had been restored, and consumers and business thereafter became more dependent on current flows to support their spending activities."[25]

Rees wonders whether there were errors in data gathering in the years 1951–53 and whether unemployment might have been underestimated, considering how much better the techniques became later. One asks, why question just those three years? Such an objection is pointless and arbitrary since it cannot be verified. Rees also suggests that higher rates in 1957–60 may have come from a change in the composition of the labor force. This alternative has already been eliminated.

Rees, like Knowles and Kalacheck, offers the 1955–57 period as more nearly corresponding "to our definition of the frictional level of unemployment. . . ."[26] He reasons that "in 1955–57 the economy was operating at near capacity levels with respect to factors of production other than labor."[27] One asks, what is there about the capacity-utilization rates in manufacturing of 90, 89, and 85 percent in the years 1955, 1956, and 1957 that makes them better than the rates 91, 90, and 93 percent which obtained in 1951, 1952, and 1953? Rees defines frictional unemployment as a rate occurring in years which ". . . from other evidence, we consider to be prosperous years."[28] But, obviously, unless one can show an autono-

[25] National Industrial Conference Board, *The Conference Board Record*, Feb. 1963, p. 5.
[26] Rees, *Studies in Unemployment*, p. 33.
[27] *Ibid.*
[28] *Ibid.*, p. 32.

mous rise in the frictional rate, the unemployment rate itself *is* a measure of prosperity and helps create it. The case does not appear conclusively proven. If major structural shifts did occur during the 1955–57 period, there is even more reason not to beg the question by choosing that very period as a comparison base.

We therefore conclude that (1) the frictional level of unemployment at full employment need not be the same as the inflationary minimum; (2) there is no evidence that there is one unique level of unemployment below which prices will rise; and (3) there is no reason to believe that unemployment rates cannot be reduced below 4 percent to 3 percent of the labor force if both structural and demand unemployment are eliminated, and certainly none if we place this objective as first in our order of priorities.

CHAPTER 11

CONCLUSIONS
AND POLICY IMPLICATIONS

CONCLUSIONS

The foregoing discussion has been more fruitful in illuminating particular aspects of labor market functioning in an economic context than it has been in setting out a neat count of unemployment in various theoretical categories. This is partly because of lack of data and partly because of the nature of existing data. The form in which unemployment data by occupation are collected, the lack of regional detail, the short length of crucial time series, and inadequate job vacancy information all hamper the analysis and prohibit a simple diagnosis and quantification of unemployment. But, of equal importance, structural and demand unemployment are so interrelated as to defy dichotomous enumeration.

The basic source of disagreement among the structuralists, the demand theorists, and this presentation is conceptual. The theoretical framework relating to technological change, the nature of technical labor requirements, and the interactions of labor skill markets with demand, prices, and unemployment are basically at issue. This study's conclusions hinge to a large extent upon assumptions with respect to whether labor skill requirements involve significant degrees of complementarity and nonsubstitutability on the labor demand side, and nontransferability on the labor supply side. For this reason the study will probably do less to change the opinions of extreme structuralists or demand theorists than to open new insights into the phenomena of structural change and unemployment.

The reader will by now have noted that most of the statistical analysis has involved little more than testing with simple regression models. There has been almost no attempt to use the complexities of multiple correlation analysis or factor analysis. Limitations in the quality of the data and the length of the time series did not seem to warrant complicated techniques. The basic conceptual points, however, have received strong support from the statistical results. Though none of the tests reported is by itself conclusive, the additive effects are, essentially, a refutation of the demand position. That is, we have shown considerable evidence to deny that inadequacies in over-all demand in the economy relative to productivity and labor force growth were responsible for persistently high unemployment rates from 1957 to 1964, independent of structural unemployment.

We generally conclude that there is evidence beginning with 1957 of an over-all inadequacy in demand relative to labor force and productivity growth, and that structural changes with respect to technology, the composition of output, and the location of industry *reinforced these demand inadequacies*. The structural changes also raised the level of structural unemployment through imbalances in labor skill availabilities and demands, involving a redundancy of some skills and educational levels and a shortage of others; these problems *have been reinforced by demand inadequacies*. Thus the structural-demand controversy has been founded on a false dichotomy and has hindered the development of a sound full-employment policy.

We believe that we have demonstrated both directly and indirectly that structural changes have occurred in the economy which affected the proportions of labor skill requirements in such ways as to penalize individuals with little education, unskilled workers, new labor force entrants, Negroes, and older men; that, in addition, shortages of specific skills have contributed to the unemployment of their skill complements.

We set out a theoretical framework which, in the first place, separated the causes of unemployment into inadequate demand, structural change, and frictional factors. This framework lifted the analysis out of the classical setting which assumes homogeneous, substitutable labor units and onto the modern stage where new technology functions with differentiated labor inputs and imperfect markets.

The evidence suggests that new technology has been substituting indirect for direct labor and the more educated and trained for the less educated and less well trained. By implication there now are greater problems of labor transfer than earlier. The evidence also points to shortages of some kinds of overhead labor. Thus, structural redundancies and shortages resulted in a drag on demand. Since there is also evidence that the new technology is strongly capital-saving, a major conclusion is *that there is an intimate connection between structural change and demand unemployment*.

The simple-minded assumption that a worker is structurally unemployed only if he is matched by a listed vacant job he cannot fill ignores the facts of economic life. The workers whose skills are complements of skills in short supply are not represented by unfilled jobs. Neither is there an available measure for new production foregone due to projects not undertaken, new research not carried out, or new firms not established because of skill shortages. Potential adequacy of demand is not reflected in achieved levels of GNP.

Direct tests of structural unemployment are hampered by the nature of the data. The skill composition of unemployment is affected by classifications of the unemployed according to "last job." Structural problems are better reflected through measures related to duration of unemployment. But, since prolonged inadequacies in over-all demand are able to produce similar evidence with respect to duration, and since prolonged shortages in specific skills can contribute to inadequacies in demand, the major contribution made here is a demonstration that the demand theorists have not proved their case. The tests they offer cannot adequately discriminate.

Evidence indicates that the labor force is adaptive and responsive to economic conditions and has not contributed to higher unemployment rates by perverse mobility responses. On the contrary, the changing patterns of migration rates and labor force participation have largely worked to hold down unemployment rates. Beyond this, the evidence suggests that unemployment is more likely being under-stated at an increasing rate as men with inadequate education stop looking for work out of discouragement and are listed as not in the labor force.

A major conclusion to be drawn from the study is that the incidence of structural unemployment provides an indictment of social and economic inadequacies in our society. It is found to have taken a disproportionate toll among Negroes, youth, and older men. It thus is an open challenge to conditions of civil rights, the nature of our educational system, and our manpower approach.

The demand theorists' position ignores these essentially political considerations, since it would apply aggregate policy measures to over-all problems. The structuralists who identify themselves with inflationary fears also ignore the human content of unemployment. The work here has attempted to extricate the full-employment problem from the trade-off dilemma between stable prices and full employment by showing that the unemployment rate need not be tied to the price level once structural blockages are attacked. The emergence of this position is indicated in a statement by Otto Eckstein, of the Council of Economic Advisers in 1965.[1] However, until the interdependence of the *causes* of structural and demand unemployment are seen, the co-ordination of the two approaches will not be seriously undertaken. Fiscal and selective measures will develop in isolation and with little attention to getting an integrated, adequate manpower policy of appropriate scale.

The decline in the unemployment rate in 1965 neither proves nor disproves the assertions made with respect to structural problems. The yearly average did not reach the 4-percent level anticipated by many demand theorists, despite a tax cut, a major increase in private investment, and an increase in U.S. military expenditures on the war in Vietnam. However, the war has relevance to the questions discussed here. The dollar volume of spending required to escalate the war was important with respect to output growth. But, in addition, the fact that this is a "conventional" war has its impact on the employment content of the spending: It is being fought by ground and air forces and has required conventional arms and a build-up of the Armed Forces through conscription. The weapons of destruction in the war call on the very skills and industries which faced structural decline, namely production workers in durable goods production.

It is no accident that in the third quarter of 1965 fabricated metals, electrical equipment, machinery, and chemicals showed significant employment increases, while transportation equipment began to revive.[2] The use of expanded draft calls rather than reliance on Reserves to build up the Armed Forces worked to lower youth unemployment; reliance on the Reserves would have been a serious drain on scarce labor skills.

The results of spending for the war in Vietnam do not refute the structuralist analysis; the war merely arrests the problems. There has been minimum inflationary pressure on the economy precisely because existing

[1] When the case for manpower policies was first presented and the programs were first instituted, some of the discussion unfortunately presented manpower policies and general economic policies as alternative roads to full employment. The Council of Economic Advisers was frequently required to defend expansionary fiscal and monetary policies against some over-enthusiastic advocates of manpower policies. . . . Today it is generally accepted that manpower policies without the job creation that only general fiscal stimulus can provide would yield a bitter harvest of educated and trained people unable to utilize their newly acquired skills. And it is equally clear that manpower policies to improve the flexibility and efficiency of the economy allow us to raise our sights on our full employment targets. [Otto Eckstein, "Statement before the Subcommittees on Employment and Manpower of the Senate Committee on Labor and Public Welfare and the House Select Subcommittee on Labor," Executive Office of the President, Council of Economic Advisers, April 30, 1965, p. 2.]

[2] The unemployment rate in durable goods reached its lowest level since the fourth quarter of 1953. More than three-fourths of the increase in manufacturing in the third quarter of 1965, as compared with the prior year, was among production workers.

capacity was not fully taxed and the producer goods industries were able to supply new investment demand. The manpower required to turn out conventional war goods was available from the pool of those structurally displaced. Significantly, popular fears of inflation were more related to problems of skill shortages than to excess demand.

Thus, the Vietnam War merely postpones the disquieting question of whether the United States will be able to face up to the problems of structural change and adequate demand in the context of a peaceful world.

POLICY IMPLICATIONS

The problem of unemployment is disturbing because the productive capacities of this country have been developed to the point where full utilization of all productive assets could make possible a reasonable provision for all. On the other hand, the lack of full utilization of those capacities places large numbers of individuals in the position of not being able to get sufficient work, the remuneration for which would provide for their maintenance.

The purpose of this section is to indicate where the findings of this study lead with respect to public policy for full employment. It is impossible to include here an over-all evaluation of current manpower policy or to present a detailed public program. Much work is already underway at the federal level directed at both structural and demand problems; an evaluation of these is a large task in a study already lengthy. Rather, this section makes explicit the broad policy implications which flow from the work and offers a series of more specific policy suggestions that have come to mind in the course of the study. The discussion is not addressed to policies designed specifically to increase over-all demand, such as tax cuts or increased expenditures of one sort or another, since this area has been amply dealt with elsewhere in the literature.

National Policy

If the economist's job is in part to promote the most efficient use of resources, then the economist's responsibility with regard to manpower policy under the Full Employment Act should be to advocate the kind of spending that will generate maximum employment per dollar. It is generally accepted that the federal government must be concerned with maintaining an adequate level of aggregate demand. But only the most vulgar Keynesian will maintain that a dollar of private investment or government spending will have the same employment content wherever it is spent. Thus government responsibility will vary as the effectiveness of the private dollar varies. After top priority expenditures are allocated, government spending should be regarded as discretionary spending and should be used for the maximum health of the economy. It is our good luck that public civilian needs with regard to social investment and services are also in harmony with the surplus labor skills for which money spent to fill these needs would generate employment.

The data indicate that labor displacement has been heavy in the goods-producing industries and among agricultural, operative, and unskilled occupations. The data also show that shortages exist in professional, technical, managerial, and certain skilled occupations. It stands to reason that government spending must take these imbalances into account. This requires a combined long- and short-run approach. Either alone would be a waste of public resources, would not substantially cut unemployment, and could be inflationary.

In the short run, unemployment can best be relieved by spending in those areas which require a minimum of skills in short supply and a maximum of skills in excess supply. Public works projects, housing, urban renewal, mass transportation, road construction, social services, and the like are well adapted to such spending, along with expenditures on various kinds of durable public equipment. The employment generated through expenditures by the Area Redevelopment Administration has involved larger proportions of redundant skills than in the economy as a whole.[3] In sharp contrast, advanced military or defense-related expenditures involve above-average proportions of professional, technical, clerical, and craft workers as compared with total manufacturing employment and below-average proportions of operatives.[4] Thus military expenditures involving advanced technology are less beneficial than a peace-time spending program of comparable size and need not be undertaken for economic benefits beyond those warranted for their primary purpose.

Government spending, wherever it is channeled, will increase aggregate demand. This includes money spent for retraining or to support education

[3] U.S., Department of Commerce, Area Redevelopment Administration, *Redevelopment*, Jan., 1965, pp. 4–5, and March, 1965, pp. 6–7.

[4] Before the escalation of the Vietnam war, the direction of change was toward increasing proportions of professional, technical, and skilled workers in defense industries and a decreasing proportion of production workers relative to the economy as a whole. Between 1958 and 1963 in five defense-related industries the proportion of production workers fell from 64 to 57 percent. In all U.S. manufacturing the fall was from 75 to 74 percent. (Joseph F. Fulton, "Employment Impact of Changing Defense Programs," *Monthly Labor Review*, May, 1964, pp. 513, 514.)

as well as for construction of highways or to build missiles. Income tax or excise tax cuts also increase aggregate demand. The content of the increase is related to the incidence of the cuts. If inflationary pressures due to bottlenecks are to be minimized and if there is to be a maximum increase in employment per public dollar, selective expenditures and/or tax policy are called for.

If government were solely to spend or cut taxes, even selectively, to utilize redundant skills and relieve pressure on skill bottlenecks, the long-run problem of continued displacement and skill shortages would still be present. A simultaneous long- and short-run manpower program is called for. In the long run the structurally displaced must be changed into employable labor and skill shortages must be eradicated. A major part of such a program would be to prepare new labor force entrants to qualify for the newly opening occupations. If this were done, the complementarity of labor inputs would then work to mop up some of the structurally unemployed who cannot easily be retrained and whose skill proportions were cut down rather than abolished with respect to output.

We suggest therefore that a government-supported training and retraining program large enough to accommodate 1 percent of the labor force annually be a permanent part of the federal manpower program.[5] As long as the trend to automation continues, the composition of output goes on changing, and industry continues to relocate, the problem of labor displacement and skill blocks will continue. If disarmament is ever accomplished there will be additional problems.

The very scale of automation technology precludes the possibility of the automatic equilibrium adjustment provided by the competitive market model. The computer can calculate the competitive solution but it cannot bring it about. It will have to be the job of federal manpower policy to ease labor adjustments and smooth out market mechanisms. The earlier these problems are spotted, the smaller the measures needed to overcome the dislocations. Certainly no other agency is in a position to do the spotting and help the adjustments.

The long-run job of the government must be to maintain short-run demand and help bring about appropriate long-run labor adjustments. It will have to be a kind of clearing house for labor markets. This is economically the cheapest way out. Since expenditures on labor training,

[5] Further support for this recommendation will be found in Joseph M. Becker, William Haber, and Sar A. Levitan, *Programs to Aid the Unemployed in the 1960's*, the W. E. Upjohn Institute for Employment Research, Jan., 1965, p. 29, and Margaret Gordon, "Retraining Programs at Home and Abroad," *Proceedings of the Seventeenth Annual Meeting*, Industrial Relations Research Association, Chicago, Dec., 1964, pp. 128–38.

location, and mass education are in themselves a form of demand, these outlays serve a double purpose and are social investments.[6]

The incidence of structural unemployment is such that the free market is ill-equipped to deal amelioratively with the problem. The labor market is hostile to Negroes, to young inexperienced youth, to older workers, and to the poorly educated. Thus private industry may be encouraged to develop its own training programs, but the federal government must take over-all responsibility to see that social injustices are not perpetuated.

A monograph written under funds provided by the Manpower Development Training Act suggested that ". . . an active manpower policy ought to aim at raising the educational levels of the labor force by reducing the number of school dropouts. . . . Substantial efforts should be directed toward increasing opportunities for workers with the lowest educational level."[7] In addition to the whole area of extending and expanding education and training, a public manpower policy will have to come to grips with the problems of civil rights, care of the aged, social legislation of all forms, and even states' rights and the dilemma of expanding trade with the Communist world.

Specific Policy Areas

PUBLIC DATA AND RESEARCH

Research for this study has provided the author with an opportunity to use and evaluate much of the public manpower data. A number of related series were also utilized. Improvements in collection, definition, and continuity were called for in several instances. The various series collected by the Departments of Commerce and Labor related to labor force, employment, earnings, unemployment, and education would benefit by a greater uniformity of industrial and occupational categories, reference periods, and definitions. The most serious inadequacies in the manpower data lie in the area of labor requirements, availabilities, and mobility.

● A very important breakdown needed is the occupational composition of industry employment by area. The area data are the most clearly inadequate.

[6] Benefit-cost analysis of retraining programs should separate out the effects of training workers who would normally be hired when there was an increase in aggregate demand as opposed to workers who would be impacted regardless of the level of demand. In addition, the benefits of filling jobs whose requirements are in short supply extend beyond the immediate placement to the creation of jobs which are complements of the primary placement.

[7] U.S., Office of Manpower Automation and Training, *Formal Occupational Training of Adult Workers*, Manpower Automation Research Monograph No. 2, Dec., 1964, p. 4.

- Next would be job vacancy data. In combination with the unemployment data by occupation, industry, and area they could be used to indicate primary and secondary employment effects and enable a differentiation of structural, demand, and frictional unemployment. (Work to this end is underway.)

- Industry hours of work by occupation within industries would aid analysis greatly.

- Data on the experienced labor reserve should be gathered regularly. This could be done with several simple questions for those not now in the labor force: "Has X ever worked? What was his major occupation and industry when he worked? When did he last work? Is he able to work now?"

- The unemployment of structurally displaced workers may be seriously under-estimated by failure to count workers who have withdrawn from the job search out of discouragement. The current method of counting only workers who volunteer such information should be replaced by a question which elicits such information. The respondents who have withdrawn out of discouragement (or not entered for the same reason) should be counted as unemployed.

- Unemployment data should be gathered by primary, or "best," occupations and industry as well as last occupation and industry. This would be useful in tracing mobility and transferability of skills and would help spot incipient structural problems.

- Job-shift data would be much more useful if they were collected every year. Otherwise the cyclical trends cannot be separated from the secular.

- Geographic mobility data could be more closely related to employment by asking respondents about their labor force status at the time of migration and one month subsequent to it.

- "Employment, unemployment, and job vacancy data on a local area basis are badly needed. Adequate manpower policy requires a picture of the skill composition, availabilities, and training of the local labor force, matched with an occupational breakdown by industry of employment and vacancies. The whole question of structural unemployment essentially revolves around skills and locations. "

- Tabulations that simultaneously provide for labor force status, unemployment rates, and duration by age, sex, color, education, occupation, and industry would permit analysis of variance and factor analysis.

A major area of investigation directly relevant to unemployment is skill complementarities. Research should be undertaken to ascertain the elasticities of substitution of specific skills by industry and the effects on these of technological change. Additional areas for investigation should include the effects of technology on entry job requirements, the range of skill families within industries, and minimum educational requirements at the entry job level and at the upper end of the skill family.

YOUTH AND EDUCATION

When a large portion of our unemployed are youth, under-educated youth, and to a disproportionate extent, Negro under-educated youth, then a policy solution must embrace the entire structure of our educational system, youth guidance, and placement facilities and reach out to the roots of ghetto existence. Such an approach is clearly in tune with the poverty program of the Johnson administration. The self-perpetuating "poverty cycle" must be broken. Justification of this kind of program is not only moral or ethical; if this problem is not solved, it will rot the very fiber of our economic structure.

A study by the President's Task Force on Manpower Conservation made the following points: A third of male youths turning eighteen would be unqualified for entry into the Armed Forces if examined. Half of these would be rejected for medical and half for mental reasons. The major causes appear to be inadequate educational and health services. This group's unemployment is four times higher and their educational level well below the average for their age. These youths were found to want and need counseling and training.[8]

The problem is not that we are suddenly getting more ill-equipped youth. It is that the gap between the least prepared youth and the minimum qualifications for the least demanding occupations is widening under the impact of technological change. It is not enough to find these men at eighteen, nor should it be forgotten that there are also girls to consider. Even a Youth Employment Opportunities Act comes too late in the life cycle. It seems little enough to ask for a federally sponsored, school-age child-registration act, which would periodically examine the health, achievement, and prospects of every youngster in our country, with remedial programs ready to correct deficiencies before they have gone too far. Why should this be different in scope from the program to wipe out polio or smallpox? At a time when educators talk easily about sex education in the schools, they must also demand courses that will provide

[8] The President's Task Force on Manpower Conservation, *One-Third of a Nation, A Report on Young Men Found Unqualified for Military Service* (Washington: U.S. Government Printing Office, Jan., 1964), pp. 1–2.

youngsters with information about their educational and vocational alternatives and the techniques of job placement. How many youngsters even learn about the existence of the state employment services?

One of the difficulties with the Manpower Development and Training Act is that training allowances for youth could encourage rather than discourage new school dropouts. What is needed in addition is a direct payment to families dependent on their children's income so that the children can remain in school and complete their education. This is surely as acceptable a form of transfer payments as unemployment insurance. The social cost of unemployment insurance for the laborer at a dead end cannot be compared to the investment in a person preparing for a needed skill. It is worth the effort to find a way to implement such a policy. Certainly the test of a free society is not the number of avenues that exist, but the ability to choose freely from among the avenues—without economic coercion.

In line with this thinking, we must pay attention to higher education as well. Not only are possible current earnings attractive to the potential high-school dropout, but they are increasingly tempting to the student who might go on to apprenticeship training, college, or graduate school. On all three levels the incomes normally generated during the study period are negative or nominal. For example, the income received by the average graduate assistant who already holds the master's degree is low enough to place him in the poverty group. Yet, increasingly, the graduate student is married and has children to support. We suggest, therefore, that a program of income support related to all levels of education be adopted in addition to other forms of income maintenance and that this be undertaken as a preventative rather than an ameliorative policy.

The role of educational and training programs in preparing workers for job openings is obvious. Just as much needed is adequate secondary education and vocational school training for youngsters who will not go on to college. Full-employment projections assume that enough schools will be available to keep young people out of the labor force and at their studies long enough to prepare them for useful employment. If the schools are not provided the unemployment rate will rise. It is an economic necessity to evaluate the ability of our educational system to channel individuals toward training that is required for future work. Edward Chase makes the point that our regular secondary schools are geared to train the minority who go on to college, and our vocational training programs are self-perpetuating centers of obsolete information and skills.[9] The unemployment figures for the young and for new labor force entrants

[9] Edward T. Chase, "Learning to be Unemployable," *Harper's Magazine,* Vol. 226, No. 1355 (April, 1963), pp. 33–40.

lend support to this disquieting evaluation. It is possible that our educational system has not kept pace with the nation's changing employment needs and may have helped aggravate the unemployment problem.

In May, 1964, the *New York Times* reported on a study by the American Council on Education. It summarized the study, stating that

> Failure of the nation's colleges and universities to respond to modern vocational needs has led to the simultaneous threat of disastrous youth unemployment and critical manpower shortages. . . . [The report] . . . places much of the blame on the emphasis and prestige given to "the college track" in the schools, which concentrate attention on about 20 per cent of the students—those who complete college.
>
> The other 80 per cent—those who either drop out of high school, fail to enter college or drop out of college without a degree—enter the modern technological world "unequipped with the tools they need for survival."[10]

Our proposal is a revamping of the vocational training system and inclusion in it of federal and local support for technical colleges. This is underway in some states. In addition, we would like to see efforts of the sort that have been pioneered in a few localities—vocational training programs jointly run by industry and unions, schools and industry, and government placement agencies and industry. That is, a combination of local industry of every sort, employment services, schools, and trade unions should be providing vocational training and apprenticeship programs with federal support. Industry has the modern machines and equipment; they already employ the skilled workers, administrators, and supervisors needed for teaching and planning. Industry will do the ultimate hiring, so it knows what it needs. Employment services are equipped to channel personnel, handle records, and supervise attendance. Schools are endowed with facilities, faculty—and more important—have access to the young people before they leave school. The unions have the confidence of their members, access to large numbers of workers, and an inside knowledge of workers' problems. Such a combination of resources requires only the funds to pay for instruction, support young workers during training, and provide social services. The chief role of the federal government should be to guarantee that the programs adhere to principles of equality with respect to race, sex, and social background.

---

[10] Fred M. Hechinger, "Colleges Found Failing to Meet Manpower Needs." *New York Times*, Sunday, May 31, 1964, pp. 1, 40. The study referred to is *Man, Education, and Work* by Dr. Grant Venn.

JOB TRAINING, RETRAINING, AND RELOCATION

Current programs for training and retraining either take accessible and easily retrained workers whose education and age make them good rehiring prospects, or they work with "hard core" unemployed and have heartbreaking results in many cases. Payments for retraining under existing legislation are limited to the equivalent of unemployment benefits and allow no additional income without cutting the benefits. Yet "hard core" retraining can take a year or more, since it often starts with teaching workers to read and write. Local programs have limited funds. Federally sponsored programs have not yet come to grips with the nature of structural unemployment problems.

The Manpower Development and Training Act of 1962 and its 1963 amendments provide the basic legislation for federally sponsored training and retraining. It serviced 199,240 trainees in 1964, or 0.3 percent of the labor force. Thus in size alone it is still inadequate. But, in addition, the amended act still does not begin to tackle the problems facing the undereducated, the youth, and the aged. It does somewhat better in its proportionate coverage of the long-term unemployed and Negroes.[11] Another problem with MDTA is that much of its training is for occupations that would normally be filled by the currently unemployed as demand increased. For example, in 1964, 16 percent of the training approved was for semi-skilled work. Training for bottleneck occupations would provide multiplier employment effects.

We propose that the federal government expand efforts (1) to provide basic reading and writing skills and long-term training for the educationally deprived, particularly adults, and (2) undertake training for occupations of skill scarcities and at the same time concentrate on individuals with the least likelihood of finding work unaided.

The federal government is in a good position to evaluate regional imbalances in labor supply and demand. Part of the problem here is relocation costs. The labor market works so that the cost of resettling an

[11] The amended MDTA provided for expanding youth participation in training programs by lowering the age of those eligible for youth training allowances from nineteen to seventeen and by permitting up to 25 percent of all those receiving training allowances to be youths of seventeen through twenty-one with little or no previous work experience. This is an important liberalization of the original act, which limited funds for youth training allowances to 5 percent of total allowances paid. To help qualify the poorly educated for occupational training, the MDTA was amended to provide for basic educational training in such subjects as reading, writing, language skills, and arithmetic. However, in 1964 only 4.6 percent of all trainees had less than an eighth-grade education, while 20 percent of the unemployed in March, 1962, were so characterized. (U.S., Office of Manpower, Automation, and Training, *MDTA Training Program: Comparison of 1963 and 1964*, Manpower Evaluation Report No. 4, Dec., 1964, pp. 2–5).

engineer and his family often is carried by the firm, while this does not apply to the bench worker. Yet someone will have to bear such costs. The worker himself is least able to do so. We therefore suggest a program that will provide relocation allowances to manual and sub-professional workers. The federal government is also in a position to maintain property values in distressed areas through special mortgages and resale insurance.

THE AGED AND NEGROES

Even if all that has been suggested is done, there will be workers who will remain unable to relocate or retrain. Many of these will be the aged. The re-employment problems of older workers require other forms of attention than those usually associated with aggregate demand solutions. For example, the Rosses suggest that

> Conventional employment service routines will not result in the successful placement of many older workers, aside from those who have scarce skills and except in a period of general labor shortages. A large percentage of older workers can be placed, however, with the use of intensive and individualized efforts beyond those made available to the general run of job seekers. Such efforts are relatively expensive—ranging from twice to 10 times the cost of routine placements—but are justified by the public interest in reintegrating the older worker.[12]

Any programs that encourage retention of older employees through seniority rules and attrition schemes are worthy of support. The block to mobility does not lie in the desires of workers but in the opportunities they face. As long as mobility is possible for younger workers there is no harm in attrition policies. It makes sense that the workers who are the best candidates for retraining are those with the longest future working lives. Employers should be encouraged to hold on to their older workers, while refresher training and graduated retirement plans might ease the problem. The long-run problem of the youth and the aged is that of providing sufficient income in the form of transfer payments to make longer periods of investment possible at the start of the working life and to make early exit attractive and desirable at the end.

The plight of the Negro worker is particularly glaring since Negroes show the effects of institutional or social barriers in addition to those of structural and demand-related unemployment. Negro youth and Negro men suffer more than white, so that the incidence of structural unemployment is greater in the Negro community. None of the approaches to youth problems, educational requirements, programs for the aged, and reloca-

[12] *Studies in Unemployment,* p. 116.

tion proposals can be adequately handled without specific confrontation of segregation and discrimination.

Nothing short of a massive program to undercut the atmosphere of futility in the Negro ghetto will do. This implies a guarantee that education and training for Negroes will be rewarded by placement at the end. This means soliciting Negro enrollments for technical schools and for higher education because Negro youth have no experience in being accepted at many institutions. It does not occur to them to apply even where they would be accepted. It also means teaching teachers how to create an atmosphere of equality and making such attitudes requisites for teaching.

All federal programs will have to deny funds to educational agencies or local governments that cannot guarantee nondiscriminatory training and placement. Private employment services will have to be regulated to rid them of discriminatory practices.[13] The Civil Rights Act of 1964 is a step in this direction. The job of salvaging human skills and dignity will require a serious commitment to reshaping those with obsolete skills, those without skills or hope of working, and those who have been able to ignore these problems for too long.

FINAL COMMENTS

Aggregate increases in over-all demand, including spending for warfare, and a manpower program, admittedly inadequate, helped reduce unemployment in 1965. The remaining unemployment problems are less dramatic and probably more stubborn in character.

As technology continues to cut down both the labor and capital content of output, will the economy generate sufficient peace-time demand to maintain production at adequate levels? The extent of the market determines the outer limit of output. The specter of the society with no workers and mass unemployment is not realistic if only because such a society will not have a market and thus no profits. The employed will either have to have incomes large enough to provide for greater numbers of non-employed dependents, or the central authorities will have to redistribute income through taxes and transfer payments.

If there ever is a society with no workers, the unemployed will have been converted to those not in the labor force—but receiving transfer payments. The question is, what are we prepared to do about the casualties incurred in the march of economic change? Continued economic growth itself depends upon the answers we find.

[13] See the article, "Wide Bias Found in Job Agencies," *New York Times,* July 21, 1963.

INDEX

American Council on Education, 226
Area Redevelopment Administration, 220
Armed Forces: migration rates, 133n; return of, 213
Automation, 221. *See also* Capital productivity, Labor displacement; Labor productivity; Technological change

Balance of payments, 204
Bell, Daniel, 211
Berman, Barbara, and David E. Kaun: quoted, 69
Bowman, Raymond, 38
Bureau of Employment Security: jobs in clearance, 137; job vacancies, 156, 160
Bureau of Labor Statistics: dropouts, 154; goods and services, 60–61; seasonal unemployment, 31–32, Stein and Kellogg, *Unemployment: Terminology, Measurement, and Analysis,* 17n; worker categories, 6; mentioned, 34
Bureau of the Census, Household Survey: estimates of unemployment, 15–17; job mobility, 115; long-term unemployment, 177–78; migrant, definition, 131; occupational data, 85–86. *See also* Current Population Survey; Household Survey
Business cycles: changes in employment, 110–12; distressed areas, 67; education, 151; employment in goods and services, 39–61; female employment, 98–99; industry employment, 55; job mobility, 115; job shifts, 118; labor productivity, 47; male employment, 102–4; male occupations, 100–2; occupational shifts in employment, 109; participation rates, 97–100; 106–7; recession unemployment, 183; related to employment by industry, 113; related to part-time work, 85; technological displacement, 55; unemployment rate, 22–23; variation of employment changes, 79–84
Business turnover unemployment, 32–34

Capital and labor coefficients, 8
Capital growth: related to output growth, 41–46
Capital productivity: and skills, 43–46; technological change, 41, 43–46

Capital spending and demand, 46
Capital stock series, 42
Census of Population: occupational data, 85–86
Chase, Edward, 225–26
Civilian Unemployment Rate: defined, 16
Civil Rights Act, 229
Clague, Ewan: 49–50; quoted 168
Consumer expenditures: by occupation, 62–63
Council of Economic Advisers: manpower policies, 218n. *See also* Heller Report
Current Population Survey: unemployment estimates, 15–17. *See also* Household Survey

Demand: adequacy, 216–17; changes in and demographic change, 37; changes in and participation rates, 37, 109–10; distressed areas, 67–68; educational requirements, 150; goods to services shift, 62–63; inadequate, defined in Knowles-Kalacheck Report, 11; income and employment, 170; job availability, 117; labor productivity, 46; mobility, 129–30; shifts in related to output growth, 59–63; technological change, 55; technological displacement, 55; theorists, minimum unemployment, 203
Demsetz, Harold: creeping unemployment, 12; occupation and income, quoted, 173
Department of Labor: job vacancy survey, 162–63
Displacement: of workers, 210; technological, 7
Distressed areas: business cycles, 67; characteristics of, 64–65; unemployment, 64–69; unemployment causes, 66–67
Dommar, Evsey D.: labor shortages, 9; quoted, 6
Dropouts: and work experience, 190–91; reasons for, by color, 199. *See also* Education

Eckstein, Otto: price level and unemployment rate 217–18; wages, 204
Education: adaptive role, 142; aged and Negro training, 228–29; changes in

231

STRUCTURAL UNEMPLOYMENT AND AGGREGATE DEMAND:
A Study of Employment and Unemployment in the United States, 1948–1964

By Eleanor G. Gilpatrick

designer: Cecilie Smith
typesetter: Baltimore Type and Composition Corporation
typefaces: Baskerville (text), Alternate Gothic and News Gothic (display)
printer: The John D. Lucas Printing Company
paper: Lindenmeyr Schlosser Company
binder: Moore and Company, Inc.